The psychology of interpersonal perception

We are making judgements about other people all the time: deciding what they are like, predicting what they will do, providing explanations for their behaviour. How do we make these judgements? What leads us to decide what a person is like? Are we accurate in our judgements? In *The Psychology of Interpersonal Perception* Perry R. Hinton sets out to answer these questions by looking at the psychological research on how these impressions arise.

He explains that our knowledge of other people is not strictly limited by the information we have about them. We process that information; we make inferences. Often these inferences concern another's personality – for example, inferring that a person who helps an old lady across a street is caring and that someone playing loud music on a public beach is selfish. Perry Hinton investigates how we make assumptions about people, how we develop explanations and expectations about their behaviour, and how these influence our judgements. Each chapter focuses on a different aspect of interpersonal perception, from nonverbal information and attraction to implicit ideas about personality and strategies of thought. Throughout the book Hinton uses practical examples – such as a job interview – to illustrate the relevance of the study of interpersonal perception to our everyday experiences.

The Psychology of Interpersonal Perception provides a comprehensive and up-to-date introduction to a fascinating subject. It will be of special interest to students and practitioners in a wide range of areas, including social psychology, communication studies, business and management, personnel and health studies.

Perry R. Hinton is a Senior Lecturer in Psychology at Coventry University.

The psychology of interpersonal perception

Perry R. Hinton

London and New York

First published in 1993 by
Routledge
11 New Fetter Lane, London EC4P 4EE

Simultaneously published in the USA and Canada by
Routledge
29 West 35th Street, New York, NY 10001

© 1993 Perry R. Hinton

Typeset in Garamond by LaserScript, Mitcham, Surrey
Printed and bound in Great Britain by
Mackays of Chatham PLC, Chatham, Kent

British Library Cataloguing in Publication Data
A catalogue record for this book is available from the British Library.

Library of Congress Cataloging in Publication Data
Hinton, Perry R., 1954–
    The psychology of interpersonal perception/Perry R. Hinton.
    p. cm.
    Includes bibliographical references and index.
    1. Social perception. I. Title.
    BF323.S63H56 1992
    153.6 – dc20   92-15272
                                                                CIP

ISBN 0–415–08451–2 (hbk)
ISBN 0–415–08452–0 (pbk)

To Anna, Anthony and Emma

Contents

Figures and tables

FIGURES

TABLES

Preface

Interpersonal perception is all about how we decide what other people are like and the meanings we give to their actions. Finding out how we make these decisions is a fascinating study that has occupied many psychologists. This book presents the outcome of much of this work.

For a number of years I have taught psychology to a range of students, from those majoring in the subject to others taking only a single course. While it is something of a cliché to say that we are all interested in people, the popularity of psychology in general and the enthusiasm of these students does lend support to this view. However, this wide appeal does mean that those who come to the study of psychology often have very different backgrounds and very different interests when it comes to applying the knowledge gained. In this book I have attempted to disseminate the findings of the psychological research in a way that allows the reader to appreciate the relevance of the material to their own area of interest without undermining the complexities of the subject matter. Each chapter begins with examples of everyday relevance and then gradually draws the reader into the more detailed psychological analysis.

I would like to express my gratitude to my colleagues and former colleagues who in their various ways have aided me in this endeavour, in particular Sue Wilkinson, Martyn Lee, Ian Connell and Rob Wilde; also the many students of Communication Studies who have attended my course entitled 'The Psychology of the Social Individual' and whose feedback has provided invaluable assistance in the writing of the book. Finally, I would like to thank my family for their constant support and encouragement.

Chapter 1

Introduction

Mary looked at the report on her desk. The company was doing very well. More orders were coming in. She felt very pleased with the first five years of MT Design. There were always problems but she welcomed the current ones in contrast to the difficulties of starting up the company. Now it was time to make some decisions. The most important one was the appointment of a new designer. It was only a small company and Peter and Susan, the other two designers, had been with her from the start. The six-member support staff were coping well with the workload. The bottleneck was definitely with the designers. It was with some relief that Susan and Peter received her decision and the three of them arranged a meeting later in the day to sort out the advertisement for the new post.

We are making judgements about other people all the time: deciding what they like, predicting what they will do, providing explanations for their behaviour. We might perceive a man who pushes past us as rude, a young woman in a business meeting as a high flyer, a child in a classroom as creative. In many instances these judgements have practical effects for the people involved: they influence whom we make friends with, who gets a job, who is suspected of a crime. We should not underestimate their importance: a jury's opinion of a man's honesty could sway the decision of guilt or innocence, a woman's career could depend on an interviewer's judgement of her competence. Yet, how do we make these judgements? What leads us to decide what a person is like? Are we accurate in our judgements? This book sets out to answer these questions.

It is not surprising that we can describe our family and friends: we know them well, we have experienced them on many occasions. We know less about acquaintances and yet it is not difficult to say what they are like or whether we like them or not. It does not take long to decide a man at a party is boring or a woman on a training course is friendly. With other people we might exchange only a few words in a brief encounter whilst waiting for a bus or in the check-out queue in a shop. And there are those whom we know about only through the mass media. Yet, despite the limited information, we are able to offer opinions about their personality and explanations for their behaviour. Think for a moment how you would describe our current political leaders. It is not difficult despite the lack of personal knowledge. It is even possible to discuss a person whom we have only read about in a newspaper article or seen briefly on television. Consider the conversations we have about those people who suddenly become 'famous for fifteen minutes', the heroes and heroines of disasters, the people with unusual hobbies, the participants in a scandal, all of whom get discussed on the bus or in the bar: 'He's a brave man'; 'She's a kind woman'; 'He's a nasty piece of work'; 'She was out for what she could get'; 'He was misunderstood'; 'I think she is better than they have made her out to be'. Sometimes the information we have can be very limited indeed, as in a fleeting glance at passers-by in the street, yet this may be enough for us to make certain judgements about them. If you pointed to a stranger and asked a friend: 'What do you think that person is like?' you might get an answer such as 'he looks like a businessman' or 'she looks like a student'. If you then go on to ask what businessmen or students are like you might get a long description. Thus it appears that even on the briefest of information we can form an impression of a person in our minds. We shall be looking in this book at the psychological research on how these impressions arise.

In a well-known quote the writer Christopher Isherwood said 'I am a camera', but a moment's thought reveals that we are more than simply recorders of information, like a camera or a tape-recorder, rather we are processors of information. We do not simply register the information that reaches our eyes and ears, we perceive it, we make sense of it. A moving pattern of different colours before our eyes is perceived to be a car travelling along the road. Similarly, our perception of a person goes beyond a simple registering of the way they look and sound: we make *inferences*. We might assume that a girl wearing glasses is intelligent or a young man in a black leather jacket likes heavy rock music. The information available to us is limited yet we can sum people up with little difficulty. But we might be wrong in our inferences: the girl might require remedial teaching and the young man prefer Mozart. This gives rise to the question: are we like Sherlock Holmes, able to interpret the most subtle of cues to a person's character and behaviour accurately, or are our inferences more like those of Dr Watson, somewhat inaccurate?

Often our interpersonal perceptions are judgements of personality: the characteristics people have, the kinds of people they are. But these judgements are more than that, they provide us with explanations of behaviour as well. If we believe that kind people help others because of their kindness, not to gain a reward, then seeing someone as kind provides an explanation for their kind acts. Furthermore, these judgements can result in expectations of behaviour: a kind person will behave kindly in the future. A personnel manager is unlikely to put in the time and effort to interview candidates to aid a decision on their competence without the belief that a person judged as competent will also be competent in the job.

As we shall see in this book, our expectations can also guide our judgements. Consider a car accident. If it involves a young man in a sports car, a witness might report that he was going too fast despite not being able to judge the car's speed. Here the witness is relying on a belief that young men drive fast. The assumptions we hold about people can therefore influence our recollection of events (e.g. Loftus, 1979). It is therefore of interest to know what assumptions we hold about people, how we group them into different types, such as young men and old men, and expect them to behave in certain ways. In this book we shall be endeavouring to explain how we develop these assumptions, explanations and expectations concerning people and their behaviour, and how they influence our judgements.

We can sum up the situation of interpersonal perception, in its simplest form, in the following manner. A person (the perceiver or observer), or persons, receives information about another person (the actor), or persons, and on the basis of that information makes inferences about them. There are a number of factors that could influence the judgement.

First, there is the information from the actor. This could be the behaviour of the actor as seen by the observer and include the actor's style of dress, hair-style, accent and other nonverbal information. The actor need not be present, the information could be a curriculum vitae, or résumé, or it might be a description by a third party, such as a friend arranging a blind date.

Second, we have the influence of the perceiver on this information. The perceiver might not be paying attention to the information or alternatively might spend time carefully considering it. The perceiver's own expectations about people can influence the judgement. These might be generally held stereotypes, such as a belief that librarians are quiet and responsible, or idiosyncratic views, such as a belief that tall people are not to be trusted. The ways in which the perceiver has learnt to explain people and events come into play here as well.

A third factor to consider is the relationship between the observer and the actor. You might view someone who creeps up behind you and slaps you on the back very differently if it happens to be a friend as opposed to a stranger. Different relationships, such as those of doctor–patient, employer–employee, colleagues, friends or lovers, will all lead to different assumptions, different expectations and different explanations concerning the information a perceiver receives. The familiarity of friends and lovers might be deemed unprofessional if displayed by doctors to patients or between employees; indeed, it might even be viewed as harassment.

There is also the social context to be considered. Interpersonal perception does not take place in a vacuum: a person singing loudly whilst taking a bath is likely to be perceived in a different way from someone doing the same in a library or at a funeral service. It is not surprising for a doctor to discuss the intimate details of a patient's medical history in surgery. Yet, we would not expect this to happen in a crowded street.

Finally, there is the cultural setting. Arabs stand closer to each other in conversation than Americans do (Hall, 1966). If they happen to be in conversation together there is the risk that the former will perceive the latter as *stand-offish* and the latter will see the former as *over-familiar*.

Thus the inferences we make about people from the information we have about them are potentially subject to each of these influences.

Each chapter in this book will focus on a different aspect of interpersonal perception, describing the psychological investigations into the topic. As we progress through the book we shall move gradually from the information concerning the actor, and how this is viewed, to a consideration of observer-related factors, how assumptions and expectations arise and how they influence judgement, to a consideration of the processes of thought a perceiver engages in. We shall also be considering the question of the accuracy of interpersonal perception, finishing with a number of examples where the results of the psychological research have important practical implications.

Each chapter will begin with the example of an imaginary small company seeking to recruit a new member of staff. Progressing through the book, we shall see the selection process develop until the successful candidate is chosen. The example has been chosen, not as a model of how selection should be undertaken, but as an illustration of the practical relevance of the study of interpersonal perception.

Chapter 2

Inferences from nonverbal information

Peter was first in the office that morning. He looked at the pile of application forms lying on his desk. He counted them and sighed. There were fifty in all. He decided to get a drink. When he sat down again he flicked through the forms as he sipped his coffee. The applicants had been asked to provide a small photograph. His eyes fell on the face of a youngish man in spectacles. He looks quite intelligent, thought Peter, picking up the form. Up close the man appeared rather bookish. Might not be dynamic enough, thought Peter, putting the form down once more. The next face was of an older woman, somewhat reminiscent of his Aunt Audrey who had been an inveterate traveller. Now she was a dynamic person, thought Peter, picking up the woman's form. He was somewhat surprised to find that the woman had not travelled widely. He was just looking at the photograph of an attractive female candidate when Susan entered the office.

'How is it going?' she asked.

'Well,' said Peter arranging the forms into a pile, 'I haven't started yet.' He divided the pile into two.

Susan sat down opposite him and a bundle of forms landed on the desk in front of her.

'Your half,' said Peter with a smile.

Susan looked down at the forms before her.

'Good grief,' she said looking at the photograph on the top form. 'He looks as if he's just crawled through a hedge.'

'Let me have a look,' said Peter moving round to look over her shoulder. 'I say, you're quite right.' The man's hair in the photograph was tousled and the collar of his shirt was crumpled. Even the expression on the man's face was one of surprise.

'I'm not sure he could find his way here for interview, let alone do the job,' said Peter with a laugh.

Susan joined in the laughter but then stopped suddenly as she glanced down the form.

'Oh, I don't know,' she said, pointing at the section on past experience. His employment record was impeccable.

'Well I never,' said Peter. 'I wouldn't have guessed it.'

Mary looked in at the door.

'Have you got all the forms?' she asked.

'Yes,' replied Susan with a wry smile, patting the pile of papers before her.

'Let me know when you've worked out the short-list,' said Mary as she left.

You are visiting friends in a strange town. You decide to do some sightseeing while your friends are otherwise engaged and as a favour you offer to take some books back to the library for them. Unfortunately, you are lost, so you decide you must ask someone the way. You approach a woman with a briefcase, she's probably a businesswoman who works nearby, but she appears in a hurry so you look for someone else. A man and a woman carrying shopping are smiling and chatting. They look friendly so you ask them. They are very pleasant but do not know the way. A bored-looking man at a bus stop shrugs his shoulders but an elderly woman behind him smiles and offers directions. On the way to the library an unshaven man in old clothes stops you and says he's lost his wallet and would you give him some money for the bus. You don't believe him but give him something. At the library, the librarian has her hair in a tight bun and looks very severe. She informs you curtly that a book is overdue. You pay the fine and on your return tell your friend what an unpleasant woman she was.

You can see from the above example how we are summing people up all the time, making snap judgements about them: what they are like, what they do, whether they are telling the truth. Yet the only information we have about these people is that gained from a brief encounter. We know nothing about them except from what we can see and hear. This shows the power of nonverbal information and the inferences we make from it. These snap judgements in turn might then influence how we behave. I once worked for a company where the computing staff were allowed to dress casually. A computer-programmer colleague and I were washing our hands in a cloak-room when a man from the 'smartly dressed' section of the company walked in and, seeing my colleague, proceeded to congratulate him on mending the sinks, having mistaken him for a plumber. My colleague was too dumbfounded to say anything and the man left unaware of his mistake. In more important encounters, such as a visit to the doctor's or an interview for a job, nonverbal information might have important consequences. If we look right for the job we might increase our chances of getting it.

These everyday examples of inferences from nonverbal information lead us to ask two interesting questions. What specific inferences do people make on the bases of different sources of nonverbal information? Are these inferences valid? In this chapter we shall be looking at the psychological research that has attempted to answer these questions.

THE TYPES OF NONVERBAL INFORMATION

When we encounter a person there are a number of sources of nonverbal information presented to us. First, there are a person's physical characteristics, such as skin colour, height or face shape. These are readily available to us, even at a quick glance. Normally these change little over time, although plastic surgery for cosmetic reasons is becoming more popular, and in this chapter we can see why this is. Then there are the more dynamic aspects of the body, the way a person moves, talks, and other characteristic actions. These require some effort to change, as Eliza Doolittle and many budding actors have found. Yet there are some things that we can change easily: how we comb our hair, which clothes to wear, our choice of jewellery. We can use these to project a deliberate image: the smart-suited business executive or the punk, for example. Finally, there are dynamic aspects of appearance, such as a smile or a frown. The combination of all these sources of information gives an observer a rich and varied set of information with which to judge us.

THE RELATIVELY UNCHANGING ASPECTS OF THE PERSON: OUR PHYSICAL CHARACTERISTICS

Throughout history people have believed that a person's physical make-up reflects their 'underlying' character. Physiognomy, the features of the face, and physique, a person's body shape, have been seen as the two key aspects of the body that reveal the personality. Fat people have been perceived as jolly and people with high foreheads as intelligent. From the ancient Greeks to the present day, many authors have claimed a link between physical characteristics and personality traits.

Physiognomy

In *Jane Eyre* by Charlotte Brontë the eponymous heroine studies her employer, Mr Rochester, as he sits by the fire:

> I knew my traveller with his broad and jetty eyebrows; his square forehead, made squarer by the horizontal sweep of his black hair. I recognised his decisive nose, more remarkable for character than beauty; his full nostrils, denoting, I thought, choler; his grim mouth, chin, and jaw – yes, all three were very grim, and no mistake.
>
> (Brontë, 1847, p.142)

This is not just a physical description of Mr Rochester's face but also of his character. But why should we assume that full nostrils indicate choler? What justification is there for assuming a relationship between physiognomy and personality characteristics? Allport (1937) lists three reasons, drawn from the *Physiognomonica*, said to have been written by Aristotle, the oldest known work on the subject. The first relies on the belief that similarity between faces, particularly human and animal, indicates similarity of character. If a face has a similarity with an animal, say a fox, then the person has the characteristics of that animal, and is foxy and sly. The second explanation relies on stereotyped beliefs about people. If a man is very dark then he must have the characteristics of dark people, such as Ethiopians, who were stereotypically seen by the the the author of the work as cowardly. Thus, the man must be a coward. The third explanation is based on the view that a person's character will leave traces in the facial expression. Hence a mouth that appears to be smiling even in repose indicates a cheerful personality.

There are two aspects to physiognomic analysis (Allport, 1937). The first is a consideration of the *bony structure* of the face, which is due to our genetic make-up. Physiognomists performing this analysis make associations between this structure and personality, say, for example, that an aquiline nose indicates nobility of character. Here we see that if these associations are made then the physiognomists are also assuming a genetic origin to personality, as nose shape, for example, is something we are born with. The second aspect of the analysis is *muscular set*. Here it is assumed that a person's experience will have influenced their facial appearance and hence experiential characteristics of personality can be read from the face. The sour man will have developed a sour-faced look, his facial muscles held taut and his mouth turned down in displeasure.

In Victorian times there were attempts to identify the criminal and other personalities from facial characteristics (Lombroso and Ferrero, 1896). Now we would question the assumptions upon which these relationships were based. Why assume a link between facial features and crime? Does this assume that people are born criminals? Without questioning the assumptions very seriously, there is evident scope for this sort of theory to be used as a justification for discrimination against the unfortunates who have 'criminal' features, despite their not actually having committed any crime.

In the present century psychologists have attempted to test out some of these physiognomic claims experimentally. Essentially the psychologists asked the following question: is the trait inferred from the physical feature revealed by other measures of personality? If a woman has a long nose (or whatever) indicating meanness but she often gives to charity and her friends regard her as generous then it casts doubt on the validity of the physiognomic inference.

A good example of this experimental work comes from Hull (1928). He selected a group of forty female students who all knew each other. He asked them to rate each other on a number of personality characteristics while looking at a photograph of the face of the student they were rating. He then had the photographs rated on the same characteristics by subjects who did not know the person in the photograph. He was interested in seeing whether the latter group, who had only the facial features on which to make their judgements, made similar ratings to the former group who had personal experience of the individuals. Within each group of raters there was a high degree of consensus as to which person had which characteristics. However, there was little agreement between the groups, so the personality judgements on the basis of the face alone did not match up to judgements made through personal experience. The only two characteristics which showed some agreement were beauty and intelligence. The agreement on beauty is understandable if we assume that both sets of raters were considering physical beauty, as the photograph would show this quite well. This leaves intelligence. Is this the one characteristic that we can accurately read from facial features?

The answer, according to the results of a study by Brunswik (1956), is no. In this experiment twenty-five subjects were presented with photographs of the faces of forty-six soldiers. The soldiers knew each other but they were not acquainted with the subjects. The subjects rated each face on a number of traits (including intelligence and likeability). These ratings were then compared with other measures of these traits. IQ was used as a measure of intelligence and the soldiers' likeability judgements of each other formed the measure of likeability. The ratings on the basis of facial features did not match the values on the other tests, implying that the subjects were not able to judge these characteristics very well. Interestingly, again, there was a high degree of consensus amongst the subjects on which faces looked intelligent and which did not. One explanation of this is that there was a shared stereotype (see Chapter 4 on the nature of stereotypes) of what makes an 'intelligent face' even though it does not correspond with other measures of intelligence.

The experiments showed that, despite the lack of support for their validity, there are commonly held beliefs associating physiognomic cues and personality and these are worthy of psychological study in their own right. Further research questions arise from this: which facial features are commonly believed to indicate which personality traits? What explanations can be proposed for these associations? This was the question that Secord and his colleagues set out to examine in the 1950s.

These researchers employed photographs of faces in their experiments. Subjects rated the faces on a range of characteristics and these ratings were then compared to the physical features of the faces to see if there was any association between the two. A consistent finding in a number of the studies was that there was a high degree of agreement between the subjects on the characteristics they attributed to particular faces, suggesting that there are commonly held beliefs about the personality characteristics that can be 'read' from the face (Secord, 1958).

Secord (1958) argued that these judgements are influenced by *cultural factors* and *expressive cues.* A woman whose hair was well-groomed and had used cosmetics appropriately was seen by the judges as attractive (Secord and Muthard, 1955). This inference appears to rely on culturally based expectations concerning hair-styles and use of make-up. Also, widely held prejudices appeared to inform certain judgements, such as the unfavourable characteristics attributed to dark-skinned faces (Secord *et al.*, 1954). The importance of expressive cues was illustrated by the high correlation found between the feature 'mouth curvature' and the judgement 'easy going'. A smile indicates friendliness and a face that appears to be smiling is inferred to indicate a pleasant person.

Secord (1958, p.305) quotes an unpublished study showing the reciprocal relationship between beliefs concerning personality characteristics and facial features. In this study the subjects were given the following descriptions and asked to rate the facial features of the two men.

A: This man is warmhearted and honest. He has a good sense of humour and is intelligent and unbiased in his opinion. He is responsible and self-confident with an air of refinement.

B: This man is ruthless and brutal. He is extremely hostile, quick-tempered and overbearing. He is well-known for his boorish and vulgar manner and is a very domineering and unsympathetic character.

The subjects had no difficulty in the task and rated the two men differently on twenty-five out of thirty-two physiognomic characteristics: the former was seen as having average features and the latter with more abnormal features. It appears that people have very clear ideas about what they expect certain personalities to look like as well as vice versa. We see this effect in the majority of actors chosen to play the heroes and villains throughout the history of the movies.

Five kinds of inference process are proposed by Secord (1958) to account for the results of his studies. The first is *temporal extension*: a momentary expression is seen as an enduring characteristic: a smiling face is seen as indicating a good-tempered person. The second process is called *parataxis* where we generalize from someone we know to someone we do not know. If your mother is warm and kind then you might infer that a woman who looks like your mother is also warm and kind. Third, there is *categorization*. This is similar to stereotyping as we categorize someone as a member of a group (such as sex, age, race) on the basis of their face and infer that they have the characteristics we believe are held by that group. The fourth kind of inference, *functional quality*, is based on the functions of the various parts of the face: the mouth is for talking, the eyes for seeing. Thin lips, pressed together, are seen as indicating someone who is 'tight-lipped' in their personality as well. Glasses indicate someone who reads a lot, so by inference they must be intelligent. Finally, there is *metaphorical generalization*, where the inference is more abstract, based on a number of physical attributes. The woman with thin lips and her hair in a tight bun might lead to a judgement of a severe personality which in turn might lead to a further judgement of censoriousness.

All five of these factors provide reasons why personality judgements from faces are common and also why there is often so much agreement about which features indicate which characteristics, despite the lack of supporting evidence. Indeed the pervasiveness of the belief that there exists a relationship between facial features and personality characteristics was supported in a survey of university students where it was found that over 90 per cent held this view (Liggett, 1974).

More recently, Berry and McArthur (1986) have studied the perception of adults based on their degree of facial babyfacedness. Not surprisingly, they found that the babyfaced adult was perceived as being warmer, more submissive, more honest and physically weaker than the less babyfaced adult, indicating a perception of child-like qualities in the person. Berry and Brownlow (1989) conducted an interesting study where photographs of faces were judged on their facial babyishness by subjects who were not acquainted with them. The people in the photographs also answered questions about their physical power, social power, warmth and masculinity. The inference of child-like qualities from a babyface would predict babyfaced individuals to be low on physical and social power, high on warmth and with more feminine characteristics. However, for male faces, only warmth showed the expected relationship with babyfacedness and, for female faces, babyfacedness correlated only with physical power. Whilst it is interesting to speculate on the reasons for these particular findings, three out of the four child-like characteristics were not found to relate to babyfacedness, again questioning the validity of the physiognomic personality inferences made by the subjects in the earlier study.

In conclusion, it has often been shown that frequently there is agreement as to which facial features indicate which personality characteristics. However, it has also been shown that these inferences have rarely been supported by other evidence.

Physique

That people have assumed a link between body form and personality is shown by the numerous occasions where it is indicated in literature throughout history. For example, in the play *Julius Caesar* (Act I, Scene 2), Shakespeare has Caesar say:

Let me have men about me that are fat,
Sleek-headed men, and such as sleep o' nights.
Yon Cassius has a lean and hungry look.
He thinks too much. Such men are dangerous.

Concern about male physique was exploited in the body-building advertisements of the 1950s arguing that the physically small, weak man, the 'seven-stone weakling', had less fun in life, was less attractive to women and couldn't hold his own in male company. Whilst people may not talk of 'seven-stone weaklings' very often nowadays, other terms have emerged. It is not difficult to picture the physique of a 'wimp', a term commonly used in the 1980s and 1990s. The wimp also has a personality which we can describe without much difficulty: introverted, little interest in sport and so on. Similarly, fat people may be assumed to be jolly or a man of athletic build as lacking in intelligence.

There is some evidence to support a relationship between physique and personality. The German psychiatrist Kretschmer (1925 [1921]) studied the physiques of his patients and classified their disorders by his system of body types. He found that schizophrenics tended to have an *asthenic* physique (long and thin) with manic-depressives being *pyknic* (short and fat). He inferred that normal individuals also had characteristics that could be linked to physique. Whilst his system of classification was quite complex, in essence he saw the asthenic as more introverted and less dominant than the pyknic. There are a number of problems with this work, such as our tendency to get fatter as we age which could well have confounded his data (Hall and Lindzey, 1985), but it is interesting to note that it appears to accord with certain common beliefs about body shape and personality.

The psychologist Sheldon was aware of Kretschmer's work and in turn developed his own theory relating physique to personality. Sheldon (1940) examined photographs of thousands of people and from this work argued that there were three main components to a body's shape: endomorphy, mesomorphy and ectomorphy, with a person's physique being some combination of the three. At the extremes of body shape were the *endomorph* (high in endomorphy and low in the other components) whose physique was rounded and fat, the *mesomorph* who was muscly and athletic and the *ectomorph* who was thin and with little muscle.

Sheldon (1942) also undertook a study of temperament, assessing the personality of some 200 men over five years. Comparing temperament to physique, he found that there were clear correlations between certain personality characteristics and body shape. Endomorphs tended to enjoy food and comfort, to be fairly even-tempered, amiable and relaxed, with a need for people: desiring affection, being sociable. The more energetic mesomorphs enjoyed physical action as well as being bold, ruthless and aggressive with a desire for power and domination. The ectomorph was more of an introvert, highly strung and restrained, seeking privacy and solitude when troubled.

Sheldon, as a constitutional psychologist, saw the relationship as arising out of constitutional factors: our hereditary biology influences both our physique and our temperament. However, there are alternative explanations. First, our physique might influence the sort of activities we engage in. The large, strong man is likely to be more successful as a rugby forward than the small man and hence to choose this activity. Second, other people's expectations of our behaviour can have a self-fulfilling effect (see Chapter 4). Ectomorphs might be stereotyped as introverted but clever and hence more likely to be selected for 'back-room' jobs despite their actual characteristics. Expecting someone to be tough or jolly might encourage them to act in that way. Also, it has been suggested (Humphreys, 1957) that Sheldon's particularly high correlations could have been influenced by his own beliefs about personality and physique. As he made both the physique and temperament ratings he could have unconsciously biased the findings in favour of his beliefs.

Despite the equivocal nature of their validity there are clearly commonly held beliefs concerning the relationship of personality characteristics to body shape. Wells and Siegel (1961) asked subjects to rate silhouettes of the three body types on various characteristics. Mesomorphs were seen as stronger and more adventurous, whereas ectomorphs were seen as more quiet, nervous and tense, and endomorphs as more good-natured and dependent. Mesomorphic men were seen as very masculine and slim ectomorphic women as very feminine. These are obviously similar to Sheldon's findings.

More recently, Ryckman et al. (1989) asked student subjects to rate endomorphs, mesomorphs and ectomorphs on a range of personality characteristics. Mesomorphs were viewed more favourably than endomorphs, with the former viewed as healthier, more hard-working and better-looking than the latter. Ectomorphs were seen positively, for example, intelligent and neat with more friends than endomorphs, possibly indicating a changing view of ectomorphy over the years. Ryckman et al. also looked at the differences between the sexes, finding that female endomorphs were seen as neater and cleaner than the male endomorphs. Male mesomorphs were perceived as less intelligent and sloppier but with more friends than their female counterparts. The female ectomorph was viewed as better-looking with more friends and less likely to be teased but less intelligent than the male ectomorphs.

The negative ratings of endomorphs can have unfortunate consequences. Fat people suffer from discrimination in jobs, salaries and college entrance (Argyle, 1988). This appears to arise from the inference people make from obesity to characteristics such as laziness, greed or lack of self-control as explanations of their size. When an alternative explanation was provided (such as a thyroid problem) the prejudice was less but still there (DeJong, 1980).

We can see, therefore, that irrespective of the accuracy of our judgements, there are definite expectations about the personalities we believe are associated with particular body shapes. Clearly, these beliefs could be influential in a range of situations from employment selection to the judgement of people one meets at a party.

Height

For men, shortness is perceived as a disadvantage in a number of respects. We have the expression 'walk tall', implying that the man of strong character stands tall to face the world. The 1989 US Presidential candidate, Michael Dukakis, stood on a raised platform in a televised debate with the taller George Bush, so that each man appeared the same height. Unfortunately it did not help him, as the taller man won the race to the White House as he has invariably done (Feldman, 1971).

The belief that the taller man is more competent than the smaller man is borne out by evidence showing that the taller man was chosen more often over a smaller but equally qualified man for a job and that taller graduate men received higher starting salaries than their smaller counterparts (Feldman, 1971). However, the accuracy of this perception is not supported by the evidence: taller men perform no better in their jobs than smaller men (Argyle, 1988).

It appears, therefore, that, irrespective of its validity, there is a strong perception of greater competence in taller men. This was also demonstrated by Wilson (1968) in a study where students judged the height of a man introduced as a student, demonstrator, lecturer, senior lecturer or professor. His perceived height rose with his increased status by over five inches!

It has been known for the smaller leading man to be positioned in a film 'take' so that he will appear taller than his leading lady. This expectation, that a man should be taller than a woman in a relationship, was borne out by Gillis and Avis (1980) who found, in their study, that men preferred a smaller female partner and women a taller male partner.

How unfair for the smaller man to be perceived as both less capable and less desirable than the taller man. There is some comfort in noting that we should be careful in isolating a single factor from the many that influence our perception of people and remember that it is not just height that is involved in job and mate selection. The actors Mickey Rooney and Dudley Moore have done rather well as leading men despite their smaller than average stature. It is also worth noting that women's height does not have the same influence on perceivers as men's height (Hatfield and Sprecher, 1986).

Stigma – unusual physical features

If we consider the question logically, the presence of scars, disfigurement, deformity and disability should not influence our interpretation of the personality of the individual. Yet the evidence, both anecdotal and experimental, shows that this is not the case. A BBC radio programme for disabled people is ironically entitled *Does He Take Sugar?*, noting the common though erroneous inference that physical disability implies a lack of ability in other respects. As Goffman (1963) has noted, people infer that some form of unusual physical characteristic indicates an abnormality of personality. The title of Goffman's book *Stigma* sums up the inference. Originally the word was used for a mark branded on a criminal or slave but now it has a connotation of a blot on one's character.

Experiments have again revealed these beliefs. Bull (1979) presented subjects with pictures of a man or woman's face either scarred or unscarred and asked them to rate the person on a number of personality characteristics. For the man, scarring led the person to be seen as less warm and affectionate, more dishonest-looking, less sincere and attractive, and with fewer friends. For the woman, scarring led to her being seen as more dishonest-looking, less attractive and more humourless. The reverse also seems to be the case: people with unpleasant personality characteristics are also assumed to have abnormal features (Secord, 1958).

Voice

At school one day, a teacher of my acquaintance, frustrated that every time he went to speak a pupil interrupted him, exclaimed: 'Every time I open my mouth some fool speaks!' It was only the explosion of laughter that made him realize the inadvertent comment on his own personality. We may not be able to detect a fool, but we can infer a person's age and sex, even from a brief utterance (Scherer and Giles, 1979), with accent revealing one's regional background. In Britain, a person with a 'home counties' accent is attributed higher status than a Cockney or Birmingham speaker (Argyle, 1988). A person's voice can also be used to characterize them with the regional stereotype associated with their accent.

During the 1930s and 1940s a number of psychological studies investigated the relationship between voice and personality. The result of this work showed that, while listeners agreed on the traits associated with different voices, these trait attributions were seldom valid (Addington, 1968). Judging a person by their voice might bring agreement from other people but not from other measures of personality. As Addington (1968, p.493) points out: 'Whether we like it or not, our voices do elicit stereotyped personality judgements.' So what is it about a voice that makes one believe that a person is intelligent, sexy or sensitive? Addington (1968) had two men and two women with voice-training experience speak passages of text in different ways. The passages were rated by one group of listeners on vocal characteristics and by another group on personality characteristics. Addington found that a faster speaking rate made the person appear more animated and extroverted, irrespective of whether it was a male or female voice. Increasing pitch made a male voice sound more dynamic, feminine and aesthetically inclined but a female voice more dynamic and extrovert. The results for the variation in voice quality are shown in Table 1.1.

Table 1.1 Personality judgements on the basis of voice quality

Voice quality (high in:)	Male voice	Female voice
Breathiness	younger and more artistic	more feminine, pretty, petite, effervescent, highly strung and shallower
Thinness	no relationships found	less mature but (curiously) increased sense of humour and sensitivity
Flatness	Similar results for both sexes: more masculine, sluggish, colder and withdrawn	
Nasality	Similar results for both sexes: having a range of socially undesirable characteristics	
Tenseness	cantankerous (i.e. older and unyielding)	younger, more emotional, feminine, high-strung and less intelligent
Throatiness	older, more realistic, mature, sophisticated, well-adjusted	more oafish (unintelligent, ugly, careless, uninteresting and others)
Orotundity (full and round)	more energetic, healthy, artistic, sophisticated, proud, interesting and enthusiastic	livelier, more gregarious, and aesthetically sensitive but also more proud and humourless

Source: adapted from Addington, 1968.

Knowledge of these voice stereotypes is clearly useful when casting for a radio play. One suspects also that certain politicians alter their voices to try and appear to have more positive characteristics. It is interesting to consider how judgements based on voice differ from other impressions of a person. Consider someone you have met after only speaking to them on the telephone. Did they look and behave as you expected from their voice alone?

OUR CHANGING APPEARANCE: THE WAY WE CHOOSE TO LOOK

Our physiognomy and shape are relatively hard to change; it takes plastic surgery, body building or dieting and even then we may still not have changed much. Yet there is much of our appearance that is relatively easy to alter, particularly the choice of clothes we wear and the style we choose for our hair.

Hair and hair-styles

Facial and bodily hair are simply biological features of being human yet they take on a social significance: young men become eager to grow facial hair to appear older (and then shave it off!) and an older balding man may purchase a toupee to appear younger. Chest hair on a man can be seen as a sign of masculinity and is often a feature of the leotarded circus strong-man who bends iron bars, yet it is removed in body-building contests. And there are products aimed at women for the removal of 'unwanted' body hair. Thus body hair can be seen as a social cue, with conventional meanings, used to impute a characteristic such as masculinity to the person. The same is true for facial hair. Bearded men have consistently been found to be perceived as more mature and more masculine than non-bearded men (Addison, 1989) but not always as attractive (Feinman and Gill, 1977).

Hair-styles are influenced by fashion and other cultural factors, but different hair-styles can also lead to the inference of different personality characteristics (Roll and Verinis, 1971). They can also be used to indicate group membership (Argyle, 1988): the oiled quiff of the Teddy boy, the long hair of the hippy, the very short hair of the skinhead, the mohican style of the punk. An observer might then use this information to stereotype the person on the basis of this group identification (see Chapter 4).

Hair length, particularly in men since the 1960s' hippies, also has an influence on the perceiver. Peterson and Curran (1976) found that female students not only preferred shorter-haired males but also saw them as more intelligent, moral and adjusted. The women preferring the short-haired men tended to be politically more conservative and those preferring the long-haired men tended to be more liberal, implying that male political views were inferred from their hair length.

Hair length also depends to a certain extent on the social group (Argyle, 1988), with different groups having different *norms*: it is not acceptable for a man to have long hair in the army but it is usually acceptable at college. Going against the expectations of a social group can have costs to the person, such as rejection by the group (Secord and Backman, 1974). In the early 1970s I recall an 'old hand' warning prospective freshmen not to go to college with short hair as they might not be talked to!

As well as hair-style, there is also hair colour with its attendant inferences. Lawson (1971) asked subjects to rate 'redheaded female', 'brunette female' and 'blonde female' on a number of personality characteristics. The results illustrated commonly held beliefs concerning hair colour and personality, with redheads seen as emotional and fiery, blondes as attractive but dumb and brunettes as sensible and dependable. Weir and Fine-Davis (1989) followed up this study, using photographs of the same woman with red, blonde and brunette hair. They found that male perceivers, unlike female perceivers, saw the blonde female as less intelligent and less aggressive than the brunette. And both sets of perceivers saw the blonde as more popular than the brunette. Weir and Fine-Davis argue that the difference between the sexes might be due to the men preferring to see blondes as dumb. With the redheaded female both male and female perceivers saw her as more aggressive than the blonde and the brunette, in accordance with the 'fiery redhead' stereotype.

Glasses

Whilst the wearing of spectacles has the obvious implication that the person has poor eyesight, this is not the only inference made by a perceiver. Thornton (1944) found that a person wearing glasses was seen as more intelligent, dependable and industrious than when not wearing them; and Hamid (1972) found that spectacles made a person less attractive. Bartolini *et al.* (1988) found that glasses gave a person a greater perceived authority, and sunglasses less authority, than no glasses at all. They also found that women appeared more honest wearing glasses and men appeared less honest in sunglasses. But they did not find a difference in perceived attractiveness with the different types of eyewear.

An important point to note here is that usually in these studies subjects rate a person in a photograph on a variety of characteristics. In some photographs the person is wearing glasses, in others not, and the ratings are compared across these categories. Thus, the subjects have only the static image from which to make their judgement. In an interesting experiment by Argyle and McHenry (1971), subjects, on viewing an individual wearing glasses for fifteen seconds doing nothing, rated them 14 points higher in IQ than when they were not, in support of Thornton's findings. However, this effect disappeared when the person was seen taking part in a conversation for five minutes. This result indicates that the effect of spectacles, like a number of the effects of nonverbal information, needs to be considered carefully in the context of other factors: wearing glasses may influence only initial or fleeting impressions.

Why should spectacles be viewed as conferring intelligence and authority on the wearer? It may be due to a false inference on the basis of the functional quality of glasses (Secord, 1958). Spectacles imply reading and reading implies knowledge. From the inference of knowledgeability one might assume high status and thence authority. Advertisers will often use an actor wearing glasses to give the impression of a scientist or expert talking about their product. The inferred knowledgeability, however, might be lost if the inference is not supported by additional information, such as what they say.

Another aspect of spectacle wearing is the inference that the wearer is conventional, unimaginative and shy (Hamid, 1968). Our stereotyped image of a bank clerk is of a timid spectacle wearer. We see this aspect of wearing glasses most dramatically in the Superman character, where mild-mannered Clark Kent throws off his glasses (and his clothes!) before flying off as Superman.

One outcome of this research is that if you are sending a photograph to a prospective employer whom you want to impress with your intelligence it might be worth-while putting on your glasses, whereas if the photograph is destined for an explorers' expedition or a dating agency, contact lens may be better!

Clothes

Clearly we wear clothes for comfort and protection: very few of us would risk a cold winter's day or a motorcycle ride without them. Yet even when we could comfortably go naked, such as on a warm day or in an air-conditioned building, we still choose to wear clothes. There are concepts of decency which we conform to. Clothes therefore have a social function: the wearer is communicating social information by their choice of clothes that a perceiver may use to make inferences about the person.

A key aspect of our clothes is that they 'tell' a social perceiver about our membership of a particular social group (Argyle, 1988; Kaiser, 1985). In some circumstances we are obliged to wear certain clothes, such as the uniforms that go with certain occupations. The clothes have a clear meaning to the perceiver: this person is a police officer, commissionaire or railway guard, for example. The uniform itself can then have an effect on the perception of the person wearing it. For the police, in uniform they are seen as more competent and reliable than when out of uniform (Singer and Singer, 1985) and having more authority when wearing a police helmet or hat than without it (Volpp and Lennon, 1988). In a hospital, clothes indicate who are the patients, nurses and doctors (Argyle, 1988). We can also choose to show our membership of a particular group by selecting certain clothes to indicate that we are a 'punk' or the supporter of a particular sports team. Even our membership of a particular social class can be determined by our clothes. Sissons (1971) had an actor ask passers-by for the time on Padding-ton Station, London. Their reactions were more positive when the actor was dressed and spoke in an upper middle-class manner than when he appeared working class.

Clothes may also be used as indicators of the wearer's personality. But this must be seen in the context of the clothing conventions of the occasion. There are socially defined norms about what clothes we are expected to wear for particular situations, such as a wedding or a funeral. These may be formal rules, as at a black-tie party. If people go against convention, they may be excluded from the occasion: a man may be refused entry to a restaurant without a tie or to a discotheque wearing jeans. There are also informal codes of dress that we learn and follow, such as dressing in one's 'Sunday best' for church. There is no formal requirement but we may be frowned on for wearing beach clothes in church. Thus, certain conventions about appropriate clothing develop for many situations and we learn to expect people to dress according to these conventions. But what happens if people dress in an unexpected way, such as in formal attire at an informal gathering or vice versa? The perceiver is left with a problem of explanation: did the person choose these clothes because of the sort of person they are (conservative or unconventional) or because of other reasons (they have just come from a business meeting without time to change)? This is a question of attribution, that we shall be looking at in Chapter 8. Unexpected behaviour requires explanation in a way expected behaviour does not. It has been suggested that, if we believe that someone has a choice in the matter and that their behaviour is unexpected, then we have a tendency to see this as indicating a character trait (Jones and McGillis, 1976). If a person chooses bold, bright colours when everyone else is soberly dressed we may well perceive them as extroverted.

How do we make sense of inconsistencies of dress, such as the smart businesswoman wearing training shoes, an example considered by Kaiser (1985)? Again we seek to explain the unexpected, the assumption being that we expect people to dress consistently. If we find out that the woman walks to work and changes her shoes on arrival we need not attribute specific personality characteristics to her as this provides us with a convincing explanation of the inconsistency (Kaiser, 1985). However, various deviations from conventional dress may be used to infer personality: the man with odd socks and a smart but crumpled suit may well be viewed as a disorganized person.

Certain clothes can also become associated with particular types of people. A man wearing a sober suit might be perceived as a conservative individual and a woman in a smock dress as politically 'green'. Evidence of this inference comes from Cahoon and Edmonds (1989) who showed male and female students photographs of the same woman dressed either in slacks and a blouse, judged as conservative, or a revealing dress, judged as sexy. The subjects rated the woman when wearing the revealing dress to be more sexually active, to be more flirtatious, willing to use sex appeal to her advantage and more willing to be unfaithful if married than when she was wearing the more conservative clothing.

Clothing styles change frequently with changing fashions and perceptions can change with them. Flared trousers and bright colours were fashionable in the 1970s but rare in the 1980s. Thus the perception of the same outfit could be very different at different times: sometimes fashionable, sometimes out-moded. When the movie star Clark Gable removed his shirt in the 1932 film *Red Dust* to reveal a bare chest the sale of vests reputedly fell. However, dressing fashionably as opposed to conservatively can have costs as well as benefits (Kaiser, 1985), particularly where a conservative style is seen as indicating competence (see Chapter 10).

Bodily adornment, such as cosmetics and jewellery, can be used to supplement clothing as a fashion style (Morris, 1977). The man with tight trousers and an open-necked shirt might also be wearing a medallion. Similarly, the chunky gold watch and other gold jewellery add to the expensive clothes of the extrovert football or boxing manager. Adornment can be functional: spectacles are usually worn to improve eyesight but the choice of black-rimmed 'Buddy Holly style' or round gold-rimmed 'granny' glasses (like those worn by John Lennon) is likely to be dictated by preferred style or fashion. False hair, eyelashes and finger-nails, like cosmetics, can all be applied to enhance the attractiveness of the individual or to project a particular style. Adornment such as a wig can be used both as a fashion accessory or, as is the case with judges, as part of a uniform. Indeed, the dress sword of the soldier is now part of a ceremonial uniform rather than a weapon to be drawn in anger. But there are other forms of adornment that cannot be removed at will: tattoos and certain kinds of body mutilation. These permanent forms of adornment are often used as signs of group membership in societies where being a member of a group has important implications for an individual, with the adornment as evidence of initiation into the group (Morris, 1977). In Japan, highly decorative tattoos mark out the gangster fraternity, to the extent that some hotels will not admit individuals with them.

THE DYNAMIC ASPECTS OF THE PERSON: HOW WE LOOK, SOUND AND MOVE

We are not mannequins, but walking, talking human beings and the dynamic aspects of the person can also be used as a basis for inference. The tone of voice of a shop assistant might lead us to view them as rude or a smile as friendly. These transient pieces of nonverbal information may be taken to indicate a more permanent aspect of the individual, possibly through temporal extension (Secord, 1958).

We can detect emotion in others quite well. The large number of facial muscles allow for a rich source of expression. Yet there are about half a dozen facial expressions that appear to be universally recognized as indicating specific emotions. Happiness, surprise, fear, anger, sadness and disgust or contempt are all 'read' quite correctly from the face. Other emotions cannot be so accurately detected (Ekman, 1982). Emotions are also expressed through the voice and we are very good at detecting these, although this does provide a difficulty for the psychologist in distinguishing the vocal characteristics of the different emotions (Scherer, 1986). With active emotions like joy and anger we speak louder and faster with a higher pitch, but we speak more harshly with anger. With more passive emotions like boredom or sadness we speak more softly and slowly with a lower pitch and when we are depressed we speak with less intonation (Scherer, 1986). Posture can also be used to judge emotion. A person slumps in their seat when bored and leans forward when interested, and we are able to detect these feelings successfully (Bull, 1987).

We also have expectations about people's behaviour in interaction. We usually smile on greeting friends. If one doesn't we will ask what is wrong. People don't smile when they are being serious and an unsmiling face can be used to indicate dominance (Keating *et al.*, 1981). Being stared at by a stranger can make us very uncomfortable (Argyle, 1988) but not being looked at enough during conversation can lead to a judgement of inattentiveness or lack of interest (Kleinke, 1986). A person who uses gaze to show interest may be viewed positively (Argyle, 1988). Coupled with other nonverbal signals, such as smiling in the right places, this can lead to a person being seen as friendly and attractive.

But there are cultural differences in the degree to which we display emotions and these can lead to judgements of character. The Japanese and English cultures have traditionally eschewed emotional expression. The traditional perception of the English as reserved, demonstrated by the 'stiff upper lip', is often seen as a stereotypical characteristic attributed to them by people from more expressive cultures, such as Americans or French. Again, it is the unexpected that requires explanation and hence the person expressing an unexpected emotion or not expressing an expected one may be taken as indicating a personality characteristic: the unexpressive Englishman is reserved, the scowling shop assistant is unpleasant.

THE OVERALL EFFECT

We must be careful in isolating different appearance factors as we usually observe a complete person, rather than just the face (Berry and Brownlow, 1989) or from the neck downwards (Cahoon and Edmonds, 1989). As we saw earlier, listening to a speaker can reduce the effect of his or her spectacles on our judgement of intelligence (Argyle and McHenry, 1971). We should bear in mind that a number of sources of nonverbal information are usually available to us and the combination of information can lead to a different interpretation than the isolated elements. Here it is the conflict or inconsistency between different pieces of information that needs to be explained and so one source of information might be preferred over another. The blonde-haired woman teaching a graduate class on relativity theory is unlikely to be perceived as a 'dumb blonde'. However, a film director casting the part of a 'bimbo' might choose a blonde to play the role so that the look is consistent with the audience's expectation of the part.

As well as conflict between different aspects of a person's nonverbal communication there is also potential conflict between a person and their setting. Being dressed as Napoleon will not be seen as odd at a fancy dress party but in a business meeting is likely to raise a few eyebrows, with the person perceived as eccentric (at best). As we shall see in Chapter 8, behaviour that goes against expectation leaves the perceiver with the problem of finding an explanation for it.

ATTEMPTING TO CREATE A DELIBERATE IMAGE: IMPRESSION MANAGEMENT

We should not assume from the preceding sections of this book that a person has no control over the inferences that others make about them. We all engage in impression management, that is, attempt to manipulate the impression others gain about us. We all 'put on a show' at times, by using our nonverbal communication to create a deliberate impression. The clothes we choose to wear for an interview or a date, wearing sunglasses even when it's cloudy as it looks 'cool', having our hair cut in a certain style, putting on a 'telephone voice', feigning interest in a boring lecture given by our tutor, behaving 'nicely' when grandparents come to visit; these are all ways of managing impressions. In many cases, such as preparing for a job interview, we are deliberately considering the impression we want to give but impression management need not necessarily always be conscious (Tetlock and Manstead, 1985): on getting a very prestigious job a friend of mine suddenly acquired a more upper-class accent which reverted back to her old one after a few days! I'm not sure how aware she was of this. Sometimes we are more concerned about our impression than others: in attending a job interview we might pay considerable attention to what we are going to wear but in preparing to meet friends we might slip on a favourite jacket, only appreciating its well-worn appearance when our friends make a joke about it.

One way of looking at how we present ourselves to others in our everyday lives is in terms of actors playing roles (Goffman, 1959). This dramaturgical framework helps us to understand the different impressions we construct. For example, a car salesman, after being charming and polite to a difficult customer, might slouch into the office, throw his arms up and confide to a saleswoman how irritating he had found the customer. To Goffman this is like slipping backstage. Similarly, we may take on different roles with different audiences: the self we present to our mothers might be very different from the self our friends perceive.

Impression management and self-presentation are often used synony-
mously, although impression management can be seen as a more general
term than self-presentation (Leary and Kowalski, 1990) as people can manage the impressions of other people and other things as well as themselves.
For example, the consultants and press secretaries working for politicians
who attempt to get their employers perceived in a good light.

Leary and Kowalski (1990) provide a model of impression management,
comprising two processes: impression motivation and impression construction. The first of these concerns the degree to which a person is
motivated to manage their impression actively. This can be affected by three
key factors: the goal-relevance of impressions, the value of desired goals and
the discrepancy between desired and current image. A woman who really
wants a job as a dental receptionist (that requires a smart appearance) will
try particularly hard to look good especially if she knows that others often
see her as rather unkempt. All three factors are important here: the impression matters, the woman wants the job and she realizes that she doesn't
usually look very smart. Another woman going to the same dental surgery
but only to have her teeth checked is unlikely to be as concerned about the
impression she presents.

A motivated person then will endeavour to construct an impression. This,
according to Leary and Kowalski, depends on a range of factors. People have
their own perceptions about themselves (their *self-concept*) and this will
influence the impression they attempt to give, whether they try to present
themselves as they believe themselves to be or not. Further to this is the
influence of how we would like to be. In applying for a job where persistence and loyalty are stressed a candidate might emphasize five years spent
in the current post to give the impression of 'good company person' rather
than the fact that he or she left college before the end of the course ('college
drop out'). Thus, individuals tend to present a *desired identity image* rather
than an undesired one, although this image is likely to be limited by what
they believe to be the truth of themselves and their lives. A third factor is *role
constraints*. We take on many roles in our lives: sister, father, doctor,
preacher, and there are expectations concerning these roles (see Chapter 4).
People attempt to construct an image that is consistent with these expectations. In applying for a job as a bank manager a woman is likely to present
herself as she expects a bank manager to be: soberly dressed, interested in
business matters, conscientious and so on, in order to fit the role. Similarly,
an actor playing the role of a bank manager in an advertisement dresses to
look and play the part, despite never having been a real bank manager. A
fourth factor is that called *target values*. We try to give an impression that
matches the values of the target audience; a young man finding his new date
doesn't like his favourite rock band might emphasize other aspects of his
music taste that are more in accord with hers. Finally, image construction
depends on both *the current and the potential social image*. Our present

image is affected by what people know about us and this may affect the way we can present ourselves to them. A student having flunked an examination through lack of application is not likely to be able to present an image of 'hard-working student' to a parent financing the studies, so new impression-management strategies might be adopted to repair the damage and keep the financial support. The failed student might make a blatant show of staying in to study instead of socializing, for the benefit of the parent.

We may not all engage in impression management to the same extent. Snyder (1974, 1979) argued that people differ in *self-monitoring*, with high self-monitors adapting their behaviour to the circumstances and managing their impression to fit the situation. High self-monitors in a job interview might attempt to adapt their impression to match their perception of the interviewer's idea of a good candidate. In contrast, low self-monitors are less influenced by the circumstances and are more likely to 'be themselves' regardless of the situation. Low self-monitors in the job interview are likely to be less adaptive in their behaviour and less responsive to the interviewer's behaviour. Thus, high self-monitors are more likely to engage in a number of image-management strategies than are the low self-monitors. Many politicians monitor their impression all the time, becoming the 'in-touch with the people politician', 'the good party candidate', 'the world leader', 'the tough no-nonsense politician' dependent on the audience and the issue, adapting their behaviour accordingly.

Leakage

As we have seen above, impression management can involve more than our nonverbal communication but nonverbal aspects play a key role in an impression as they are often the most obvious signs of what we are like, and they can invoke the kind of categorical judgements that we shall be looking at in Chapter 4.

Sometimes, however, our impressions do not really come off. We end up 'giving the game away', apparently letting our 'true' feelings slip out. This is known as *leakage* (Ekman *et al.*, 1969). Many people are required by their occupations to manage their impressions and not show their emotions: newscasters must keep an unemotional expression despite the content of the news they are reporting. Similarly, doctors dealing with horrific accidents or informing patients of the death of loved ones are obliged to keep their emotions in check and present an image of calm concern. Research has found that we are able to control facial expression better than our extremities (Ekman *et al.*, 1969). A nervous interviewee might present a calm face but there might also be nervous movement of the feet or hands. However, the reason for this is that we are usually less aware of these parts of the body than of the face (Ekman *et al.*, 1969) and with practice people can learn to control their extremities better.

CONCLUSION

Our encounters with other people are often brief. Employing inferences about the nonverbal aspects of the person 'tells' us so much more about them. Advertising in the media involves presenting us with essentially nonverbal images: people may appear on the screen for only a few seconds yet by their looks and actions we have made inferences about their status, lifestyle and personality. These inferences might help us to explain the behaviour of others rather than seeing them as unknown and unpredictable. However, our judgements might be stereotypical rather than based on valid relationships. We shall be developing these ideas throughout the book.

Chapter 3

Interpersonal attraction

In their office, Peter and Susan were working their way through the job application forms. Peter was looking at the photograph of an attractive woman accompanying one application. He began to read the information below it. Her qualifications were good but her experience was limited. He tossed the form to Susan.

'Should we short-list this one?'

Susan read it carefully.

'Well . . .' she answered uncertainly. 'She seems quite good. I suppose it's not her fault she's not been in the industry long.' Susan could see nothing unfavourable on the application form.

'OK,' she answered more positively, 'put it on the pile for further consideration.' She was unaware that she had rejected a similar, though less attractive candidate a little earlier.

They read on through the forms.

'Hey!' said Peter. 'This is the person!' He looked up with a smile, handing Susan the form. She looked at it carefully. It certainly didn't look like a good candidate. The man's past experience was not very applicable. Then she noticed it. Under the section on personal interests was written 'scuba diving', Peter's favourite hobby.

'We certainly cannot have this person,' she said. 'Two people going on about diving would be just too much!'

'But,' said Peter, 'he sounds perfect. He's bound to fit in.'

'Bound to,' replied Susan ironically but also with a smile, 'apart from the fact that he's got the wrong qualifications, the wrong experience and is applying for the wrong job!'

'Pity,' said Peter good-naturedly as Susan put the form on the reject pile. He liked working with Susan: at least she appreciated his sense of humour.

The depiction of beauty has been a rich seam in the history of Western culture. In Greek myths beauty often led to love and tragedy, and these legendary beauties have remained alive through the works of some of the greatest of artists. The goddesses Aphrodite and Persephone disputed the love of the beautiful youth Adonis who was required to spend part of the year with each. Shakespeare chose this love for his play *Venus and Adonis*. Michelangelo took for a subject the god Zeus and his love for Ganymede, the most beautiful of youths. The famous judgement of Paris is brilliantly depicted in the painting by Rubens. For his choice of Aphrodite as the fairest of the three, Paris suffered the displeasure of goddesses Hera and Athene but was rewarded by the love of the most beautiful of all women, Helen. Their love sparked the greatest of heroic tragedies, the Trojan War. Human beauty had the power to inflame the passion of the gods and incite armies to war.

Beauty might arouse passion in others but beauty itself has been seen as indicative of an internal goodness, a purity and grace. The beauty of Botticelli's Venus radiates her divinity. The perfection of the Madonnas of Raphael is both physical and spiritual. To the poet Keats, in his *Ode on a Grecian Urn*, beauty is synonymous with truth.

If beauty is good then ugliness is bad. In our fairy stories, the Sleeping Beauty and Cinderella suffer from people ugly in both looks and deeds, the wicked witch and the ugly sisters, and end up with handsome princes whose beauty matches their own. Even when ugliness is good, as in 'Beauty and the Beast', it turns out that the Beast is but an enchanted prince whose beauty returns once the spell is broken.

In this chapter we shall be looking at the psychological studies of physical beauty: both what it entails and also what inferences we make from physical beauty to personal characteristics. But interpersonal attractiveness is more than just a question of physical attractiveness (so we hope!) and proverbs provide us with folk wisdom as to who is attracted to whom. Unfortunately the relevant proverbs – 'birds of a feather flock together' and 'opposites attract' – appear to conflict! So, in this chapter we shall consider this apparent contradiction in terms of the psychological investigations into liking and the development of friendships.

PHYSICAL ATTRACTIVENESS

What makes a person attractive?

If we look through the history of images of attractive people we can see that judgements of what is attractive appear to change both over time and across cultures. Paintings depicting female beauty in previous centuries show a fuller, more curvaceous figure than might be deemed beautiful today. Looking at the recent past we can see that the hourglass figure of Marilyn Monroe is not shared by the actresses noted for their physical beauty in the cinema today. And, as Kaiser (1985) points out, a more muscular female body has been more acceptable since the 1980s. We can see this typified in the physique of Madonna, who is arguably the iconic woman of the 1980s and 1990s to contrast with Monroe of the 1950s. If we include differences between individuals in their judgements of what makes a person beautiful then we can see why Berscheid and Walster concluded:

> There exists no compendium of physical characteristics, or configuration of characteristics, which people find attractive in others, even within a single society. It appears, however, that the culture transmits effectively, and fairly uniformly, criteria for labelling others as physically 'attractive' or 'unattractive'.
>
> (Berscheid and Walster, 1974, p. 186)

This *cultural hypothesis* does not mean that we cannot investigate physical attractiveness, simply that the findings may well reflect generally accepted norms rather than any *absolute* criteria of attractiveness. It would be rare to find a person who could not say whether they found a particular person attractive or not. Psychologists have studied the topic by presenting subjects with a scale from attractive to unattractive and asking them to mark off a point on the scale corresponding to the attractiveness of the person presented, usually in the form of a photograph or a drawing. The pictures presented are varied along one or more dimensions, such as thin–fat, and the position on the dimension that is judged to be the most attractive is noted. In this way the generally agreed characteristics of an attractive person can be discovered for the particular group of subjects performing the ratings.

In contrast to the cultural hypothesis, we can consider attractiveness in evolutionary terms where the success of an animal is viewed with respect to its potential reproductive potential: those who breed succeed! If we apply this idea to the human form then, for a female looking for a successful mate, an attractive male should be one who is big, strong and healthy, in order to compete with other males for resources; and a male should prefer a woman with good child-rearing qualities, so youthfulness and nurturance should be attractive (e.g. Buss, 1987), along with an hourglass shape (Furnham *et al.*, 1990). We can term this the *reproductive fitness hypothesis* of attractiveness.

Finally, we have a third possibility in the explanation of beauty and that is the *average hypothesis* (e.g. Langlois and Roggman, 1990). It has been suggested that holders of average physical characteristics are more able to adapt to a range of environments and less likely to carry harmful genetic mutations than those with abnormal features (Symons, 1979). Symons also suggests that we are able to detect the average with respect to physical characteristics; thus, we should view those of average features as the most attractive. This hypothesis is also an evolutionary theory, as average characteristics are seen to offer a good chance of the production and survival of progeny.

We can see whether the psychological evidence supports any of these ideas.

The attractive body shape

Studies on the most attractive shape of the male body have shown that an extremely well-developed body of the Mr Universe type is not seen as attractive to women. According to Beck *et al.* (1976), a moderately large chest and small buttocks were generally seen as more attractive in a man by their female subjects. Variation in attractiveness ratings was found for different types of women by Beck *et al.*: larger men were preferred by women who enjoyed sport and physical activity, medium-sized men were chosen by more traditional feminine women and thin men were preferred by more reserved women from higher socio-economic backgrounds. However, there does appear to be a preference for a mesomorphic physique in judgements of attractiveness of men by males as well as by females (Beck, 1979). Complementary to this, Ryckman *et al.* (1989) found, in a study with both male and female subjects, that a male mesomorphic physique was seen as more attractive than ectomorphy which in turn was more attractive than endomorphy. Indeed, Kaiser (1985) suggests that mesomorphy appears to be a 'ideal' physique for men in Western culture.

In the studies of female physique, men have been shown to prefer a medium-sized physique in women, with a preference for medium (Kleinke and Staneski, 1980; Furnham *et al.*, 1990) or larger breasts (Beck, 1979; Kaiser, 1985). Again there were differences between groups of men. Larger breasts were preferred by more aggressive and independent men with the smaller-breasted female form preferred by more passive, self-deprecating and indecisive men (Beck, 1979). Women themselves tended to prefer the moderately small-breasted shape (Beck *et al.*, 1976). Women also have a preference for a female figure that tends towards thinness, related, possibly, to a common desire in women for a reduction in their own body size (Kaiser, 1985). When mixed groups of men and women have rated the attractiveness of female body shapes, endomorphy is seen as significantly less attractive than mesomorphic or ectomorphic shapes, with the thin woman (ectomorph) no less attractive than the larger mesomorph (Ryckman *et al.*, 1989). The positive view of thinness in women found in this study and others (e.g. Spillman and Everington, 1989) might be related to changing views of health with thinness seen as a positive attribute (Ryckman *et al.*, 1989) and to the frequency of thinner women presented in the mass media (Kaiser, 1985; Spillman and Everington, 1989).

Men tend to want to be larger than they are and women smaller than they are (Calden *et al.*, 1959). Satisfaction with one's body size was found to be greater for the larger than average man and the smaller than average woman (Jourard and Secord, 1955) and men wish to be tall and women do not (Berscheid and Walster, 1974), possibly indicating their desire to get closer to a cultural 'ideal' of the larger than average man and the smaller than average female. Extremes of body shape are not seen as attractive (Furnham and Radley, 1989), with obesity being seen as particularly unattractive in both sexes (Ryckman *et al.*, 1989). The thin (ectomorphic) woman was also seen as more attractive than an equally thin man (Ryckman *et al.*, 1989).

The data provide some support for the evolutionary hypothesis: medium body shapes are liked, with attractive deviations from average tending to follow the predictions of the reproductive fitness hypothesis. However, we should be cautious about the generality of the above findings, given that the perception of the large woman as unattractive is not shared by other cultures: Kenyan (Furnham and Alibbai, 1983) or Arab (Argyle, 1988), for instance, and apparently not by our own in past times if we are to judge by the painters of the Renaissance. Differences across individuals and cultures provide problems for the universality expected of an evolutionary explanation.

The attractive face

Secord (1958) found that subjects asked to describe the facial features of a 'warmhearted and honest' man assumed this man to have average features, whereas a 'ruthless and brutal' man was seen as having more abnormal features. It does appear that abnormal features are seen as indicating abnormal personality (Clifford and Bull, 1978; Goffman, 1963) and hence the average face is viewed more positively. In an experiment that demonstrated the attractiveness of an average face, Langlois and Roggman (1990) digitized photographs of faces and combined 2, 4, 8, 16 or 32 of these images to produce composite or average faces. Subjects were asked to judge the attractiveness of individual faces as well as composites. The results showed that an averaged face, composed of 16 or 32 individual faces, was judged to be significantly more attractive than the average of the individual faces. Langlois and Roggman concluded that an attractive face is an average face. They suggest two possible reasons for this preference for the average face. The first is the average hypothesis, noted above. The second explanation is a cognitive one: through our experience of faces we have come to view the average face as a prototypical face (see Chapter 4 on prototypes) and the average face is therefore the most 'facelike' of faces: it is essentially our ideal face.

However, while an average face might be attractive, it can be argued that there is more to the very attractive face than simply an absence of abnormality or irregularity, particularly as in Langlois and Roggman's experiments some individual faces were rated as more attractive than the composites (Alley and Cunningham, 1991). Research on the specific features that make up an attractive face has shown that it is not always the average feature that is seen as the most attractive (Cunningham *et al.*, 1990). Keating (1985) tested the reproductive fitness hypothesis that a more dominant-looking man (with facial features indicating strength and maturity) and a more nurturant-looking woman (with facial features indicating youthfulness) will be the most attractive. She asked subjects to rate the dominance and attractiveness of identikit faces that differed on four physical features: eyebrows, eyes, lips and jaw. These features could be mature (thick brows, small eyes, thin lips and square jaw), average or immature (thin brows, large eyes, thick lips and round jaw). The faces were made male or female by the specific choice of hairline.

In sum, the results supported the view that the more dominant-looking male was also seen as the most attractive. Also, immaturity of features in a female led to increased attractiveness judgements despite the unexpected finding that thin lips were attractive. Keating suggests that this might be due to the thick lips in the experiment being too extreme and hence reducing the attractiveness of the face. Large eyes in females were a particularly good indicator of attractiveness (as we shall see below on facial babyishness). As Keating (1985) points out, this type of evidence provides some support for a sociobiological rather than a cultural origin to perceptions of beauty.

Further support for the view that immaturity of facial features leads to an increased rating of attractiveness for women and a reduced rating for men comes from the studies of facial babyishness (cf. Berry and McArthur, 1986). Characteristics of a babyface are a round face, with a relatively large forehead and small chin, large eyes and smooth skin. As we grow older the facial dimensions change to produce a mature face. However, some adult faces retain some of these immature characteristics and are viewed as babyfaced in comparison to the faces of their contemporaries. As Berry and MacArthur (1986) note, the attraction to an immature female face and a mature male face may be related to the extent people prefer faces typical of their gender. The adult female face tends to retain more immature features than a male face and hence immature characteristics in a female face indicate a strongly female face and mature characteristics in a male face indicate a strongly male face.

Cunningham (1986) performed detailed measurements on the photographs of faces of Miss Universe competitors and female college seniors to see which facial features correlated with judgements of physical attractiveness made by a group of male students. Attractiveness ratings were related to the immature features of higher, wider and more separated eyes, a small chin and a small nose. The mature features of wide cheekbones and narrow cheeks were also seen as attractive. The combination of immature and mature features in the most attractive faces could be explained by the immature features eliciting feelings of caring and cooperation, with the mature features suggesting status and eliciting respect rather than condescension (Cunningham, 1986). Essentially the face is seen as that of an attractive young woman rather than a child.

Judgements of attractiveness may be due to more than simply features indicating young adulthood. If we believe that we can perceive personality characteristics from facial features (and Chapter 2 indicates that we do) then a face might appear attractive if a range of positive characteristics can be 'read' from it. A combination of mature and immature features can lead to a judgement of attractiveness due to the inferred personality contained in those characteristics. A man who is seen as dominant and strong from his square jaw may be seen as more attractive if wide eyes also make him appear vulnerable and innocent. Cunningham *et al.* (1990) have proposed a multiple motive hypothesis of physical attractiveness. Women are influenced in their judgements of male physical attraction by multiple motives. A dominant male is useful in conflict with other males but may not be nurturant in family relationships. So a male is not attractive solely on the basis of his perceived dominance; other motives influence the decision. Thus a combination of motives, including dominance, sociability and status, may all operate in a woman's judgement of male facial attractiveness.

In an experimental test of the multiple motive hypothesis Cunningham *et al.* (1990) presented facial photographs of male college seniors to a group of female raters, also college students. It was found that the immature features of large eyes and small nose coupled with the mature features of prominent cheekbones and large chin were seen as attractive, conveying both 'cuteness and ruggedness' (Cunningham *et al.*, 1990, p.65). Attractiveness appears to be more complex than simply maturity of features in men and immature features in women. Babyishness and maturity of features may be just two of the important dimensions that combine with other characteristics such as hair-style and length, facial hair, grooming and cosmetics in an overall judgement of facial attractiveness.

Making our faces more attractive

One way we can improve an unattractive face is to try to cover it up! Facial hair is an indicator in men of maturity and masculinity and as such may be seen as either attractive or unattractive. As we have seen above, mature features can lead to a judgement of attractiveness in men but beardedness can also be seen as an extreme masculine feature and hence less attractive. Feinman and Gill (1977) found that female college student subjects rated beardedness less attractive than a moustache or no beard. It is therefore of interest to investigate differences in background or character between women who find bearded men attractive and those who do not (Addison, 1989). Baldness, another characteristic more common of men, has been found to be less attractive than a head of hair (Cash, 1990). People also tend to overestimate the age of a bald man (Cash, 1990). Cash went on to compare the judgements of younger women (mean age 20.3 years) with older women (mean age 35.2 years), on the assumption that the former may not have had the experience of balding men amongst their friends and acquaintances. Both groups regarded the balding men as less physically attractive than non-balding men and were in agreement with their rather negative judgements of older balding men. However, the older women regarded the younger balding men as more likeable and intelligent than the younger non-balding men, whereas the younger women rated them as less likeable and less intelligent. It could be that the apparent increase in age due to hair loss for these younger men gave them an appearance of maturity that was more appealing to the older women (Cash, 1990). Yet, it is not surprising that a number of bald men resort to hair-pieces in their attempts to appear younger and more attractive. Sean Connery in his movie role as James Bond was obliged to wear a hair-piece. However, as we shall see later, there is more to attraction than this one aspect of our physical appearance and the actor Telly Savalas in the television series *Kojak* made baldness a trademark that did not appear to harm his physical attractiveness.

Hair is obviously something we can change and there is some evidence that women are perceived as more attractive with well-groomed hair (Secord and Muthard, 1955) and experimenters may well reject photographs for judgement if hair is particularly out of place (Cash, 1990). Hair colour may lead to the evocation of the stereotypes such as 'dumb blonde' mentioned in the previous chapter, yet the attractiveness research has not shown a clear preference for a specific hair colour (Feinman and Gill, 1977). Hair length and style may influence an attractiveness judgement but there are obviously cultural influences, as these aspects of our appearance are influenced by fashion and hence may be interpreted in those terms.

Interestingly, most of the experiments on facial attractiveness deliberately choose faces without spectacles, because it is assumed that glasses will influence the judgement of the attractiveness of the face, as research has shown that a bespectacled face may be seen as less attractive than the same face without glasses (Hamid, 1972). But this is not always the case (Bartolini *et al.*, 1988).

For a woman an 'appropriate' use of cosmetics can enhance her attractiveness as judged by men but not necessarily as judged by women (Secord and Muthard, 1955; Cash *et al.*, 1989). Cosmetics can be used to cover up blemishes and enhance facial characteristics. Thus, a face can be made to appear more regular or eyes to appear larger and so more attractive. However, there are cultural meanings to cosmetics and a particular style or quantity of cosmetics may have different effects on a perceiver. A highly made-up face that looks stunning at a party might lead to a different perception in a business meeting (Cash, 1985).

Despite the effects of grooming, one finding clearly stands out in the literature on the attractiveness of faces. The simplest way to appear more attractive for both men and women is to smile (Mueser *et al.*, 1984; Cunningham, 1986; Cunningham *et al.*, 1990). Even when the judges were asked to compensate for the facial expression in their ratings, Mueser *et al.* still found that the face with the happy expression was rated the most attractive. One explanation for this is as follows. People usually smile when they like us and it is a pleasant feeling being liked. This in turn can lead us to see them positively and we judge them to be attractive (as we will see in the reinforce-ment-affect model later in this chapter).

A second aspect of facial expression that influences judgements of attrac-tiveness is pupil size, possibly because a large pupil indicates interest or sexual interest (Argyle, 1988). Hess (1972) discovered that men found photo-graphs of women more attractive when the women's pupils were dilated, even though the men were unaware of the difference. Cunningham (1986) also found wide pupils were related to males' judgements of female attrac-tiveness. Pupil width in this study also correlated with the men's judgements of the women's brightness (on a scale from *very dull* to *very bright*). Pupil size might operate like smiling on the male judges: the woman's perceived interest leads in turn to a positive judgement of attractiveness.

Context effects on judgements of attractiveness

It might be tempting to see our judgements of physical attractiveness to be based simply on the physical characteristics of the person being judged and independent of any other factors. Yet this would be false. In a study by Kendrick and Gutierres (1980) a group of male students were interrupted while watching television by two others (confederates of the experimenters) and asked to make a judgement of the attractiveness of a yearbook photo-graph of a young woman, purportedly to help resolve an argument about arranging a blind date for a friend with her. The interesting aspect of this study was that the students were deliberately interrupted during the screen-ing of the programme *Charlie's Angels* which starred three very attractive women. Kendrick and Gutierres found that the *Charlie's Angels* students rated the photograph as less attractive than other students interrupted during a different programme or asked when not watching television. It appears that the contrast between the attractiveness of the women on the television and the woman in the photograph led to the lower rating of the latter's attractiveness.

The context of more attractive people does not always reduce the attrac-tiveness of an individual. Geiselman *et al.* (1984) asked subjects to rate the attractiveness of pairs of high school yearbook photographs of female faces. The results showed an assimilation effect: a face was seen as more attractive in the context of a more attractive face and less attractive in the context of a less attractive face.

Why does a contrast effect occur sometimes and an assimilation effect at others? Wedell *et al.* (1987) argued that the way the information is pre-sented is crucial. If information is presented *successively*, then contrast effects occur as the judge is trying to decide on the attractiveness of each new face relative to the previously presented faces. However, if the information is presented *simultaneously* then assimilation occurs as the judgement of one face is not separated from the other and the less attractive face gains from being 'averaged' with the more attractive face. The results of their experiments supported Wedell *et al.*'s view, although they do make the reservation that assimilation may occur only with this type of material (pairs of adjacent photographs of faces), as the simultaneous presentation of several items or the use of other types of material has led to contrast.

Practically, if only physical attractiveness counts in a judgement, it is better to be seen after a less attractive person or at the same time as a more attractive one. (As we shall see later, there are also other benefits of being seen in the company of an attractive person; for example, Sigall and Landy, 1973).

Conclusion to physical attractiveness

In searching for the source of physical attractiveness researchers have looked at both the body and the face. If anything, the face is the more powerful influence of the two (Alicke *et al.*, 1986). None of the three explanatory hypotheses has received unequivocal support from the evidence. Indeed, the research of Cunningham *et al.* (1990) indicates that multiple motives might underlie judgements of attractiveness. We should also be aware of the limitations of this research. The standard experimental set-up entails a group of subjects, usually from the same culture, looking at drawings or photographs of people (or occasionally people standing briefly before them). The subjects then rate the people on attractiveness and these ratings are combined for specific subject groups (e.g. male raters, female raters). Differences in ratings are noted between the subject groups or between the physical features. The effect of this design is that the experiments focus on agreement between raters rather than individual differences between raters. Thus the results tell us about 'the male subjects' preferences' or 'the female subjects' preferences' but not John Smith's or Mary Brown's preference. Also, the studies often focus on a limited cultural group, such as a group of students from a particular college. Cultural differences are often indicated, as above, by non-experimental evidence, such as images of beauty presented in different cultures. The question of cultural differences is quite a complex one, given the development of the mass media. Cunningham (1986) found that black, Oriental and Caucasian Miss Universe contestants shared many common facial features. Given that each contestant was chosen by people from their own country and the final judging panel was multinational then this could indicate universal ideas of attractiveness, supporting an evolutionary hypothesis. However, as Cunningham also points out, these contestants could have been chosen according to Western standards of beauty, as the contest received a substantial income from Western television companies.

A second point to note is that the standard experimental design provides the subject with only the physical features of the person and hence can

discover only what people find physically attractive, not the relative importance of physical features compared to other factors in making someone
attractive. Different people might have different opinions as to the importance of physical features in making a person attractive. Evidence for this
comes from a study by Morse *et al.* (1976). Subjects observed a person for
thirty seconds and rated them for attractiveness. Morse *et al.* found no
difference between the male and female subjects in their ratings of attractiveness. However, when the subjects were asked to give the importance of
various characteristics in judging members of the opposite sex, differences
between men and women emerged. The male subjects were more concerned with physical appearance (such as hair, shape, face, weight) than the
female subjects, who were more concerned with personal qualities (such as
intelligence, independence, sense of humour, manners) than the men. Despite this difference in emphasis, both men and women were concerned with
a mixture of physical and personal qualities in their judgements: the face,
intelligence and sense of humour were amongst the top five characteristics
for both groups. However, as Morse *et al.* argued, the word 'attractive' may
mean something different when a man judges a woman to be attractive than
when a woman judges a man as attractive.

A number of non-physical aspects of a person have been shown to
influence judgements of attractiveness. Competent people are seen as attractive. Yet we can be put off by someone who appears 'too perfect' and
therefore the near-perfect person who commits a blunder gains in attractiveness, such as President John F. Kennedy after the abortive 'Bay of Pigs'
invasion of Cuba in 1961 (Aronson, 1976). Surprisingly, being done a favour
to, rather than doing someone a favour can also make us more attractive
(Aronson, 1976). The explanation is that the person performing the favour
concludes that we must be deserving of the favour (or why else would they
be doing it) and therefore we must be an attractive person. So if you want
someone to like you, one strategy is to get them to do you a favour!

Despite the points made in this section, physical attractiveness can have a
powerful influence in a whole range of social settings, and how we are
responded to by others, even in crucial social environments such as the
place of work, classroom, the hospital and the courtroom, can be influenced
by physical attractiveness (as we shall see in Chapter 10). In the following
section we shall endeavour to answer the question why this occurs.

THE 'WHAT IS BEAUTIFUL IS GOOD' STEREOTYPE

It is tempting to argue that physical attractiveness should not affect our
judgements of other characteristics: what does it matter whether someone
looks physically attractive or not in our judgement of their friendliness,
honesty or competence? Unfortunately, the evidence suggests that it does
matter and that there exists a commonly held belief that physically attractive

people also have a number of positive personality characteristics as well. This has been termed the 'what is beautiful is good' stereotype after the seminal paper by Dion *et al.* (1972).

In the experiment by Dion *et al.* (1972) college-student subjects were asked to rate three other students on twenty-seven personality characteristics and to rank order them on five further traits. The subjects were given only a year- book photograph from which to make their judgements. The three photo- graphs were selected by the experimenters so that one person was physically attractive, one average in attractiveness and one unattractive. The results clearly supported the research hypothesis: physical attractiveness had a major effect on the personality judgements. A subset of personality traits was chosen as a measure of *social desirability*. There was a clear finding that the physically attractive individuals were seen as having most socially desirable characteristics. This was found irrespective of who was rating whom: men rating women, men rating men, women rating women or women rating men. Attractive people were also expected to get better jobs, be better spouses and have happier marriages, have better prospects for happy social and pro-fessional lives and be, overall, happier people. Not only were attractive people seen as having a range of positive qualities but they were also seen as having greater potential success and happiness than the less attractive.

Surely, we might argue, these beliefs are both unfair and unjustified. So why do people hold them? Dion *et al.* suggest they are not so illogical if either of the following two processes occur: first, if personality did affect outward appearance in some way, such as an inner calmness leading to less physical tension and, hence, fewer lines or wrinkles. Second, cultural expec-tations that an attractive person is virtuous could lead them to behave accordingly (see Chapter 4 on the self-confirming nature of stereotypes). Even if neither of these processes actually occur it is quite possible that we believe that they do occur. We saw in Chapter 2 how people infer per-sonality from physical characteristics, irrespective of the validity of those inferences. There is also a wealth of cultural material providing us with 'evidence' for a relationship between beauty and goodness, as we saw at the beginning of this chapter. Dion *et al.* (1972) cite Sappho and Schiller whose writings include this view. In films and television the heroes and heroines are usually very attractive and villains are invariably ugly as well as nasty. It is not surprising that, if we learn by observing these role-model characters (Bandura, 1977), we might develop a belief that the physically attractive are also attractive in personality, no matter how erroneous this is in real life.

INFERENCES ABOUT ATTRACTIVE PEOPLE: THE BENEFITS OF BEAUTY

The results of much research into physical attractiveness have shown 'that the physically attractive – across age, sex, race, and all socioeconomic stations – receive numerous preferential treatments' (Berscheid, 1985, pp. 453–4) These effects can have an important influence on the lives of individuals. Teachers can have expectations that physically attractive children will achieve greater success (Clifford and Walster, 1973). In a study by Landy and Sigall (1974) male student subjects were given an essay to evaluate. The essay was either well written or badly written. Information was also given about the supposed student writer of the essay along with a photograph of her from a college yearbook. The information was always the same, but for some subjects the student in the photograph was attractive, for others she was unattractive and for the control group there was no photograph. The results showed that the less attractive the student the poorer her evaluation. Interestingly, writer attractiveness had a much greater effect on the assessment of the bad essay than the good essay. One possibility is that an attractive student, being expected to do well by assessors, gets given 'the benefit of the doubt when performance is substandard or of ambiguous quality' (Landy and Sigall, 1974, p. 303). If this occurs, we will find that the marks appear to confirm the view that the physically attractive perform better. However, this is due to the marker's bias rather than genuine differences in ability related to physical attractiveness. Here we see the self-fulfilling nature of a stereotype (see Chapter 4).

One of the advantages of being attractive is being attributed a higher status than an unattractive person, and seen as having a better job, to have been to a better college and earn more money (Kalick, 1988). Interestingly, Kalick found that subjects in a task of matching photographs with personal history descriptions assumed that there was a stronger relationship between attractive people and ascribed status than attractiveness and achieved status. The subjects associated physical attractiveness more with people whose high status from attending a prestigious college arose through factors such as family connections compared to those whose high status came about as a result of outstanding performance. As Kalick notes, 'Attractiveness appears more strongly associated with the perception of having had a good life handed one than with that of earning it' (1988, p. 481).

With the attractive person appearing to gain the advantages of life effortlessly, what can the rest of us do to acquire some of these advantages? Apparently, one way is to make friends with an attractive person! In an experiment by Sigall and Landy (1973) subjects entered a waiting-room where a man and a woman were sitting next to each other. The woman was either attractive or unattractive. In one condition the woman said the man was her boyfriend, in a second condition she indicated that she was sitting there waiting for someone else. After a minute or so the subject entered the experimental room and was asked to give their first impressions of the man in the waiting-room. Regardless of whether the subject was male or female, the man was viewed most positively when he had an attractive girlfriend and least positively when his girlfriend was unattractive. When the man and woman were not seen as together, her attractiveness did not affect the subjects' rating of the man, and his rating fell between the two girlfriend conditions. In a repeat set-up male subjects were placed in the role of the man sitting next to the woman in the waiting-room. They were asked to predict how they would be rated by another subject observing them with the woman. The ratings showed that the subjects believed that they would be rated highest when they were seen as having an attractive girlfriend and least highly with an unattractive girlfriend, indicating that the 'attractive partner effect' was held by the man in the relationship as well as by an unrelated perceiver. The positive effects of an attractive friend also occur with friends of the same sex: friends of an attractive person are seen more positively than friends of an unattractive person (Kernis and Wheeler, 1981). One explanation of this effect is that perceivers attribute positive qualities to friends of an attractive person on the assumption that they must have something that makes the attractive person like them (Sigall and Landy, 1973).

PHYSICAL ATTRACTION IN SOCIAL INTERACTION

Up to now the information on attractiveness has concerned the inferences about physical attractiveness from photographs or people we see. However, what happens when we go beyond this and actually meet people and talk to them? Does physical attractiveness have any influence on our social interaction?

Over four periods of ten weeks Reis *et al.* (1980) asked a group of male and female first-year college students to note down all their social interactions lasting ten minutes or more. At the end of the test periods the students were photographed and the photographs were rated for attractiveness. Reis *et al.* then set out to analyse the interaction data to see if a person's physical attractiveness correlated with aspects of their social interaction. The results showed that it did, especially for attractive males, in terms of with whom they interacted, who initiated the interaction and how satisfied they were with it. These males spent more time socializing with females than the less attractive men and these interactions were also longer and more frequent. In contrast, the attractive males spent less time with other males. More of the attractive males' interactions with the opposite sex were mutually initiated rather than self or other initiated. The interactions were more likely to be conversations rather than pastimes or tasks for the attractive males. Attractiveness was not found to relate to the amount of social interaction or to the initiation of the interaction for the females. But attractive females did spend more time on dates and party interactions and less on tasks than the less attractive females. Attractiveness affected the satisfaction with the interaction for both males and females, the more attractive being more satisfied, with the relationship between attractiveness and satisfaction increasing over time, particularly with opposite-sex interactions.

Interestingly, these results imply that it is male attractiveness rather than female attractiveness that is an important influence on social interaction. This goes against the commonly held view that attractiveness is more important to a woman's social interaction than to a man's. Reis *et al.* (1982) suggested that, as the study had been undertaken with first-year students, a market-place economy effect could explain the results. Given the college expecta-tion that first-year males date only first-year females but that first-year females can date a male from any year, coupled with the greater proportion of males compared to females attending the college, then it can be argued that attractiveness is less relevant to first-year females' interactions than their relative scarcity. However, the relative abundance of first-year males might lead to attractiveness influencing the interaction. To test this, Reis *et al.* (1982) repeated the earlier study but this time with college seniors. Despite the plausibility of the hypothesis, the results supported the earlier findings and the hypothesis was rejected.

A further finding by Reis *et al.* (1982) helps explain these results. Attrac-tive men were more assertive and less fearful of rejection by females than less attractive men. In contrast, attractive women were less assertive and less trusting of the opposite sex than the unattractive women. For men, therefore, attractiveness and assertiveness combine and the attractive man can initiate opposite-sex interactions that are likely to be successful. An unattractive man's fear of rejection may lead him to regard attractive women as more likely to reject him and approach fewer or less attractive women with whom his fear of rejection is less, in accordance with the matching hypothesis (see below). For women, attractiveness and assertiveness may partially balance each other, with the less assertive but attractive women and the more assertive but unattractive woman both engaging in a similar number of interactions (Reis *et al.*, 1982).

There is also the question of what one hopes to obtain from a relationship. Deaux (1977) proposes that males tend to seek an increase in their status whereas females tend to seek closeness from a relationship. A man gains in status from a high-status partner, such as an attractive woman (Sigall and Landy, 1973; Kalick, 1988) and might assess his chances of acceptance as greater the more attractive he is. However, for a woman seeking a good relationship, partner beauty may simply be one factor out of many that could lead to a satisfactory relationship (Reis *et al.*, 1982).

PHYSICAL ATTRACTIVENESS AND THE MATCHING HYPOTHESIS

When we meet strangers, especially potential dating partners, what makes us try to continue the relationship? Much of the work described above leads us to assume that the physical attractiveness of a potential partner is a key factor. We all would like a beautiful partner. However, does the beautiful person want us? If we are not attractive and our potential partner is, might they not reject us for someone more attractive? Similarly, if our partner is less attractive than ourselves, couldn't we do better? If this logic is followed we will then seek out a partner of similar physical attractiveness to ourselves in the belief that we are the 'best' the other can get. This has been termed 'the matching hypothesis' (Berscheid and Walster, 1974).

To test this out, Walster *et al.* (1966b) arranged a 'computer dance' for new college students: purchasers of tickets fill in a form about themselves and the organizers arrange date pairs using this information. For this dance, however, Walster *et al.* randomly generated the male–female pairs. During the dance the students filled in a questionnaire about their partner. The analysis of these questionnaires showed that a person's liking for their partner and their desire to see them again was based solely on one factor: physical attractiveness. The more attractive the partner the more they were liked.

This lack of support for the matching hypothesis might have been due to the nature of the computer dance itself. In this event the risk of rejection by one's partner is minimized. What would happen in a situation where this risk was greater? In an experiment by Huston (1973) male subjects chose one of three possible dates differing in physical attractiveness. When they believed that they would be accepted for the date they selected the most attractive woman. When acceptance was not guaranteed, the male subjects still preferred the most attractive woman but their estimate of their chance of acceptance by each woman was related to their own perceived attractiveness.

Again the evidence is more supportive of physical attractiveness *per se* influencing the results rather than matching, although Huston's data indicate that fear of rejection might play a role in choosing a partner and this could lead to matching. But these data do not inform us of longer-term choices outside the psychology laboratory or the computer dance. In an experiment by Murstein (1972) the members of ninety-nine couples engaged in long-term relationships were independently rated on physical attractiveness. The difference in attractiveness between partners was then compared to the difference in attractiveness between randomly paired individuals from the group. The results showed that the members of a couple were significantly more similar in physical attractiveness than the randomly paired individuals.

It does then appear that couples do end up with a partner approximately similar on attractiveness, although, as Murstein (1977) points out, matching need not necessarily take place on physical attractiveness alone (as we shall see below). A further complication comes from work on self-esteem (Stroebe, 1977). Individuals may well match with a partner who matches their own perceived physical attractiveness rather than their attractiveness as judged by others (Duck, 1988). Confident in your own attractiveness you may try to match with an attractive partner, despite the judgements others would make of you.

PHYSICAL ATTRACTIVENESS IN THE MAINTENANCE OF RELATIONSHIPS

The lure of the physically attractive appears to imply that, if an available, more attractive potential partner were to appear on the scene, we would be tempted to switch to them at the expense of our current partner, for all the advantages the physically attractive brings. Clearly we should not forget that there may be other factors that maintain a relationship, yet, surprisingly, the attractive alternative might actually appear less physically attractive to someone in a relationship than to someone on their own. Simpson *et al.* (1990) presented subjects with magazine advertisements of opposite-sex persons and asked the subjects to rate them on physical and sexual attractiveness. The results showed that, for both men and women, those involved in a dating relationship found the people in the advertisements less attractive than those not in a relationship. In a subsequent experiment it was shown that the difference in judged attractiveness occurred for pictures of young, opposite-sex persons, rather than same sex or older people, the most likely group to pose a threat to a relationship, indicating that some form of relationship maintenance process may be operating.

We should not ignore the influence of physical attractiveness in the development of relationships, but findings such as the above should make us wary of a simplistic belief in its effects. As Stroebe (1977) points out, if everyone wants a physically attractive partner only a few can be satisfied, which 'divides the world into a few beautiful and happy people who get the partners they want, and the average who have to take second best, and thus should, according to this view, never be completely happy. While this may be true for one's choice of car it does not seem to be true for one's choice of partner' (Stroebe, 1977, p. 88). And, as Murstein (1977) suggests, it is not necessarily physical attractiveness that both partners require for a viable relationship; different qualities may be offered by each partner which can result in a satisfactory relationship: it is not unknown for one partner to be rich and the other attractive, such as Aristotle Onassis and Jackie Kennedy. It is therefore worth looking beyond the purely physical and considering other factors, such as personality and attitudes, to see how they might influence our attraction to others.

MAKING FRIENDS

Meeting people

Of all the people we meet in our lives why do we become attracted to some who become friends whereas others remain acquaintances? We have already looked at physical attractiveness as a positive quality in others. Yet if we look at a group of friends can we determine what it is that brought them together and leads them to like each other? Consider your own friends. Where did you meet them? Why did they become your friends and not others? We often make friends at school, college or work, and there may be a reason for this. Festinger *et al.* (1950) looked at a group of married students all of whom had moved into the same housing project, made up of a collection of small houses at the Massachusetts Institute of Technology. They found that friendships developed between people living close to each other. Indeed the distance between residences was a good predictor of friendships. It seems, as Festinger *et al.* predicted, that the chance of repeated brief encounters can lead to friendship. Indeed, those who occupied an end house of a group that didn't overlook a grassy court like the rest, had fewer friends than the others. Clearly proximity gives individuals greater opportunity for contact, but why should this lead to friendship? An answer comes from the work of Zajonc (1968): familiarity can lead to an increase in attraction. This has been termed the 'mere exposure' effect. Simply seeing the same person in the lecture room or the office on repeated occasions can increase your attraction to them.

Mere exposure doesn't always increase attraction: someone who is unpleasant is unlikely to be seen more positively over time (Swap, 1977). In a social relationship reciprocity appears to play an important role (Byrne, 1971). We tend to like those who like us, and dislike those who dislike us. A friendly overture is more likely to yield a friendly response. A person's attraction to us can be rewarding and hence lead us to like them. Similarly, if we are pleasant, smiling and friendly we may well find others respond in kind, as receptionists around the world will know.

Getting to know each other: self-disclosure

After a superficial contact with another person we must then learn about each other if a relationship is to develop. We engage in self-disclosure. Reis *et al.* (1982) found that the attractive male was more self-disclosing than the less attractive man. Self-disclosure can also make us more attractive. However, how much we disclose at a particular stage of a relationship is important. Disclosing too much or too little may have the reverse effect if it is inappropriate to the level of intimacy of the relationship. On a first date a couple may swap information about their music preferences but telling a partner, at this stage, about one's sexual desires might lead to a rapid distancing. Yet, disclosing the same information at a more intimate stage might lead to a deepening of the relationship. Duck (1988) notes that we self-disclose when we wish to be liked. Initially we do not disclose too much information but the amount and the intimacy of the information changes to match the changing intimacy of the relationship. There is a risk to self-disclosure in that we are providing another person with information that could be used to harm us in some way and so a further important element is the reciprocity of the disclosure: mutual disclosure at the same level of intimacy allows a relationship to develop successfully (Duck, 1988).

THEORIES OF ATTRACTION

We have seen that physical characteristics play a role in deciding who we like. However, as we learn more information about a person, through spending time with them and disclosing aspects of our lives, we may become friends or decide that we don't like each other after all. A physically attractive person who hates everything about us may well lose some of their initial appeal. So what factors lead us to like someone beyond the purely physical?

Similarity

We all know the proverb 'birds of a feather flock together' and, intuitively, it appears a powerful force in our society. Consider your friends. I suspect that many share the same interests and attitudes as you. They may well be from the same background as well. Why is it that we end up with friends who are very like ourselves? In this section we will be considering two psychological explanations of this proverb.

Liking and similarity: reinforcement

In *the reinforcement-affect model* of attraction (Byrne, 1971; Byrne and Clore, 1970; Clore and Byrne, 1974) our liking for other people depends on how we are feeling when they are around. We like a person who makes us feel good and dislike someone who makes us feel bad. If we find a person's company rewarding by being interesting or amusing then it reinforces our liking for them. Consider how people act when inviting a new date home for the first time. They try to choose the right music, make a good meal, be entertaining in their conversation: essentially set up the rewards that will reinforce their date's liking for them. When it doesn't work, the meal goes wrong, the conversation is boring and the music is not liked, the relationship may well suffer.

Interestingly, the people we like are not only those who make us feel good but also those who just happen to be around when we are feeling good. Imagine you have just passed a difficult examination and you celebrate with a fellow student who just happens to be around as you get the results. The good feelings from the examination success then become associated with the other student. Alternatively, if you failed the examination, you might dislike the fellow student you meet when you are feeling bad. This may explain the tendency to shoot the poor unfortunate messenger who brought bad news in former times!

Once a person has been associated with rewards that have led to positive feelings in us then the person alone can make us feel good. We look forward to seeing our friends even when they do not wine and dine us. Similarly, someone associated with punishment can make us feel bad even when the punishment is no longer present. A school pupil might dislike a teacher who punished them in a previous class, despite the fact that they have not been punished again.

One very reliable finding is that friends have a greater similarity in their attitudes and opinions than randomly paired individuals (e.g. Duck, 1988). This could be due to similar attitudes leading to liking or that liking leads to similar attitudes. In a test of this, Byrne (1971) asked people to fill in questionnaires to discover their attitudes to a range of topics. He then gave them the completed questionnaires from strangers and asked them to indicate how much they liked that person. The stranger-questionnaires were actually completed by the experimenter and deliberately varied to be either similar to or different from that of the subject. The results showed that the greater the similarity of attitudes the greater the degree of liking, supporting the view that attitude similarity led to liking. It was also found that the proportion of similar attitudes, rather than their number, predicted the degree of liking: I will like someone more if I learn that I agree with 6 out of 10 attitudes rather than 10 out of 20. In the second case the number of similar attitudes is greater but the proportion is less: 50 per cent compared to 60 per cent. Specific attitudes were also relevant to the degree of liking: the more important the attitude to the subject the greater the liking when there was agreement with the stranger. The most important attitude was the stranger's view of the subject, with the subject liking a stranger who liked them.

Why should attitude similarity lead to liking? The explanation from Byrne and Clore is that we have a 'learnt drive to be logical, to interpret the environment correctly, and to function effectively in understanding and predicting events' (1970, p. 118). According to this view, we want to know whether our understanding of the world is accurate or not. With the physical world it is possible to check some things out quite easily. If I think today is colder than yesterday I can check the temperature readings. I cannot check out my belief that John is an aggressive man in the same way. So in order to evaluate the accuracy or appropriateness of my social knowledge I compare our views with those of other people. Finding a consensus in agreement with my views provides a validation for my views and, not only that, it also makes me feel good about those people who are in agreement with me. Discovering that Sarah also thinks that John is aggressive gives me a degree of social validation for my view of John. It also results in an increase in my liking for Sarah. Thus Sarah's attitude similarity reinforces my liking for her.

In a complete reversal of the above theory Rosenbaum (1986a) argued that it was not attitude similarity that leads to liking but attitude dissimilarity that leads to repulsion. A person with dissimilar attitudes is aversive, argued Rosenbaum, and so is avoided. Thus, we end up with those people who have similar attitudes who, in contrast, become more attractive. Rosenbaum (1986a) demonstrated this in his experiments by including a neutral or no-attitude condition along with the similar-attitude and dissimilar-attitude conditions. The findings showed that dissimilar attitudes led to less liking than both of the other two conditions, with no difference in liking between the no-attitude and similar-attitude conditions.

Byrne *et al.* (1986) were critical of Rosenbaum's experimental designs, arguing that it is not possible to produce a neutral or no-attitude condition as people assume that, unless informed otherwise, others share a high degree of attitude similarity with them, as shown by *the false consensus bias* (see Chapter 8). Therefore, the no-attitude condition is simply another attitude-similarity condition and the results follow from the reinforcement-affect model. However, Byrne *et al.* did agree that attitude dissimilarity could play a role in relationship formation. They proposed a two-stage process in relationship formation. Attitude dissimilarity plays a role in the first stage, along with other negative evaluations of a person, leading to that person being rejected from the pool of potential friends. In the second stage, attitude similarity, along with other positive evaluations, results in increased liking towards certain people from within that reduced pool of potential friends.

Despite further critical analysis on both sides (Rosenbaum, 1986b; Smeaton *et al.*, 1989), both sides acknowledged the importance of studying dissimilar attitudes as well as similar attitudes when investigating inter-personal attraction.

Condon and Crano (1988) questioned whether consensual validation was the crucial factor in attitude similarity leading to liking. They suggested an alternative explanation in terms of 'inferred evaluation': whether we believe another person likes us or not. According to this view, when we discover that someone has similar attitudes, we assume, on the basis of our past experi-ence of people, that this person will also like us. Believing that someone will like us then leads us to like them as we have learnt that people who like us usually reward us, by food, care, help, sex, interest or even consensual validation of our views. Here consensual validation is only one way in which a liked person may reinforce our attraction to them but not the only factor. When two people like each other there is an expectation of mutual gratifi-cation of needs but these may be different for different people: one friend might help to explain a complex topic of study, another might be good company on a night out. Condon and Crano (1988) suggested that infor-mation about another person related to their likelihood of satisfying a need is the major determining factor in our liking of them. (We shall take up this point of need satisfaction later in the chapter.)

Liking and similarity: balance

A second theory that provides an explanation for the liking and attitude similarity relationship is *balance theory* (Heider, 1958; Newcomb, 1961). According to this theory we seek a balance in our attitudes and relationships. If we share similar attitudes to someone we like, or disagree with someone we dislike, it produces a harmonious or balanced state. If we agree with some-one we dislike or disagree with someone we like, a state of imbalance reigns and we are motivated to change our beliefs to restore balance, possibly by changing our attitude or deciding we don't like the person after all.

Newcomb (1961), in a study on the acquaintance process, investigated the attitudes and developing friendships in a group of male students who shared the same house. All were initially strangers to each other. Newcomb (1961) found that those with similar attitudes made friends in the later stages of the sixteen-week test period. Presumably they were learning the attitudes of each other over this time. Also those who liked each other tended to share opinions about other residents.

He also found that a balanced relationship where two people liked each other was different from one where they disliked each other (Newcomb, 1968). Balance strain was relevant only when there was disagreement with a liked person rather than agreement with disliked person. Agreeing with a liked person resulted in pleasant feelings. Disliking another person tended to result in unpleasant feelings despite the balance of disagreement. It appears that we are motivated to agree with people we like but not so concerned with people we dislike, as the unpleasantness exists whether they agree with us or not.

There is a further complication to the balance model of attraction. Some attitudes are more important than others in the production of balance strain. A married couple are unlikely to be less attracted to each other if they disagree on the books they like to read but may well have problems if they disagree on where they like to live. Thus, an imbalance is unlikely to be a problem if the attitudes are of little importance.

Newcomb (1981) re-analysed the results of his 1961 study and discovered two specific groups within the house when he looked at the liking and agreement of each pair of students. Only in the first group, Group A, was there the expected balanced pattern of liking and agreement. In the second group, Group B, the relationship was reversed: people tended to like those who disagreed with them. Newcomb looked for differences between the groups. Amongst the differences, Group A members were on the whole from small midwestern towns studying engineering whereas Group B members came from cities and were studying liberal arts. These results indicate that other factors may be involved in liking as well as balance. Commitment to one's own values may have been more important to Group B subjects than balance in their liking and so they were attracted to others with a commit-ment to certain values despite these values being different from their own.

Exchange: liking and mutual satisfaction

Similarity is not the only concept that we can use to explain how attraction arises. A second concept is that of 'exchange'. In any relationship we can consider what each person gains by it. Often a relationship does not continue if someone believes they are not getting enough from it. As an example, Maureen is asked out for a meal by Paul. Each can calculate their profit from the evening by looking at the benefits gained, such as a pleasant restaurant meal and amusing conversation, compared to the costs, such as their share of the price of the meal and the loss of important time studying. If Maureen has a great evening, the profit she gains will encourage her to see Paul again, maybe by returning the favour and asking Paul out. But if Paul turns out to be rather dull and his habit of waving a forkful of food at her becomes very irritating she might decide not to see him again as the encounter has not been very profitable for her. We can also see whether Paul has profited from the evening. He might have found Maureen interesting or boring. If one of them has enjoyed the evening and the other found it tedious, then their different profits might again lead to an unsatisfactory relationship. If both of them have had a good time, then their mutual satisfaction is likely to lead to increased attraction and the relationship will continue. We can sum up the idea of exchange in attraction by the saying: 'You scratch my back and I'll scratch yours'; attraction within a relationship develops with mutually profitable encounters.

Social exchange theory uses basic economic concepts in the model of social interaction. We have already introduced profit as rewards minus costs, but there are also assets and liabilities (Murstein, 1977). A popular teenager is often the one with the asset of a car. A younger brother or sister you must take to the movies with a date is certainly a liability! In economic terms we are looking to make a profit on the exchange, gaining rewards in excess of our costs. In social encounters, just as in business, a relationship is not likely to last long if one person makes a profit and the other a loss. Only if they both come away with a suitable profit is the relationship going to succeed.

Exchange theory: interdependence theory

A classic exchange theory of social relationships is *the interdependence theory* of Thibaut and Kelley (1959, 1978). Essentially individuals look at the outcomes of the various behaviours available to them in terms of the benefits they gain from each. In a relationship each person will have different choices of what they can do. A successful relationship will occur if two people can choose behaviours so that each of them maximizes their own profit. This can be represented in an interaction outcome matrix. As an example, let us consider the relationship of David and Linda deciding what to do for the evening. We shall simplify matters by assuming that they have to stay in this evening due to lack of money and have only two options: study or watch television. They both prefer studying when it is quiet; if the television is on it will make study harder and less rewarding. Also, they both enjoy watching television more when the other is there to comment on the programmes. The interaction outcome matrix in Figure 3.1 illustrates their satisfaction with the various outcomes.

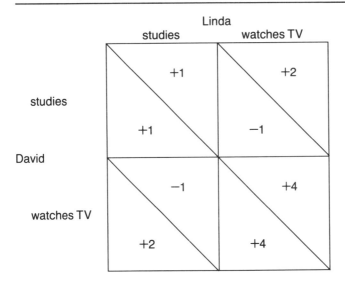

Figure 3.1 An example of an interaction outcome matrix

We can see here that the action of one will influence the satisfaction the other gets out of their chosen activity: their actions are not independent but interdependent. We can also see that there is one cell in the matrix where both maximize their rewards, so if they decide to watch television both of them will achieve maximal satisfaction. This bodes well for their relationship (but they might not get much studying done!).

If we consider the same couple but in this second case assume that David does not like watching television very much but enjoys studying much more then the matrix in Figure 3.2 might result.

Now there is not a cell in the matrix that maximizes rewards for both of them. If they end up watching television, David would rather study and if they study Linda would prefer to watch television. You can imagine the arguments they could have as a result: there are no actions that can bring mutual maximal satisfaction.

In some relationships one person is more dependent than the other. Imagine Linda's profit is unaffected by David's behaviour, she enjoys watching television regardless of what he does. However, David's satisfaction is strongly influenced by Linda's behaviour: he prefers studying but cannot concentrate if she watches TV. Potentially Linda is more powerful here as she can control David's level of profit. But note that, as soon as Linda wants something from David, such as help with her studies, the power balance swings and he now potentially has power to influence her satisfaction: he can choose to help her or not. Within relationships, Thibaut and Kelley (1978) argue, there is a strong tendency for the participants to become *interdependent* as the power between them becomes balanced.

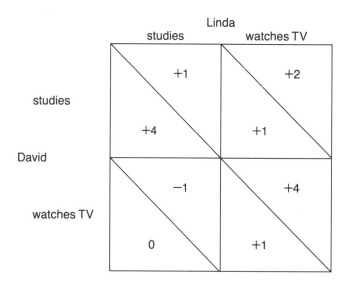

Figure 3.2 An example of an interaction outcome matrix

Life does not seem to be quite as simple as this: we encounter people who give up what appears to be a good relationship and others who stay within a seemingly unsatisfactory one. One reason for this is that we may be unaware of the mutually satisfying reasons that the couple stay together (they could both be secret Scrabble fanatics). Alternatively, it might be due to the expectations people hold about relationships and the alternatives available. Thibaut and Kelley suggested that the rewards of the current relationship should be seen in terms of a person's past rewards. Each of us has a comparison level (CL) for judging the present relationship, which is the average level of rewards we have learnt to expect from past experiences. If the outcome of behaviour in the present relationship exceeds CL then the relationship is seen positively and the other person as attractive, if it falls below CL then we become dissatisfied. If our CL is very high we might appear never satisfied, seemingly wanting the moon or finding no one capable of matching up to a former lover. But having a partner less unattractive than CL does not necessarily mean we will end the relationship; that depends on our comparison level for alternatives (CL$_{alt}$): that is, the level of satisfaction in our present relationship compared to the alternatives available. A person might remain in an unsatisfactory relationship due to the lack of alternatives or in the presence of worse alternatives. CL$_{alt}$ can be seen as a level of commitment. If the level of satisfaction is above CL$_{alt}$ we will remain in the relationship but if it drops below CL$_{alt}$ we will choose the more attractive alternative. On a desert island with few alternatives, CL$_{alt}$ might be low and even a poor relationship results in satisfaction that exceeds it. Yet for the lottery winner CL$_{alt}$ might become greater than the present relationship can offer.

Complementarity

As well as the proverb that 'birds of a feather flock together' we also have the alternative that 'opposites attract'. There appears to be a contradiction here in that the two proverbs seem to be completely opposed to each other. In this section we shall be considering, first, the psychological work on the validity of 'opposites attract' and, second, how the two proverbs can both retain some validity in human relationships.

Winch (1958) proposed that we are attracted to others who satisfy our needs. If we are to satisfy a need to be assertive then the most attractive person becomes one who is receptive, one whose needs complement our own. Who better for the dependent person than someone who is nurturant? Winch himself studied a group of twenty-five married couples and argued that need complementarity was more important than need similarity in partner selection.

An interesting finding in support of need complementarity comes from Kerckhoff and Davis (1962). They asked a group of over one hundred college couples contemplating marriage to fill in two questionnaires: one concerning certain family values (to test similarity of values) and one concerning preferred kinds of behaviour expressed and received (to test need complementarity). The couples were asked over six months later how their relationship was progressing. The results showed that for couples who had been together for a short period of time (less than eighteen months) the more similar their attitudes (about family values) the more likely their relationship was to become more permanent. However, for the longer relationships (over eighteen months) need complementarity was the better predictor of the move towards greater permanence. From this it was argued that couples progress through a relationship in stages: early in a relationship attitude similarity is important but later need complementarity becomes more crucial.

Unfortunately, carefully designed later research has not been able to repeat the earlier findings in support of the need-complementarity hypothesis (Berscheid and Walster, 1978). Indeed, this later work indicates that need similarity is more important than complementarity in long-term relationships. However, as these authors remark, 'psychologists are reluctant to completely abandon the complementarity-need hypothesis. It sounds so reasonable' (Berscheid and Walster, 1978, p.80). One reason why complementarity has not been found could be that complementarity and similarity of needs could exist together (Seyfried, 1977). Experiments often contrast complementarity and similarity and, as Seyfried (1977) argued, the effects of complementarity might be cancelled out by similarity. Partners might offer each other both complementary and similar needs.

Attraction in a developing relationship

Murstein (1977) has produced an exchange theory of attraction that postulates three stages in interpersonal attraction. These stages are indicated by the name of the theory: *stimulus–value–role theory.* At first we have only a limited amount of information about a person. This is the 'stimulus' stage and it is here that physical attractiveness can have a strong influence. When we meet new people their looks are often the only information we have. However, other stimulus information might make a person attractive: wealth, fame, intelligence, for example, and so in the process of exchange it is not just physical attractiveness that leads to an equitable exchange. Learning that someone works in television might make them attractive to some people. In the beginning of a relationship we learn lots of stimulus information about a person: how they dress, where they work, whether they are humorous or not, and each of these factors might influence our attraction to them, but as the relationship gets deeper a partner's 'values' become more important. These are a person's beliefs and attitudes. As we get to know a person we learn more about their view of the world. Initially, a woman might find the physical attractiveness of her partner an adequate reward to maintain the relationship but after a while his different political opinions begin to make him less attractive. Similarity of values is important to relationship development for three reasons (Murstein, 1977): our partner confirms our view of the world, accepts us as we express ourselves through our values and finally is likely to enjoy the same activities as us. Finally, a couple might enter the 'role' stage if they have maintained their relationship for long enough. In a relationship each of us fulfils a number of roles, such as husband, wife, lover, confessor. While there may be cultural expectations about behaviour in a certain role, Murstein (1977) argued that it is the couple's perception of a role that is important to a relationship. If their perception of a role is compatible then the relationship will be both rewarding and maintained. Let us consider the husband and wife roles for example. If a man and a woman both hold traditional, or even old-fashioned, views of the husband and wife roles then they are likely to have a happy relationship. Similarly, if they both agree that a paid occupation, child care and domestic chores are characteristic of either role, seeing 'husband' and 'wife' as simply indicating 'male partner' or 'female partner', then again the relationship can be successful. Yet role incompatibility can lead to problems for a relationship: a man who sees child care as the woman's role may find himself in conflict with a partner who sees it as something they should share. The consideration of roles can also help in the understanding of the problem of need compatibility versus need similarity. For a traditional couple with a dominant man and a submissive woman, role compatibility can indicate need compatibility because of the way the partners perceive the roles. For a less traditional couple, role compatibility could indicate need similarity. Thus, role compatibility in the perception of roles and the changing perception of roles is important in the maintenance of a long-term relationship.

Chapter 4

Person types and stereotypes

Susan was reading through one of the many job application forms.

'This seems to be the sort of person we are looking for,' she said.

She passed the form across to Peter.

'Humm,' he said, 'she seems pretty dynamic.' He read on down the form. 'There is some very good experience here. Looks good.'

'That's what I thought,' said Susan.

'My only concern is she could be too dynamic,' continued Peter handing Susan back the form. 'I couldn't stand another Jane Robinson.' Jane Robinson had been a former colleague neither had got on with.

Susan raised her eyebrows. 'Me neither!' she said with feeling. 'Even so, this one is for further consideration?'

Peter nodded as Susan put it on the appropriate pile.

'I think that's it,' said Susan with relief.

'Good,' replied Peter. 'How many have we got?'

Susan counted them. 'There're six "definites" and five "possibles".'

'Good,' said Peter. 'Can you remind me who we've got in the "definites" list?'

Susan leafed slowly through the forms. 'In the definites we have the woman with all the qualifications . . .'

'Ah yes, the Einstein.'

'. . . the Scotsman, the skier . . .'

'I'm not so sure about him now,' said Peter. 'He could be a bit of a show off.'

Susan ignored him '. . . the man who used to work for Helmsworth and Dyer. . .'

'Those H&D people are usually pretty good,' said Peter, 'but, sometimes, don't they know it!'

'. . . the woman working in France, and finally the older man from T, S and C. Do you want reminding of the "possibles"?'

'No,' said Peter. 'Let's take them to Mary.'

Susan looked at her watch. It was one o'clock. 'No, let's leave it until after lunch.'

'Excellent advice,' said Peter beginning to rise from his chair.

We have already seen how information, such as nonverbal information, can be used to categorize a person as a specific type: taking an open-neck shirt and medallion to indicate a 'macho man', for example. It is not just nonverbal information that leads to typing. When we describe our friends we often use character descriptions that include details of the type of person they are: Linda is a 'happy-go-lucky-sort-of-person', Barry is something of a 'stick-in-the-mud'. From these descriptions a listener would then be able to predict how Linda or Barry might behave in certain circumstances. We might expect a change in working practice not to bother Linda but to upset Barry.

Imagine that you read in a newspaper that a Jonathan Morris has been elected to serve on the local council. The only information about him is that he is a 45-year-old lawyer, married with three children and living in a large house in an expensive part of town. Can you imagine what he is like? What his political sympathies will be? What his views on a range of issues will be? What he might look like or talk like? We actually know very little about him and, if we see him as a unique individual, we cannot judge his personality, attitudes or behaviour. However, if we assume that he falls into a certain category of persons, a type, such as 'middle-class lawyer', then we can fill in the missing information with our expectations and he is no longer unknown but predictable. Of course we could be wrong in our typing. We now learn that Jonathan Morris earns very little working for a child-care charity and lives in a rented house shared by four different family groups. Is this new information about his lifestyle unexpected? Does it change your view of his personality despite having received no specific information about his personality at all? If so, then it shows that you did have specific expectations about him.

Stereotyping can be seen as a more extreme form of typing where we see a whole group of people as homogeneous, with the same characteristics. Assuming that, say, lawyers are all the same implies a stereotypical view of them. Assuming that an entire social group are, say, all intelligent or all unintelligent can have a major influence on how people holding those stereotypes behave towards the members of the social group. And it is not difficult to see why stereotypes have been taken to be an important factor in prejudice and discrimination.

In this chapter we shall be looking at the psychological studies investigating how interpersonal perception is influenced by the categorization of people into types and stereotypes.

USING PERSONALITY TYPES

Many attempts have been made throughout history to discover the number and nature of human types. This work has usually made the assumption that there are genuine types to be uncovered. The astrologers fit us into twelve broad types corresponding to the sun's position in the zodiac when we were born. To the Greek physician Galen, in the first century AD, there were four main types of people: sanguine, melancholic, choleric and phlegmatic. We might question the explanation of these typologies: in the first case, that the state of the heavens influences personality and, in the second, that personality is linked to amounts of bodily fluids. However, it is interesting to note that, irrespective of the validity of these types, people continue to use them in their character descriptions: 'You are a typical Aquarian', 'Maurice is melancholic'. For me 'phlegmatic' sums up many of the stolid characters portrayed in the British wartime propaganda movies of the 1940s. Yet I am not using the word in terms of its ancient psychological explanation, that these people have an excess of phlegm in their bodies!

With the advent of psychology as an independent discipline psychologists took up the task. Jung argued that people had either an introverted or an extroverted attitude to experience and Eysenck has developed the introvert-extrovert distinction in terms of personality types (Hall and Lindzey, 1985). As we saw in Chapter 2, Sheldon related personality to body type. While there has been much debate in the psychological literature about the validity of any of these typologies as explanations of human personality (Mischel, 1968, 1973), it does appear that people find it very useful to label others as a 'type'. Indeed, the words extrovert and introvert are now part of our everyday vocabulary, with very few people employing them in terms of Jung's theory. We don't need to. Labelling someone an introvert is immediately understood by others: an introvert is quiet and prefers their own company to that of others.

It is important to make a distinction between the psychological theories of person types and our everyday categorization of people. The former area of work concentrates on the psychological evidence for and against human personality types and will not be covered here. It is the latter area, the use of types in our everyday descriptions, which this chapter will focus on, exploring how and why they are used.

Consider the usefulness of perceiving people in terms of types rather than viewing them in terms of their individuality. A descriptive label can serve to evoke a range of expectations about the person so labelled. First, we can see people in terms of their occupation: police officer, shop assistant, bank manager and so on. Usually we are interacting with these people for a specific purpose: we want to buy something from the shop assistant. We are not really interested in them as individuals or in getting to know them 'as people' but in terms of the *role* they serve. We expect shop assistants to describe the goods on offer and engage in the process of assisting our purchase. As we categorize them according to their role, we have expectations about their actions. When these expectations are fulfilled, then our interaction with them operates to our mutual satisfaction. If we do not have these role expectations then there can be a breakdown in interaction. If we didn't expect shop assistants to take our money for the goods we might end up arrested by the store detective!

Clearly, treating people in terms of their roles can result in a successful interaction. However, we often go beyond that and give personality types to occupational roles. A bank manager might be seen as responsible and concerned with money and nurses as kind and helpful, because of our tendency to see behaviour as emanating from personality characteristics rather than the requirements of the role (see Chapter 8). Role behaviour may be used to infer a personality type or even a stereotype, such as seeing all bank managers as interested only in finance.

A person's occupation is only one label we can use for typing and people may be typed according to a range of other information. These might be nonverbal, based on obvious physical information such as skin colour, sex or age. We might also categorize people by a range of less permanent characteristics, such as judging men by the length of their hair, from skin-head to hippy, or women by their choice of clothes. Each categorization allows us to expect the people whom we put into that category to behave in a similar way, so skinheads will act aggressively and old people will like sedentary pursuits. On p. 68, we shall consider how seeing a group of people as all having the same characteristics can lead to misperception and prejudice: the mild-mannered skinhead and the active old person may be rightly offended by the way they are treated.

As well as making the world more predictable through our expectations, the use of types helps us to explain people and their behaviour. An ageing college lecturer wearing youthful fashion clothing might be summed up by the students by the label 'trendy professor'. Suddenly a person is 'known' when the type is applied. They are no longer an unknown quantity but a type, with the attributes of that type of person. Note that different groups of people may use different types. Each of us learns and employs a set of types that are useful to us in our social environment. For example, Forgas (1983) found that in a Sydney university the students identified sixteen common types amongst their number, including 'radicals', 'studious students', 'lazy bludgers', 'sporty types' and 'surfies'.

In this chapter we shall see how types and stereotypes are learnt, understood and used.

TYPES, PROTOTYPES AND SCHEMATA

As well as the word 'type', the terms 'prototype' and 'schema' are also used in the research in this area to describe a categorical description of persons. The term 'type' is often used as a general term, like class or category, sometimes, as we have seen above, with the implication that this reflects a genuine category of people; whereas 'prototype' and 'schema' are viewed by psychologists as cognitive structures, the organization of information in the mind of the perceiver without any assumption that these reflect the genuine characteristics of the people being typed. The three terms are described below to illustrate the differences between them.

A *person type* is a class of people, with the assumption that they have certain characteristics in common. The implication of typing is that people can, if only broadly, be categorized into groups. Placing someone into a group allows the perceiver to infer certain characteristics of the person on the basis of group membership. You might decide from experience at a college that there is a group of people whom you classify as the 'bookworm' type. These people tend to be rather serious and studious and engage in similar behaviour such as 'reading a lot' and 'spending all day in the library'. Describing Nigel as a bookworm carries with it all the implications that follow about Nigel's character and behaviour.

A *prototype* is an original form or an ideal instance of a category. For example, you might decide that your friend Nigel is a prototypical book-worm. He is exactly your idea of a bookworm: he loves to read, spends all his time in the library, is socially inept and doesn't like parties. As a real instance of the category we can list all of Nigel's characteristics even though some are less relevant than others to our 'bookworm' judgement: he is also twenty years old, has blue eyes, brown hair and lives with his parents. Not all bookworms will share every one of Nigel's characteristics: they won't have the same hair-style or wear the same clothes but they will share certain characteristics, such as liking to read and not enjoying company. (You may be tempted to joke: 'When they were making bookworms, Nigel was the original!' This reflects the use of the term 'prototype' in product manufacture. Car manufacturers, for example, create a prototype of a new model to test before it enters production. When the product range comes out, the cars have the same model name but they will not all share the same features as the original prototype, such as colour or engine size.)

A *schema* is an organized set of knowledge (Fiske and Taylor, 1984). In psychology the term schema was introduced by Sir Frederick Bartlett (1932) to describe the way information is organized in memory. This link to memory has persisted and a person schema is essentially the associative links in memory between certain items of information about people. For example, the information 'likes to read', 'studies in libraries', 'not very sociable' are all linked together in memory to form the schema for a bookworm.

A number of experimenters (e.g. Mayer and Bower, 1986) use the terms prototype and schema interchangeably. However, we can make a distinction between them. As Fiske and Taylor (1984) note, a schema can be more efficient than a prototype as not all characteristics need to be specified. Consider the characteristics of a film cowboy: carries a gun, wears a hat, drinks whisky in the saloon and rides a horse. These form your schema. You might regard John Wayne as the prototypical film cowboy and his charac-teristics include his style of walk, his height, his broad shoulders, the colour of his hair as well as wearing a hat, carrying a gun, drinking whisky and riding a horse. Hundreds of other actors have starred as cowboys in films and fit your schema without having all the characteristics of the prototype. Some actors have been very different from John Wayne but are still identified as film cowboys.

Prototypes

Clearly, some people are harder to fit into a type than others. You might describe another friend, Roseanne, as a bit of a bookworm but add that she is really interesting and fun at parties. She doesn't exactly fit into your bookworm schema and she deviates from your prototypical bookworm Nigel on a number of characteristics. It appears that person categories are like categories of other objects (Cantor and Mischel, 1979a) in that they are *fuzzy sets* with no clear category boundaries. The prototype approach allows for a range of objects to be included in a category with some more prototypical than others (Rosch, 1978; Rosch *et al.*, 1976). For example, think of a typical bird – something small like a robin or a canary will probably come to mind. You are unlikely to have thought of a chicken or an ostrich. These latter two are still birds but they deviate from your prototype and are more on the periphery of the category. Similarly, there might not be a hard and fast boundary to your bookworm category, simply a prototype that sits in the centre of the category and everyone else differs to varying degrees from this prototype. In theory, anyone could be included in this category but there probably comes a point where they differ so much from your prototype that you decide that they are better described by another category. So it is not the boundaries between categories that define them but the prototypes. The decision to include a person in a category depends on the degree of similarity they share with the prototype.

Cantor and Mischel (1979a; following from Rosch and Mervis, 1975) suggest that prototypicality is determined by looking for *family resemblances* between category members: that is, the more characteristics an instance shares with other members of the category and the fewer items it shares with members of other categories then the more prototypical it is. So Nigel is a more prototypical bookworm than Roseanne as he shares more characteristics with other bookworms than Roseanne and fewer characteristics of related categories like 'hard worker'. When we have a lot of information about a person our judgement of prototypicality is likely to be based on three factors: breadth (how many of the category attributes do they share?), dominance (to what extent do the category attributes stand out from their other attributes?) and differentiation from other categories (do they have attributes incompatible with this category?). With people we have only limited knowledge about, we have to decide on whether they genuinely fall into this category by looking for evidence of the central or important characteristics. We are more likely to label someone a bookworm if our limited knowledge about them contains the information that 'they always have their head in a book'.

Cantor and Mischel argued that prototypical people are easier to categorize, recognize and recall. It is also easier to predict their behaviour as we can employ all our expectations about the category in our predictions. (Whether they actually follow our predictions is another matter!) In an experiment to test this, Cantor and Mischel (1979b) asked subjects to form impressions from descriptions of people that differed in their prototypicality. They found that the prototypical descriptions were easier to remember than the less typical descriptions.

Support for the prototype approach has come from a number of researchers. For example, Buss and Craik (1983) considered personality traits such as *dominance* as categories and behaviours as instances of these categories. They found that certain behaviours were seen by subjects as more prototypical of a trait than others, so for the trait of *agreeableness*, 'doing the dishes after dinner' was a more prototypical behaviour than 'arriving on time for a meeting'. Thus it appears that we have prototypes for traits: certain behaviours typical of particular personality traits. We might use these in judging the character of others. If I see someone picking a fight with a stranger at a party and this is behaviour I regard as prototypical of *quarrelsomeness* then I am likely to see this person as quarrelsome. Interestingly, however, Beck *et al.* (1988) found evidence for differences between subjects in their judgements of the prototypicality of behaviours, implying that different people might have different prototypes for the same trait, and you and I might disagree on what we regard as prototypical behaviour for *quarrelsomeness*, for example (see Chapter 6).

Further evidence for prototypes in person perception was found by Mayer and Bower (1986). In their experiments they constructed a category of persons based on a prototype comprising personal details and personality characteristics. Their results showed that subjects could learn this complex prototype from exposure to information about specific individuals. They presented subjects with brief personality descriptions, comprising details of sixteen different characteristics. Apart from sex (male or female) and marital status (single or married), at each point in a description where a characteristic occurred there were four alternatives, for example, sociable/unsociable/warm/cold. A prototype was set up by selecting one of the alternatives for each of the sixteen characteristics. A person whose description contained nine or more of the prototype characteristics was deemed by Mayer and Bower to be a member of the group based on this prototype and a person whose description contained seven or fewer of these characteristics was not deemed a member.

In the test of prototype learning, a subject read through sixty descriptions (thirty members of the prototype group and thirty non-members) and after reading each description had to indicate whether the person was a member of the group or not. They were then given the correct answer and moved on to the next description. Mayer and Bower found that the subjects were accurate in over 70 per cent of their judgements of group membership for the last twenty descriptions, indicating that prototype learning had taken place and that the subjects had extracted out the prototype from the instances despite the complexity of the information presented.

In one experiment, Mayer and Bower (1986) followed the prototype learning with a incidental memory test. Subjects were given the description of four additional people and were asked to decide whether the person was a group member or not. Next came an unexpected memory test for the characteristics of these people. The results showed a tendency to allocate prototypical characteristics erroneously to a person whom they had previously classified as a member of the prototype group. It appears that not only were the subjects learning the prototype but also influenced by it in their memory performance.

Schemata

A person schema is an organized set of 'knowledge' about the traits and goals of a person, either a known person or a particular type (Fiske and Taylor, 1984). If someone asks what a friend, Maryanne, is like, you answer in terms of your person schema. She's friendly, hard-working, ambitious and a little pushy, you might answer. Similarly, if you are asked what an 'ambitious person' is like you can use a schema to list the characteristics you believe they have. But your schema gives you more than just a list of characteristics. As it is the organized knowledge about a person, such as Maryanne or an 'ambitious person', you can also predict how they might behave in specific circumstances. A person schema contains information about people's goals as well as traits. Fiske and Taylor (1984, p.150) view goals as person-in-situation schemata. We can predict what Maryanne, or an 'ambitious person', would do in specific situations. For example, we are likely to predict that an ambitious person would try to make a good impression in an interview for promotion at work.

The goals and traits within a person schema specify the relevant information in a particular situation. Maryanne is ambitious and wants to get on at work. Certain aspects of her clothing, manner and behaviour become relevant in the interview for promotion. Did she dress in smart clothes or slovenly? Did she try to appear pleasant and competent or rude and lazy? Other aspects are less relevant: whether she travelled to work by bus or taxi or whether she wore a brooch or not. Also, certain behaviours become consistent or inconsistent with the schema. Consistent behaviour for Maryanne would be to try to appear pleasant and competent in the interview. As noted above, information consistent with a prototype is highly memorable and this can be explained (Fiske and Taylor, 1984) by the person schema making certain information more relevant. This detailed schematic knowledge leads us to recall the information that she did indeed try to behave pleasantly and competently much better than other less relevant information.

Person schemata, therefore, contain the knowledge we have about specific individuals or certain types of people. This knowledge can be seen to include prototypical information (Fiske and Taylor, 1984), in that our knowledge of an 'ambitious person', for example, is essentially the characteristics and goals of a prototypical 'ambitious person'.

MEMORY FOR ATYPICAL INFORMATION

As we have seen above, it is relatively easy to recall schema-consistent information about a person when we see them as prototypical, such as remembering that a person categorized as an extrovert was outgoing. It appears that schemata can influence our memory both at the initial perception of a person and in our retrieval of information about them (Fiske and Taylor, 1984). Thus information consistent with our 'extrovert' schema, such as being outgoing, is most likely to be remembered, even when it may not have been given (Cantor and Mischel, 1977). But does this mean that inconsistent information will be less easily recalled?

Research by Hastie and Kumar (1979) found that, surprisingly, information inconsistent with a schema is particularly well remembered. They presented subjects with a list of traits, such as *intelligent, clever, bright, smart, quick, wise, knowledgeable, decisive* to generate the impression of an 'intelligent person' and then gave the subjects twenty behaviour descriptions of the person. Some were consistent with 'intelligent person', such as 'won the chess tournament', some were neutral, such as 'took the elevator to the third floor' and some were inconsistent with 'intelligent person', such as 'made the same mistake three times'. Hastie and Kumar (1979) found that the inconsistent items were very well recalled, with the neutral behaviour descriptions being least well recalled. A further finding showed that inconsistent items were better recalled when there were only a few of them in the list, compared to when there were equal numbers of consistent and inconsistent items.

One explanation of these findings is that we pay more attention to inconsistent information (Hastie, 1981). If we know someone to be an extrovert then our schema for extrovert will lead us to expect them to like parties, be sociable, dislike solitary pursuits and so forth. We are unlikely to be surprised by information that fits into this schema but if we learn of inconsistent behaviour, such as 'did not go to the party on Saturday', we pay particular attention to it, in an attempt to explain this seeming anomaly: were they exhausted after a long trip? was there something else happening that evening? do they really not like parties? This extra consideration of the information will help its recall. However, if there is lots of schema-inconsistent information we might simply decide the person is not really an extrovert after all.

Fiske and Taylor (1984) argue that normally schema-consistent information is well remembered as it forms part of our knowledge of the schema. However, when faced with schema-inconsistent information we are faced with a problem requiring time to explain: how can we make sense of the information in terms of the schema? If we decide that the extrovert didn't go to the party in order to go to a dance instead, our memory for this information will depend on the time it took to produce the explanation. If it was clear and given fairly quickly, the information might not be remembered especially well as the explanation fits in with our schema. However, if the person appears genuinely not to like parties this is likely to be very well remembered as it might even cause us to reconsider our extrovert schema.

In an experiment by Wyer and Martin (1986) subjects were given a list of behaviours performed by a man who was presented as being from a hostile group (Nazi) or an intelligent group (Nobel prize winner). After reading the behaviours the subjects were either distracted or allowed to think about the information they had been given for five minutes. When they had been distracted they recalled the inconsistent behaviours better than the consistent behaviours. However, when they had had some time to think about it, consistent behaviours were recalled better than inconsistent ones.

The 'distracted' subjects were having to rely on their 'on-line' judgements, that is their immediate judgements, and may well have attended more to the inconsistent behaviours to try to make sense of them as they read them. Wyer and Martin suggest that the results from the 'thoughtful' subjects indicate a different effect. Given that all the behavioural information was there for them to consider, it is possible that these subjects thought more about the consistent behaviours, in an attempt to confirm the validity of the person type: that someone presented as a Nobel prize winner does indeed perform some intelligent behaviours. Thus, it appears that different judgements can emerge when they have to be made 'on-line' as opposed to judgements made with the benefit of memory (Hastie and Park, 1986).

In the Wyer and Martin study there were equal numbers of consistent and inconsistent behaviours. When there are only one or two inconsistent behaviours the subjects might accept that the person type is valid but have a problem understanding these anomalous behaviours. However, when there are equal numbers of consistent and inconsistent behaviours they might need to consider whether the behavioural information is sufficient to confirm that the person really is of the type described (Wyer and Martin, 1986).

Finally, Hamilton *et al.* (1989) found that when the person category was defined by three traits (friendly, intelligent and adventurous) rather than one (such as friendly) then the recall of inconsistent and consistent behaviours did not differ. With a single trait they found, as expected, the superiority of inconsistent behaviour. They argued that with a more complex categorization each behaviour might have to be considered in terms of other behaviours (both inconsistent and consistent) to check that it had been categorized according to the most relevant trait. (The impression gained of a person described by a number of traits will be taken up in the next chapter.)

In sum, if we classify a person as a particular type we are likely to recall behaviours consistent with this type. However, inconsistent behaviours will require explanation and may be better remembered, particularly if they appear to be due to the personality of the individual and the judgement has to be made on-line. When inconsistent behaviours are as common as consistent behaviours, and there is time to review all the behaviours, we might check that the person is actually behaving according to type and consider the consistent behaviours more fully. With a person categorized in a more complex way, each behaviour might require thought to decide how it fits in with the various characteristics listed for the person.

We can illustrate these research findings as follows. If we believe Mary to be a friendly sort of person it would be a surprise to learn that she had been nasty on one occasion. We would look for an explanation of this behaviour as it is inconsistent with our view of her. If we learn that she is behaving inconsistently on a number of occasions we might begin to question whether we should still view her as friendly. To answer this we look back on what she has done, focusing on the behaviours consistent with a friendly person to check the validity of our impression of her.

INFLUENCING JUDGEMENTS OF TYPICALITY

In an interesting paper, Schul and Bernstein (1990) compared two sorts of judgements: instance-first and category-first judgements. In the instance-first judgements the subjects were given information about a person (the instance). An example of this information is as follows: 'is knowledgeable about symptoms of ailments, receives invitations for media events, has average height, highly sensitive to slight changes in his health, knows people at key power positions, likes classical music'. They were then given a category, in this example either 'local politician' or 'hypochondriac', and asked to imagine what this type of person would be like. Finally, they were asked to rate how typical a member of this category the instance was. In the category-first judgements the subjects were given the category information first, then the instance and, finally, asked to judge how typical the instance was of the category.

They found that, regardless of whether the subjects had to make an immediate (on-line) judgement or a memory-based judgement, an instance was seen as more typical of the category in the instance-first condition than in the category-first condition. As Schul and Bernstein point out, a good strategy for getting a job is to present yourself to a potential recruiter even when they do not have a job on offer. When a job does come up you will be seen, according to their results, as more suitable for the position than if you had presented yourself in response to an advertised position. They do note, however, that more specific categories (such as 'a Daley-of-Chicago type of mayor') rather than the ones they used ('local politician') might be less influenced by an instance-first in the judgement of typicality. So you should present yourself to a future employer for a job that, when it does come up, is not so specific in its requirements that your early interest has little effect.

INTRODUCTION TO THE DEFINITION AND NATURE OF STEREOTYPES

The term 'stereotype' was popularized by the columnist Walter Lippmann (1922) in his book *Public Opinion* and since then has been one of the most popular terms in social psychology. Over the years its usage has varied but the modern view has retained Lippmann's point that the 'real environment' is too complex for us to understand it fully directly and therefore we perceive the world more simply: stereotypes are part of this process of simplifying the world in order to be able to deal with it. This idea that we simplify the world through categorization has already been discussed in the previous sections on types and the same logic, discussed there, applies here, as stereotypes are seen as a more exaggerated form of typing (Secord and Backman, 1974). Whereas typing is not necessarily indicative of prejudice (it may be necessary to categorize people and events in some way in order to interact with them), stereotyping has usually been agreed to be a 'key variable' in any theory of prejudice (Cauthen *et al.*, 1971).

Stereotyping involves three stages (Secord and Backman, 1974). The first is identifying a set of people as a specific category. The defining characteristic(s) might be almost anything: people have been classified by skin colour, sex, age, height, religion, nationality, occupation and so on. The second stage involves assigning a range of characteristics to that category of people. These characteristics define the stereotyped view of that group. At one time the English were seen as sportsmanlike, intelligent, conventional, tradition-loving and conservative by US college students (Katz and Braly, 1933). While this example appears fairly positive many stereotypes comprise a range of negative characteristics: lazy, ignorant, mercenary, grasping, sly, and treacherous were all applied to certain social groups in the Katz and Braly study. The final stage is the attribution of these characteristics to every member of the category. It is this over-generalization that brings out the prejudiced nature of stereotyping as all group members are placed in the 'strait-jacket' of the stereotype: consider the treatment of, say, an intelligent, caring person by others who respond to him or her on basis of a stereotyped view of their race or religious group as ignorant and boorish.

The social stereotype

We can make a distinction between *social stereotypes* and *personal stereo-types* (Secord and Backman, 1974). A social stereotype is a consensus view of one group of people about another, such as the general American stereo-type of the English as *reserved* and *tradition-loving*. The research has been undertaken by studying the agreement between a number of people. The personal stereotype is the idiosyncratic view of a group by an individual, so one particular American might perceive the English as *wild* and *exciting*, although this view is not commonly held. This is studied by looking at individuals and the differences between individuals in their perception of groups. In this chapter we shall be considering only the social stereotype, the personal stereotype is considered in Chapter 6.

Social categories, roles and stereotypes

In any society people are categorized on the basis of a whole range of factors, as noted above. Many of these categories are examples of *role categories* (Secord and Backman, 1974). People are grouped into a role category on the basis of their common position in a social system. There are a vast number of roles in society from occupational roles to that of 'school bully'. Role expectations arise from our beliefs about the characteristics and behaviour of the individuals in the role category: firefighters are expected to put out fires and grandparents are believed to spoil their grandchildren. Shared expectations may be held by many members of society or by only a few. There may be more widely held views of doctors than, say, machine-shop supervisors, where a common view might be held only by people within a particular industry. A social role can therefore be defined as both the role category and the role expectations that accompany it (Secord and Backman, 1974).

We can make a distinction between two types of role: achieved roles and assigned roles (Fiske and Taylor, 1984). Some roles we strive to take on, such as teacher or member of the football team. These are achieved roles. Other roles are thrust upon us, in that they are assigned by others on the basis of the role category we inhabit such as 'young woman' or 'old man'. Expecta-tions also accompany these roles, thus an 'old man' will be expected to behave in certain ways or believed to have certain characteristics, despite him having no choice in being assigned this role.

It is here that we can now make a link between social roles, stereotypes and schemata. A number of researchers view stereotypes as cognitive con-structions concerning the personal attributes of a social group (cf. Snyder *et al.*, 1982) and investigate stereotyping in terms of the work on prototypes and schemata. Fiske and Taylor (1984) see stereotypes as a form of *role schema*. This is a schema that we have for a particular group of people, categorized on the basis of broad socially defined categories such as age, race, sex, occupation, nationality and so forth. With a role schema we have an organized set of knowledge and expectations about the characteristics and behaviour of a person within this role.

THE FALSENESS OF STEREOTYPES

It has been argued that stereotypes are fundamentally inaccurate as they underestimate the differences between the members of the stereotyped group. Campbell (1967) identifies four further areas where stereotypes do not accurately reflect the characteristics of the group. First, it is assumed by those holding the stereotype that it has arisen from genuine characteristics of the group. However, a stereotype might be influenced by those doing the stereotyping as well as those being stereotyped and, as we shall see later in this chapter, this could lead to a false view of the stereotyped group. Second, the overlap between groups is not appreciated. Even if one group is, on average, less intelligent than another, the stereotype held by a member of the 'clever' group might lead them to believe that they were more intelligent than all or almost all of the 'dull' group. However, an averagely intelligent member of the 'clever' group is likely to find anything up to half the 'dull' group more intelligent than him or her. (Our inability to appreciate probability in social perception is considered further in Chapter 9.) A third error is the assumption that differences between groups arise from characteristics of the group rather than from environmental conditions: a person attributes a group's lack of material wealth to personality characteristics such as laziness rather than to the social conditions within which they live. This is particularly the case if the group is identified by an obvious characteristic, such as skin colour. Finally, Campbell (1967) notes that the holder of the stereotype blames the characteristics of the group for the hostility he or she holds towards that group: for example, 'If only they were not so grasping they wouldn't be so bad.' However, the inverse is likely to be the case, that hostility towards a group leads to that group being seen in pejorative terms.

THE MAINTENANCE OF STEREOTYPED BELIEFS

At one time it was argued that the prejudiced person thought in a rigid stereotypical way and the tolerant individual was more flexible in viewing other people (Allport, 1958). There have even been campaigns telling people that stereotyping is wrong and that those who stereotype are showing a lack of thought, a simplicity of thought or indeed a rigidity of thought, all of which should be changed (Brown, 1965). However, if we take the view that stereotypes are part of the normal processes of cognition, that is, they are schemata, similar in their structure and development to our knowledge of other categories of objects, such as trees or birds, then why is it that people end up with what is essentially an inaccurate view of a social group?

In interacting with people as in dealing with objects we need to make generalizations and in doing so it has been suggested that we develop schemata, as noted above. It is, therefore, not the process of generalization that is the problem but why we maintain particular generalizations that are invariably inaccurate. Given that it is reasonable to assume that people wish to have an accurate view of the world, how is it that stereotyped views are maintained? If we assume that people are not being simple-minded or deliberately rigid in their thought but are genuinely seeking to test out their perceptions against the evidence available to them, the question that follows is: how is it that people do not detect the inaccuracies in their stereotypes? Below we shall consider a number of reasons why stereotyped views might be maintained by individuals, despite a wish for accurate perception.

A kernel of truth?

How do we decide that a stereotype is accurate or not? Consider, for example, the stereotype that the English are reserved (the 'stiff upper lip'). We would have to decide on how to measure the quality of stiff-upper-lip-ness. Then we would have to see whether the English have it. Finally, we would have to see how the English compare to other nationalities. This could entail a complicated or time-consuming piece of research. Also, it would require us to make a number of controversial assumptions about the nature of personality characteristics. And, without agreed criteria for judging group characteristics, the question of whether a stereotype contains an underlying 'kernel of truth' cannot be answered (Brigham, 1971).

Why do people believe in the validity of their opinions given the problems of testing them out? Often we look to other people as sources of information (Deutsch and Gerard, 1955). If we find widespread agreement on a stereotype, this can lead to the belief that it must contain an element of truth: 'If all these people believe it then it must be true.' Without the information to test the accuracy of a stereotype people may therefore rely on others to confirm or disconfirm their views. Furthermore, they may also look to their own experience, thoughts and memories of certain groups and group members as evidence to bring to bear on their beliefs. As we shall see below, this evidence, like that of common agreement, may not lead to an accurate perception.

Attribution of causes to behaviour

A stereotype of a social group might include the characteristic 'athletic', implying all group members are good at sports. Indeed, a number of group members may have achieved fame in this activity. Also, in recalling members of this group we are likely to remember its most famous members (see the 'availability heuristic' in Chapter 9, p. 164) and the association of the group with sporting prowess is made. Therefore, the stereotype of the group as athletic *descriptively* contains an element of truth. However, the stereotype is more than a description in that it 'explains' the athletic success, and this may well be in terms of the group members' 'athletic nature' rather than in terms of social and environmental factors (Campbell, 1967; see also Chapter 8). Yet, this particular social group might be deprived of access to success in society in a number of areas due to prejudice and discrimination, and so sport becomes one of the few activities that genuinely allows them opportunities for success. Here, then, the sporting success does arise from environmental and social factors but is attributed in the stereotype to an inherent and enduring characteristic of the group. With this stereotypical attribution of their success, individual group members could suffer further discrimination by being perceived as athletic when they are not, and as athletic at the expense of other characteristics. Unfortunately, studies by Bodenhausen and Wyer (1985) and Macrae and Shepherd (1989) have shown that people do judge individuals as behaving more in character when they behave according to their stereotype than when their behaviour is unrelated to the stereotype of them.

The self-confirming nature of stereotypes

One consequence of holding stereotyped views is that they can lead to expectations of the behaviour of those stereotyped. For example, a teacher holding a stereotype about a racial group that includes an expectation of low intelligence is unlikely to encourage a child of that race. The intelligent child, given little attention and assistance, is likely to find the material dull and difficult and subsequently not perform to his or her abilities, thus reinforcing the teacher's erroneous view that people of this race are unintelligent. To the teacher the child's behaviour is a confirmation of the accuracy of a stereotyped belief, yet it was the teacher's own behaviour that constrained the child to behave in this way.

The self-confirming nature of stereotypes was clearly demonstrated by Snyder *et al.* (1977). They found that male students who were going to engage in a 'getting acquainted' conversation with a female student expected her to be more sociable, poised, humorous and socially adept when they believed her to be physically attractive rather than unattractive, indicating that the males held an 'attractiveness is good' stereotype (Dion *et al.*, 1972). The conversations took place using headphones and microphones so that the pair could not see each other (and hence could not learn their partner's true physical attractiveness). These conversations were tape-recorded and independent raters listening only to the female student's contribution to the conversation rated her on a range of characteristics. It was found that females believed to be attractive by their male partner were judged as more friendly, likeable and sociable by the raters.

The amazing thing about this finding is that the female students who were assumed to be attractive by their partner (and independently of their actual physical attractiveness) behaved in conversation in accordance with their partner's physical attractiveness stereotype. Snyder *et al.* explain this as follows. The male student, believing his partner to be attractive, attributed characteristics to her in accordance with his stereotype of physically attractive women. Similarly, a different set of characteristics were attributed to a woman believed to be unattractive. The men therefore engaged in different styles and patterns of interaction with their partners when they expected the woman to be attractive as opposed to unattractive. The different conversational behaviours of the men in turn elicited different patterns and styles of interaction in the women. Thus, the women perceived as attractive actually behaved in a more friendly and sociable way, providing behavioural confirmation to the men of their physical attractiveness stereotype.

In a similar telephone experiment Goldman and Lewis (1977) had each subject engage in a telephone conversation with three partners. In this experiment the subjects were not told about the attractiveness of their partners. After the conversations the partners rated the subject on social skill. Goldman and Lewis found there to be a correlation between social skill and the physical attractiveness of the subject: the more attractive subjects were more socially skilful, in support of the 'attractiveness is good' stereotype. This evidence for the 'truth' of the stereotype can still be explained by the self-confirming nature of stereotypes. The physically attractive have learnt to be more skilful through a lifetime of being treated differently from the unattractive, as demonstrated by Snyder *et al.* (1977). Thus, attractive individuals end up behaving in accordance with the stereotype of them.

Evidence for the self-confirming nature of stereotypes with respect to race, religion and sexual identity has been found by Christensen and Rosenthal (1982). Thus, inaccurate stereotyped beliefs may well persist, as they are apparently being confirmed by the perceivers' own influence upon the behaviour of the stereotyped group.

The logic of testing beliefs

A fourth area of investigation pertinent here comes from research on how people test out their beliefs about the world. If I believe that all swans are white it does not matter how many white swans I seek out, I can never prove that only white swans exist. However, if I look for and find one black swan it immediately disproves my belief. Following this logic, scientists appreciate that the appropriate way to test out their hypotheses is not to look for evidence that simply confirms their views but to seek out disconfirming information. However, when people are asked in psychology experiments to undertake tests of hypotheses they tend to seek out confirming information and not look for disconfirming information (e.g. Cohen, 1983). This may be occurring with stereotypes (Snyder *et al.*, 1982): the accuracy of a stereotype may appear to be confirmed by the evidence due to our over-emphasis on confirming information and under-emphasis on disconfirming information. If I believe that all sportsmen are unintelligent, the tendency to emphasize confirming information might lead me to concentrate on evidence indicating the lack of intelligence of sportsmen ('and look at so-and-so on TV last night, he could hardly be called bright!') rather than seeking out the evidence indicating intelligence, such as the academic attainment of a range of sports stars. And so I, erroneously, believe my stereotypical belief to be demonstrated.

THE DEVELOPMENT OF STEREOTYPES

Up to this point we have concentrated on the reasons why a certain stereo-typed belief is maintained. This may explain why an inaccurate belief is perpetuated but it begs a second question: why is the stereotyped group perceived inaccurately in the first place? In this section we shall be looking at the psychological studies of the perception and classification of groups and group members. This work has shown that in the perception of social groups stereotyped beliefs can emerge.

The accentuation of group differences

Some interesting work about the perception of groups of objects or people has been undertaken by Tajfel and his colleagues. Tajfel and Wilkes (1963) conducted an experiment where subjects were asked to judge the length of eight lines of different length. The four shortest lines were labelled with the letter A and the longest four with the letter B. The lines were presented a number of times in random order. It was found that the subjects over-estimated the differences between the lines in the two groups: the difference between lines four and five was seen as much greater by the experimental subjects than by control subjects who did not have the labels A and B. This also occurred for subjects who had the labels reversed: A for the longer lines, B for the shorter. Even though the category labels A and B were not relevant to the judgement, their presence resulted in an accentuated difference at the category boundary. Tajfel (1969) argues that this overestimation of the differences between groups occurs in social perception as well: difference between the groups will be accentuated.

As well as differences between groups being accentuated, members of a specific group are perceived as being similar. Tajfel *et al.* (1964) found that subjects' ratings of two Canadians and two Indians placed the Canadians as more similar on attributes linked to the Canadian stereotype and the Indians more similar on attributes associated with the Indian stereotype. The perceived similarity of group members was also found by Hensley and Duval (1976) in an experiment using group discussion where one group of people had opinions similar to the subject (Group S) and another group had dissimilar views (Group O). As the differences between the subject's opinions and those of Group O increased, the perceived similarity of opinion between the subject and Group S increased, as did the perceived similarity of opinion amongst the members of Group O.

McGarty and Penny (1988) found the accentuation both of inter-group differences and intra-group similarity in the same experiment. Subjects were asked to rate a number of political statements on a scale of 1 to 100 indicating left-wing to right-wing. In the Uninformative label condition half the statements (the right-wing half) were labelled Author A and the other (left-wing) half were labelled Author B. In the Informative label condition Author A was described as right-wing and Author B as Marxist. In the control condition there were no labels. The ratings of the left-wing group of statements were compared with the right-wing ones. The use of a label led to an accentuation of inter-group difference compared to the control condition. Furthermore, the Informative label led to the smallest range of scores within the group, indicating the greatest perceived similarity within a group.

It seems, therefore, that, in judging other people, the presence of a known categorical difference between them and us can lead to an accentuation of inter-group difference and of intra-group similarity, particularly on characteristics associated with stereotypes of the groups (Tajfel, 1981). Knowing someone to be a member of a particular group, say British, we might then overestimate their similarity to other British people (including ourselves if we happen to be British too) and overestimate the difference between them and people from other groups, say French or Germans.

Social identity and group membership

Our personal involvement in a social group also affects our perception of our own and other groups due to the influence of the group membership on our social identity. We are all members of social groups, such as nationalities, occupational groups, even groups such as 'sixties music fans' and these provide us with aspects of who we are, our social identity. Tajfel and Turner (1979), in their *social identity theory*, have proposed that we all have a desire for a positive social identity, and a way of achieving this is to see the group to which we belong (the *in-group*) as being better than other, comparison, groups (the *out-groups*), particularly on relevant dimensions. This is sometimes called in-group favouritism. In a college the arts students might regard themselves as better than a relevant comparison group, science students, and the science students view themselves as better than the arts students.

Both students end up with a positive social identity. In this way, group members are perceiving their group as separate from relevant other groups both to establish their identity ('We are different from them') and also evaluating themselves positively to enhance that identity ('. . . and we are better'). The arts students might think that creativity and freedom of expression are important characteristics and that arts students are superior in these compared to science students. However, a science student, seeing logicality of thought and clarity of ideas as important, might regard these as characteristics of a science student but not an arts student. Interestingly, in-group favouritism might not extend to all dimensions of comparison: indeed an out-group might be seen as better on a certain dimension, so long as it is not seen as important to the identity of the in-group (Mummendey and Schreiber, 1984). For example, arts students might accept that science students are more numerate than themselves, but not regard numeracy very highly.

The need for a positive social identity leads therefore to a perception of one's own group and other groups in stereotypic terms as, again, we see that perceived differences between groups are emphasized and these perceived differences are evaluated in favour of the in-group: 'We are better than them on the things that matter!'

The categorization of people and objects

As a basis of their studies, Taylor *et al.* (1978) argued that the stereotyping of people occurs by the same processes as the perception of objects; that is, we use the categories by which objects and people are classified to aid our organization and recall of information about them (see earlier work on schemata). The categories in which we place people and objects can be linked to their *salience* in the context in which they are perceived (Fiske and Taylor, 1984). In a roomful of friends an unknown individual might stand out, so the 'friend–not friend' category is salient. Where all the people are unknown, obvious physical differences might be salient, for example, age, sex or skin colour.

In a series of experiments Taylor *et al.* (1978) studied the memory of subjects who had watched or listened to group discussions where the participants were either men and women or black men and white men. In support of their predictions it was found that sex and race were used by the subjects in their recollections of who said what in the discussion. Furthermore, subjects made more intra-group errors than inter-group errors. For example, in deciding who said a particular statement from a discussion involving three men and three women, the subjects were more likely to accurately recall that it had been said by a woman but were less able to recall which one. In one experiment the proportion of men to women in the discussion group of six was varied from 5 to 1 through to 1 to 5. When the subjects rated the discussion group on a number of characteristics it was found that the behaviour of the individual participants was interpreted in stereotypical terms with, for example, the men seen as more competent but less sensitive than the women. The group as a whole was also seen in a stereotypical manner, with a group being judged as less competent the more women there were within it. Additionally, the relative numbers of men and women in the group affected the subjects' judgements. The fewer men (or women) there were, the more likely it was that those members were judged as more stereotypically male (or female) as well as being seen as more prominent and less warm, implying that a minority group is more salient to the perceiver.

Taylor *et al.* (1978) concluded from their results that stereotyping and object perception occur through similar processing, that the process of stereotyping is influenced by the context in which the person is perceived and, finally, that the *content* and the *process* of stereotyping should be viewed separately. They argue that the process of categorization is required by the cognitive system in order to make sense of the world but that the questions of content, how and why specific stereotypes arise, is another matter.

Illusory correlation

How is it that a certain social group gains a reputation for certain charac-teristics or behaviour despite the fact that they do not differ from other groups in these respects? One explanation, based on the concept of an *illusory correlation,* was proposed by Hamilton (Hamilton, 1979; Hamilton and Gifford, 1976). Events are said to correlate if they vary together: for example, ice-cream sales are correlated with temperature, with more ice-cream sold when it is hot than when it is cold. An illusory correlation occurs when we believe that two events are correlated when they are not. Chapman (1967) showed that in a memory test on pairs of words subjects inferred that distinctive items (the longest words) had been paired more frequently than they had been. Hence, *distinctive* events might be falsely viewed as correlated.

Hamilton and Gifford (1976) tested this out in a study of social perception. They gave subjects statements about two groups of people, Group A and Group B, with twice as many statements about members of Group A than Group B. Of the statements, there were nine positive ones for every four negative ones. Thus, statements about Group B were rarer than about Group A and negative statements were rarer than positive statements, making Group B and negative statements more distinctive. As predicted, the subjects overestimated the number of negative statements referring to members of Group B. The experiment was repeated with more negative statements than positive statements and an illusory correlation again occurred, this time between the minority Group B and positive statements.

The implication is that when we learn of a distinctive behaviour by a minority group member, the frequency with which this behaviour is performed by the minority group is overestimated. It is not difficult to see how minorities can be stereotyped as thieves and vagabonds despite being no less law-abiding than the majority group. Hamilton argues that this distinctiveness attracts more attention and is therefore better remembered (Hamilton *et al.*, 1985). As we shall see in Chapter 9, the availability heuristic also implies that we overestimate the frequency of events that are easily brought to mind.

In a study concerning nuclear power, Spears *et al.* (1985) presented subjects with pro- or anti-nuclear statements that were said to come from the residents of two towns, A and B, that were possible sites for a nuclear power-station. Town A was said to be bigger than Town B and so twenty-four of the thirty-six statements came from its residents but only twelve from those living in Town B. Half the subjects received more pro-nuclear statements from both towns and the other half received more anti-nuclear statements (sixteen from Town A and eight from Town B).

In this study the subjects' own attitudes to nuclear power were also measured. Spears *et al.* found that only those subjects whose own opinion corresponded to the minority opinion in the statements made an illusory correlation (overestimating the minority opinion in the small town). Those with strong opinions corresponding to the majority opinion in the statements showed the least effect. Spears *et al.* explained this finding by suggesting that opinions corresponding to one's own are more relevant and hence more distinctive, leading to the illusory correlation.

In an analysis of previous research, Mullen and Johnson (1990) showed that the illusory-correlation effect had been demonstrated on a number of occasions indicating its importance in stereotyping. The illusory correlations were also found to be greater when the distinctive information was negative. This might help to explain how minority groups are seen as having negative characteristics: observing a minority-group member engage in a negative act could lead to a stronger illusory-correlation than if the act was positive. It was also found that the illusory correlation effect increased with the number of examples. As Mullen and Johnson note, in our real-life experiences we may encounter many more exemplars than the number presented in the laboratory, indicating that, if anything, illusory-correlation effects are likely to be stronger outside the laboratory, than in it, in the development of stereotypes.

THE INEVITABILITY OF PREJUDICE?

The above studies on categorization and illusory correlation have helped to develop the explanation of stereotyping in terms of cognitive processes (Fiske and Taylor, 1984). Unlike the earlier view (Allport, 1958) that prejudiced people are more rigid in their thinking than the tolerant, the view that stereotyping is an aspect of normal cognitive processing appears to have the depressing consequence that, as stereotyping is inevitable and as stereotyping is linked to prejudice (Cauthen *et al.*, 1971), then prejudice is inevitable.

However, Billig (1985, 1987) questions this view of the perceiver. By focusing only on the categorization process the important questions of prejudice are being ignored. Why is it that some people are more prejudiced than others? Why are they categorizing people along, say, racial lines rather than in other ways, say, friendly or unfriendly? Up to now we have been considering the nature of categorization and the influences upon it. However, Billig (1985) argues that *particularization* is just as important as categorization. Further, we need to consider how individuals discuss and argue for their views. To maintain a prejudiced view, a person might engage in particularization in the face of counter-evidence. The sexist presented with a woman successful in business might adopt a subtle particularization that retains the prejudiced view of women. In this case, business success would have to be divided along lines of sex, making a distinction between the successful businessman and the successful businesswoman. The sexist might claim, for example, that success for the businessman arose from business acumen whereas for the businesswoman it was due to 'womanly wiles', thus making a particularization in the category 'successful businessperson' on the lines of sex to defend a certain view of men and women. Interestingly, Billig (1985) notes that a prejudiced person might concede the generality of a category to retain the prejudiced view. A sexist might accept that successful businesswomen succeed by business acumen but that they are a special case of women, a subtype (see Weber and Crocker, 1983, discussed below), and hence an exception to all other women who are still seen in terms of the sexist stereotype. Billig (1985) maintains that there is a similarity of thought between the prejudiced and tolerant person but that they differ in terms of content.

According to Billig's 'rhetorical approach' to thinking (Billig, 1987), it is not that people mechanically follow procedures in thinking but that they can debate the beliefs they hold. We only need to see the heated discussions going on in bars and clubs to see people are willing to argue their point of view. As Cauthen *et al.* (1971) point out, stereotypes are essentially linguistic behaviours. They are descriptions of others that we express through language. It is most interesting to see how language is used in the description of one's own group and those of others, because, so Billig argues, these discussions should be considered in an analysis of prejudice. What is the *rhetoric* of this discourse: how do people *use language* in their attempts to defend their own positions? What do people choose to argue about? When we consider these factors from the point of view of the rhetorical approach, prejudice is not inevitable if people choose arguments against it.

DURABILITY OF STEREOTYPES

The persistence of stereotypes across a period of thirty-five years was investigated in a series of studies looking at the stereotypes held by students at Princeton University in the years 1932, 1950 and 1967 (Katz and Braly, 1933; Gilbert, 1951; Karlins *et al.*, 1969). The studies followed the same method. One hundred students were given ten ethnic groups and chose those characteristics, such as *intelligent, lazy, honest*, out of a list of eighty-four words, that they believed applied to them. Then they selected the five main characteristics for each group.

The most important finding is that there was a high degree of consensus on the characteristics of each group: subjects appeared to have a specific view of the characteristics of a nationality, indicating that a stereotype did exist. For example, Americans were characterized as *industrious, intelligent, materialistic, ambitious, progressive* and Italians as *artistic, impulsive, passionate, quick-tempered, musical*. Furthermore, many of the characteristics were consistently chosen across the years, indicating a durability of the stereotype over a considerable time. The perception of Germans as *industrious* was held by 65 per cent of students in 1932, 50 per cent in 1950 and 59 per cent in 1967. The key characteristics of the English stereotype (*sportsmanlike, intelligent, conventional, tradition-loving* and *conservative*) were chosen by at least 19 per cent of students on each occasion, a significantly higher figure than expected by chance.

The stereotypes of a number of groups did shift over time, implying that social changes were slowly reflected in the stereotypes. The stereotypes for Jews and blacks improved. World War II had a significant effect on the stereotypes for Japanese and Germans but not for English and Italians. It does appear that changes in stereotypes arise from changes in the relationship between groups. When a nation becomes an enemy the stereotype of that nationality takes on negative connotations: it is as if a new perception arises: 'We are at war with them, they must be bad.'

STEREOTYPE CHANGE

We have seen above that, despite their durability, stereotypes can change over time. But how? Does the gradual accumulation of counter-stereotypical information lead to a person changing their beliefs about another social group or is it a dramatic event that leads to greater change, like a war or a key piece of important legislation like a law against discrimination? This was the question that Weber and Crocker (1983) set out to test.

They proposed three possible models of how stereotyped beliefs could change. In the first, *the bookkeeping model*, stereotype change occurs through the gradual accumulation of counter-stereotypical information. Each piece of information relevant to a stereotype is used to 'fine-tune' the stereotype and, incrementally, counter-stereotypical information will lead to significant change. In this model each small instance of Scottish generosity will 'chip away' at the stereotypic belief that the Scots are mean, ultimately changing the belief concerning Scottish people. In contrast, *the conversion model* predicts that significant stereotype change occurs through a dramatic salient instance rather than through the accumulation of lesser examples. According to this model, learning that a Scot has given vast sums to charity might lead to a radical revision of the stereotypic belief; whereas small amounts of counter-stereotypical information, such as minor instances of Scottish generosity, are unlikely to affect the stereotype at all. The third model, *the subtyping model*, proposes that, as counter-stereotypic information is acquired, the stereotyped beliefs do not change but that a subgroup or subtype, with the counter-stereotypic characteristics, is differentiated from the group. For example, learning about generous Scottish behaviour might lead to the differentiation of Scots into the majority, 'most Scots', with meanness as a stereotypical attribute and a subtype, 'generous Scots', with the attribute of generosity. As long as the subtype is seen as unrepresentative of the whole group then the group stereotype will not change.

Weber and Crocker (1983) set out to test these three models using the occupations 'librarian' and 'corporate lawyer', the former stereotypically neat, quiet and responsible and the latter well-dressed, industrious and intelligent. Subjects were given cards with a name, occupation and three of the person's characteristics written on it. They received information either about six or about thirty members of an occupational group. Also, the counter-stereotypic information was either concentrated in a few members or dispersed throughout the group. Finally, change in the subjects' beliefs about the groups was measured.

The experimental results showed that dispersed rather than concentrated information was more effective in leading to change in the stereotype. This is consistent with both the bookkeeping and the subtyping models but not the conversion model. There was greater change in the stereotype with the dispersed information when the sample size was large rather than small, indicating that change was occurring through the bookkeeping model. However, when the counter-stereotypic information was concentrated in a few individuals, there was evidence that subtyping rather than stereotype change was taking place. These results imply that both bookkeeping and subtyping were occurring, with dispersed information gradually leading to a change in the stereotype and concentrated information leading to the subtyping of the counter-stereotypic individuals.

We can predict from these results that the stereotype of women, for example, will change and develop as more women are seen in non-traditional roles, particularly if these women are seen as representative of women as a whole. However, if these women are seen as an unrepresentative minority then subtypes emerge, such as the 'career woman', without necessarily changing stereotypical beliefs about women in general.

TRAITS AND STEREOTYPES

The question of when a category is a type or a stereotype is a difficult one as there is no clear separation between our definition of type and stereotype; the latter is simply a more extreme form of the former. However, a slightly different question can be studied: are there differences in the sort of information available with different types of category labels?

Andersen and Klatzky (1987), following from the work of Cantor and Mischel (1979a), studied the differences between trait terms (abstract categories according to the previous study), such as 'extrovert', and stereotypes (more concrete categories), such as 'bully', as category labels. They argued that traits are associated in memory with a number of stereotypes (or even people), so a 'bully', a 'clown' (and John Smith) are all viewed as extrovert. Stereotypes are associated with behaviours and other characteristics as well as having links to certain traits; a 'bully' is violent to people as well as being extrovert. Categorization by stereotype rather than by a trait term therefore allows a greater degree of social prediction: that is, having labelled a boy as a bully we are likely to predict that he will push other children around. However, perceiving a boy to be extroverted does not allow us to predict his behaviour with such specificity. Where trait terms are predictive, it is due to their associative links to a number of stereotypes. Predicting the behaviour of a boy perceived as extroverted is possible indirectly, through the stereotypes that extroversion is linked to, such as 'bully' or 'clown'. In a series of experiments, looking at the trait terms 'extroversion' and 'introversion' and the stereotypes 'comedian', 'politician' and 'bully' associated with the former and 'brain', 'neurotic' and 'guru' associated with the latter, Andersen and Klatzky (1987) compared the attributes of trait and stereotype categories. They found that trait terms were associated by the subjects with a range of different stereotypes, that stereotype labels generated more attributes than trait terms and that, whilst stereotypes have distinct attributes, trait categories share almost all their attributes with related stereotypes.

In conclusion, Andersen and Klatzky (1987) argue that traits and stereotypes are different in their representations in memory, the latter being richer (having more attributes), more vivid and with more distinctive attributes. Even though there might be more of an overlap of attributes between stereotypes (such as between a comedian and a politician) this is unlikely to diminish the specific predictions that we can make from stereotypes about behaviour. There is a temptation to see stereotypes as more useful in social perception due to their predictive quality. However, for people we do not know at all and for people we know very well trait terms may serve as more useful descriptions (Andersen and Klatzky, 1987). On a brief encounter with a woman we may be able to report only that she seemed 'nice'. We simply do not have enough information to evoke a stereotype. With a close friend, Linda, describing her in stereotypical terms does not do justice to her, whereas describing her as nice (and other characteristics) allows for her individuality. We are therefore more likely to use stereotypes to categorize those people we know well enough to fit into one but not so well that the stereotype is clearly invalid.

Stereotypes are also more efficiently processed than trait terms (Andersen *et al.*, 1990). Trait terms (such as extroverted) or stereotypes (such as politician) were combined in sentences with mundane acts (such as 'closed the door') or states (such as 'felt hungry'). Subjects had to decide if it was likely that this type of person would do or experience what was written in the sentence. The results showed that subjects responded more quickly to the sentences including stereotypes compared to those including trait terms. According to Andersen *et al.*, this increase in speed indicates a greater efficiency of processing, suggesting that subjects can employ information from stereotype categories more quickly than trait information in their inferences about people.

This work helps us to explain, in part, why we use stereotypes. We have seen that stereotypes help to simplify the diversity of individuals by providing categories within which we can place them. With a rich, vivid set of attributes we can make inferences about the behaviour of other people that might aid us in our perception of them and in our interaction with them, as we can make specific predictions about their behaviour and characteristics. The greater efficiency of processing also gives us a rapidity of processing to combine with the possibility of prediction. However, we should not see specific stereotypes as immutable and prejudice as inevitable. We do not have to support prejudiced views. Stereotypes can change, old ones die out and new ones emerge.

Chapter 5

Impression formation

Mary sat back in her chair. She was confident that all the chosen candidates satisfied a number of criteria, such as having relevant past experience, but the list was still too long. Peter and Susan entered with the collection of references.

'These might help,' said Peter, laying them out on the desk so they could all read them.

'How about this one?' said Susan, holding up a reference. The other two looked up. She scanned the paper: 'determined. . .industrious. . .skilful. Sounds pretty good?'

'Yes,' said Mary, a little hesitantly, 'although could be a little dull. Anything on creative ability?'

'No. . . not really. The only other comment is that he's friendly. That's it. Sounds nice enough.'

'Yes, keep that one for the moment. He's promising. But he does sound more of a good solid bet than a dynamic sort of person.'

'I'm not sure about this one,' said Peter. 'It says he can be aggressive. Shall I reject him?'

'I think so,' said Susan.

'Anything else?' asked Mary. 'Unusual for a referee to put that. Do you think it means personally aggressive or business-wise. Someone who'll fight tooth and nail for this company shouldn't be ignored.'

'Hard-working. . .unsociable. . .rather pushy. That's about it. Reject it?'

'OK,' said Mary. 'He doesn't sound very appealing. Not the sort of person our clients would take to.'

'Or me,' joined in Peter.

'This one looks good,' said Susan. 'Innovative. . . pragmatic. . . intelligent.'

'Yes,' said Mary, standing to read the rest of the reference over Susan's shoulder, 'keep that one.'

We do not always learn about people from direct experience. We often find out about them from descriptions. A mutual friend might describe someone we are about to meet: 'William is fun-loving and kind.' Application forms often provide space for a candidate to provide an account of themselves and their interests. References in support of a job application seek to describe the person: 'Elizabeth is conscientious and thorough.' Usually a description includes a number of trait terms and from the characterization a perceiver gains an impression of the person described. As an example, imagine that a friend, Robert, is taking you to meet his mother and you want to know whether you will get on with her, so you ask him to describe her.

> Well, Mum's pretty dynamic, always on the go, both at work and at home. In fact she's a bit of a workaholic. I think it's because she gets bored easily, but she's really creative. Diane, my sister, and I have always found her quite exciting, thinking up interesting things to do when we were kids. She's really imaginative that way. But she expects everyone else to be as clever and dynamic as herself. We've both found it hard living up to her expectations. She doesn't suffer fools gladly but can be really charming if you come up to her standards.

There is very little information here beyond a list a personality traits. Yet I am sure that you gained an impression of Robert's mother. Can you suggest other characteristics she might have? Do you think you would like her? Can you even guess what she looks like?

In this chapter we shall be considering how an impression is formed from a description based on character traits, asking how we combine the information from the various characteristics into an overall impression of the person.

ASCH'S KEY WORK

The seminal work on impression formation was undertaken by Solomon Asch, a social psychologist who followed the Gestalt approach to psychology. The Gestalt psychologists, working mostly in the first part of the twentieth century, argued that psychological experience has a quality beyond the simple addition of the individual elements of that experience. A melody is more than a collection of individual notes, a film is more than the sum of the individual frames. The overall experience is a Gestalt (from the German meaning a shape or form): we hear a tune or see a moving image, even though the tune is not contained in the individual notes nor the movement within the individual frames of the film.

Asch (1946) gave his subjects a list of seven personality traits (called the stimulus list) and asked them to form an impression of a person with these characteristics. The first thing he noted was that the subjects were able to form impressions quite easily, and suggest other characteristics of the person, as well as indicating what sort of job they might do or even what they might look like! Asch then asked his subjects to indicate on a further list of characteristics, the checklist, which other traits the person would have. This was also performed quite easily, indicating that the subjects had a clear impression of the person described that went beyond the seven traits given in the stimulus list, thus supporting his prediction that the impression forms a Gestalt, a global impression of the person.

In a series of experiments, Asch (1946) investigated aspects of impression formation by changing his trait list. To one group of subjects he gave the list: *intelligent, skilful, industrious, warm, determined, practical, cautious.* To another group he gave the same list except that the trait *warm* in the first list was replaced with *cold* in the second. However, this had a massive effect on the impression as shown by the subsequent checklist. Subjects in the first group had an impression of a generous, happy, good-natured, sociable person whereas the second group had the opposite impression: ungenerous, unhappy, irritable, unsociable. The *warm–cold* trait was called a *central trait* by Asch as it appeared to be central to the impression. In a further experiment Asch replaced *warm–cold* with *polite–blunt*. In this case there was nothing like the same effect on the impression and so Asch termed *polite–blunt* a *peripheral trait*. These results demonstrated that not all traits contribute equally to the overall impression.

However, the surrounding traits in the list were found to have interesting effects on the meaning of other traits in the list. Consider the impression formed by the following list: *obedient, weak, shallow, warm, unambitious, vain*. Now compare your impression with that produced by this list: *vain, shrewd, unscrupulous, warm, shallow, envious*. Asch's subjects reported that the first impression was of someone who had the warmth of a follower whereas the second impression was of a person who appears warm but in reality is not. Even though both lists included the word *warm*, there was a change in the meaning ascribed to that characteristic. Not only that, but in the first list *warm* was important to the overall impression whereas in the second list it was not, the impression was not of a genuinely warm person. Asch followed this up with an experiment looking at the effect of the *kind–cruel* trait on the perceived meaning of the characteristics *calm* and *strong* by noting the differences in synonyms chosen by subjects for these words after being given one of the following two lists: *kind, wise, honest, calm, strong* or *cruel, shrewd, unscrupulous, calm, strong*. After the first list *calm* was seen as serene but following the second list it was seen as cold. *Strong* changed from fearless and helpful to ruthless and hard. Asch concluded that the meaning of a trait is determined by its surrounding traits, with central traits having the most influence upon the others. This has been termed *the meaning change hypothesis*.

Another important effect found by Asch (1946) concerned the presentation of the traits. The list: *intelligent, industrious, impulsive, critical, sullen, envious* resulted in a different impression from that formed by the list in reverse order: *envious, sullen, critical, impulsive, industrious, intelligent*. In the first list the 'good' qualities are first and the 'bad' qualities later; in the second list these were reversed. The good qualities dominated the first list giving an impression of 'an able person with some shortcomings' and the bad qualities dominated the second list, with the person seen as having 'serious problems that affected their abilities'. Asch (1946) called this the *primacy effect*. It appears therefore that the subjects are building up an impression by integrating the new traits with the old, by finding a relationship between them. For example, consider the trait *fun-loving* following the trait *cruel*. The person may be seen as liking nasty practical jokes as this relates the characteristics in a way that they can apply to the same person. However, *fun-loving* following *kind* might lead to the impression of someone who likes to make others happy and is also a joy to be with. Asch found support for this idea in experiments that showed that subjects found it hard to integrate one contradictory trait at the end of the list with the impression being formed, or to combine contradictory impressions. The implication of this finding is clear. If you want to make a good impression through a description of your characteristics, make sure the better ones come first!

Asch (1946) had clearly discredited the notion that an overall impression comprises the sum of the impressions of the individual traits. The meaning change and primacy effects argued against that. He concluded that the subjects form a global impression of the person, organized in terms of the relationships between the traits. Each trait is understood in terms of the others, with some traits, the central traits, having the strongest influence on the overall impression. The checklist results showed that the impression went beyond the seven stimulus traits. The organization of the overall impression and the inferences being made from it can be seen in terms of the schema concept that we considered in the last chapter (Fiske and Taylor, 1984), with the trait list evoking a particular schema which provides a framework for understanding the person described.

TRAIT DESCRIPTIONS: APPLICABLE TO REAL LIFE EXAMPLES?

Kelley (1950) looked at the effect of Asch's *warm–cold* trait list on the perception of real people. A student class was presented with some brief information about a new instructor. For half the students the description included the final sentence: 'People who know him consider him to be a very warm person, industrious, critical, practical and determined.' For the other half, the final sentence was the same except that 'very warm' was replaced by 'rather cold'. The new instructor came into the class and led a twenty-minute discussion. After he had left the students were asked to write a description of him as well as rate him on a checklist of fifteen other traits. The *warm–cold* difference in the information given to the students led to very different impressions of the instructor, despite the fact that all students had seen the same man. The 'warm' group of students found him much more sociable, popular and humorous. More of these students (56 per cent) entered the discussion than the 'cold' group (32 per cent). These results show the applicability of Asch's *warm–cold* result to real people as well as clearly demonstrating the powerful effect the descriptions had on the students' impressions of the instructor before them. It is well worth college professors having themselves described as *warm* in the student literature if they want to make a good impression!

In another study, Warr and Knapper (1968) made the personality description realistic by constructing a newspaper report about the manager of a football team. This was then given to two groups of students, the only difference in the report was that one contained the word *warm* and the other *cold*. On a checklist of thirteen traits there was a clear difference in the impression formed of the football manager, in agreement with the findings of Asch. Indeed, in one of their experiments, the description ran to 450 words with the only difference being the phrase with *warm* or *cold* in it, yet still significant differences were found.

WHAT IS A CENTRAL TRAIT?

Asch (1946) had defined a central trait as one which produced large differences on the checklist when the trait was shifted from one extreme to the other, for example *warm* to *cold*. However, he could not predict in advance which traits would be central and which peripheral before he had tested them out on his subjects. This led Wishner (1960) to investigate what makes a trait central or peripheral in a stimulus list. He argued that we need to know something about the relationship between traits. What is the relationship of *warm–cold* to *strong–weak* or *ruthless–humane?* In his study he examined how people combine character traits when they judge real people. He selected fifty-three of the traits used by Asch (1946) in his stimulus lists and checklists. Then he asked students to rate their instructors on these traits. From these data Wishner calculated the correlations between traits. If the students who rate someone as *determined* also rate that person as *persistent* and those who rate someone as *indecisive* also rate them as *wavering* then the traits of *determined–indecisive* and *persistent–wavering* are highly correlated. If there is no consistent relationship between two traits then those traits are not correlated in the data.

Wishner's important result was that the *warm–cold* trait correlated with those traits in Asch's checklist that showed the greatest differences when *warm* was changed to *cold* in the stimulus list. This meant that a trait will be a central trait if it correlates with the traits in the checklist and it will be a peripheral trait if it does not. If we know the relationship between the stimulus trait and the checklist traits we can predict whether it will be central or peripheral in advance of the impression formation. From Wishner's results we can see the importance of the traits chosen for the checklist as well as those chosen for the stimulus list, as it is possible to make any trait in the stimulus list a central trait by selecting appropriate (correlated) traits for the checklist.

The result of this study developed Asch's work by showing that central traits can be predicted as long as we know which traits are correlated. But which traits do people believe go together? What inferences do people make from the traits they are given? The answer to these questions has been studied under the topic called *implicit personality theory* which we shall be looking at in the next chapter. For the present chapter we shall concentrate on how we combine the stimulus traits to give an overall impression.

TRAIT COMBINATIONS

Asch (1946) had argued that a simple summation of the individual traits did not predict the final overall impression. However, other researchers sought to examine whether an impression could be predicted from the individual trait values. Bruner *et al.* (1958) studied the traits *considerate, independent, intelligent* and *inconsiderate*. Subjects were asked to rate the traits individually, in pairs or as triples on a checklist of further traits. From their results they were able to show that knowledge of the individual trait ratings could predict the effect of the traits in combination. For example, when two traits individually have the same direction of inference on a checklist trait then their combination will lead to the same direction of inference: if *intelligent* and considerate lead separately to an inference of *reliability* rather than *unreliability* then their combination will also lead to an inference of *reliability* rather than *unreliability*. With three traits, even when the direction of inference on a checklist trait is not the same for all three individually, their combined effect can still be predicted: it will be the same direction as the two traits that agree.

In Asch's experiments the effect of an impression was discovered by the use of a number of traits in a checklist. A simpler method is to employ only one checklist trait. This allows for a more detailed analysis of the effect of the impression on this trait. In addition, rather than deciding whether a person is either *considerate* or *inconsiderate*, the subject can be asked to give a rating value, from, say, −5 for *extremely inconsiderate* to, say, +5 for *extremely considerate*, with a value of 0 in the middle. The reason for setting up this method is that the impressions given by individual traits can be compared with traits in combination on the same rating scale. For example, how does the value of the impression from the trait combination *intelligent* and *ruthless* compare with the individual ratings of *intelligent* and *ruthless* on the *inconsiderate–considerate* scale?

Anderson (1965) used this method to study trait combinations on a single checklist trait, *dislike–like*. He considered two possible rules for trait combination: summation and averaging. He called these two models of trait combination the additive model and the averaging model. The *additive model* predicts that a subject's impression will be the sum of the traits presented. Using the scale −5 to +5 for *dislike* to *like*, let us assume that the following traits, when presented individually, give the following values on the scale: *truthful*, 4; *conscientious*, 2; *industrious*, 1; *unpopular*, −1. If a subject is given the traits *truthful, conscientious* and *unpopular* the additive model predicts a liking of +5 (the total of 4 plus 2 plus −1). Note that, importantly, according to this model, liking will increase in a trait combination with each new trait that individually has a positive value. Thus, the impression from the combination of the three traits *truthful, conscientious* and *industrious* will be more likeable than any one or combination of two of them.

The *averaging model* predicts that the value of the overall impression on the *dislike–like* scale will be the average of the individual traits given. This model predicts a liking of $+1^2/_3$ for *truthful, conscientious* and *unpopular* (4+2−1, divided by 3). Note that in this model liking will increase only if a new trait has a value greater than the average of the previous combination. For example, *conscientious* and *industrious* give an overall average of $1^1/_2$ (2+1, divided by 2). Adding the trait *truthful* to *conscientious* and *industrious* gives a new average of $2^1/_3$ (4+2+1, divided by 3). An increase in liking has arisen as the individual value for *truthful* (4) is greater than the previous average (1.5). However, when a subject is told that someone is *truthful* and *conscientious* the model predicts an overall value of 3 (4+2, divided by 2) but when they are given *truthful, conscientious* and *industrious* the average drops to $2^1/_3$. When the individual value of a new trait is lower than the previous average a drop in liking results.

This leads to the interesting test of the two models. The additive model predicts an *increase* in liking of *truthful, conscientious* and *industrious* compared to only *truthful* and *conscientious*, whereas the averaging model predicts a *decrease*. This is the test Anderson (1965) performed. He first asked subjects to rate 555 adjectives on a seven-point *dislike–like* scale. He then selected adjectives from the high values (denoted H, liked a lot), medium positive values (M⁺, liked a little), medium negative values (M⁻, disliked a little) and low values (L, disliked a lot). Subjects were then asked to rate adjectives in pairs and in groups of four. The critical comparison was between a high-value pair (HH, for example, *reasonable* and *truthful*) and a high-value pair coupled with a medium-positive-value pair (HHM⁺M⁺, for example, *reasonable, truthful, painstaking* and *persuasive*). The additive model predicts a higher rating for the HHM⁺M⁺ quadruple whereas the averaging model predicts a higher rating for the HH pair. Anderson's results supported the averaging model and contradicted the additive model. (He also found, in agreement with the averaging model, that an LL pair yielded a greater amount of disliking than an LLM⁻M⁻ quadruple.)

The weighted averages model

A secondary finding which neither model predicted was that a quadruple led to a more polarized rating than a pair of the same type, so an HHHH quadruple gave a higher liking value than an HH pair and a LLLL quadruple gave a lower value (more disliked) than an LL pair. This is called the *set size effect*: the larger the set size the more polarized the rating.

Anderson (1965) suggested two additions to the averaging model to incorporate this finding. First, he suggested that we have an initial impression that we bring to the situation. As an example, on one day you might be feeling very positive towards people in general and the next day you are a little grumpy. This will affect your subsequent judgement of the character traits. The initial impression is therefore like another trait to be included in the averaging process. Anderson also argued that the traits could have different *weights*, that is, each trait does not necessarily contribute to the impression to the same extent. In the Asch (1946) experiment *warm–cold* was a central trait and *polite–blunt* a peripheral trait. This is the same as saying that *warm–cold* had a greater weight than *polite–blunt*.

This new model is called the *weighted averages model*. Each trait (and the initial impression) has an individual rating value (its value on the *dislike–like* dimension) and a weight (how large a contribution it makes to the overall impression). The value of the trait combination can be expressed by the following formula:

$$R = \frac{Iw_0 + T_1w_1 + T_2w_2 + \ldots + T_kw_k}{w_0 + w_1 + w_2 + \ldots + w_k}$$

where R is the final impression, I is the initial impression, w_0 is the weight of the initial impression, T_1 is the first trait and w_1 its weight, and so on, with k being the number of traits in the list.

This model can account for the set size effect. Assume that the four traits *truthful, warm, happy* and *generous* all score 4 on the –5 to +5 scale of *dislike–like* and the initial impression has a value of, say, 2 (assuming the perceiver starts with a moderately positive view of people). We now need the weights. Let us assume that the initial impression doesn't contribute very much to the overall impression, so we give it a weight of 0.2, with *truthful, warm, happy* and *generous* contributing more, say, 0.5 each, for ease of calculation. (They could in reality have different weights.)

Now we can calculate the impression of *truthful* and *warm* by slotting the values into the formula.

$$R = \frac{Iw_0 + T_1w_1 + T_2w_2}{w_0 + w_1 + w_2} = \frac{(2 \times 0.2) + (4 \times 0.5) + (4 \times 0.5)}{0.2 + 0.5 + 0.5}$$

$$R = 3.67$$

Now we calculate the impression of all four traits:

$$R = \frac{Iw_0 + T_1w_1 + T_2w_2 + T_3w_3 + T_4w_4}{w_0 + w_1 + w_2 + w_3 + w_4}$$

$$R = \frac{(2 \times 0.2) + (4 \times 0.5) + (4 \times 0.5) + (4 \times 0.5) + (4 \times 0.5)}{0.2 + 0.5 + 0.5 + 0.5 + 0.5}$$

$$R = 3.82$$

Thus, with traits of equal value, the result becomes more extreme with increasing numbers of traits, and the weighted average model is able to account for both of the effects found by Anderson (1965).

The weighted averages model and the primacy effect

As noted earlier, Asch (1946) had found a primacy effect in impression formation: the earlier traits in a list dominated the later ones. He explained this by saying that the meanings of the later traits were changed to fit into the overall impression being built up by the earlier ones, so the trait *strong* would have a different meaning after *kind* than after *cruel*. This change-of-meaning explanation is impossible with the simple weighted averages model as the scale value of a trait does not change whether it is presented on its own or in combination: the value of *crafty* of, say, +1 on a *dislike–like* scale will be the same regardless of the other traits in the list. How then can the model explain the primacy effect? One thing that can change is the contribution of a trait to the overall impression formed, its weight. If the weights of the earlier traits in a list were greater than those of the later traits then a primacy effect would occur. This provides an explanation in terms of the theory but begs another question: why do the earlier traits in a list have a greater weight?

One explanation, tested by Stewart (1965), is called the *attention decrement hypothesis*. This suggests that subjects pay less attention to the later items in a list when forming their impression. This seems reasonable, given that we can form an impression from very little information. Maybe we get an idea of the person from the first few traits and simply don't bother that much with the later ones. Stewart asked his subjects to listen to a list of traits and to rate their impression on a *dislike–like* scale. With one group he used the traditional test and asked the subjects to give a rating at the end of the list. The second group were required to give a rating after each trait was read out. It was assumed that this would require them to attend to the later traits as well as the earlier ones. The first group had the expected primacy effect but the second group did not. Indeed, they had a recency effect, with the later traits influencing the rating more than the earlier ones. Therefore, it does appear that the attention paid to the various traits can influence their relative importance to the impression formed. To make a good impression, make sure the audience attends to your good points!

ASCH OR ANDERSON?

The ability of the weighted averages model to explain a number of effects led to a debate between the supporters of the Asch view and the Anderson view as to which model was superior in understanding impression formation: that of Asch, where the impression was an overall Gestalt or schema (Fiske and Taylor, 1984) that led to a change of meaning of certain traits in the list, or Anderson's model where traits were averaged in a piecemeal fashion (Fiske and Pavelchak, 1986) to produce an overall impression.

Context effects, explained by meaning change by Asch, provided a problem for the weighted averages model. It was found that, when a trait was part of a list that produced an overall positive impression, that trait was judged more positively than when tested on its own. Similarly, a negative context reduced the scale value of a trait (Anderson, 1966, 1971; Anderson and Lampel, 1965). As noted previously, the simple weighted averaging model assumes that the scale value of a trait does not change in the context of other traits. Anderson produced a variation of the model to take account of this, and allow the overall impression to influence the scale value of a trait. If a trait, say, *fun-loving*, had a scale value of +1 when presented on its own, then the context (the overall impression produced by the weighted average of the traits) modifies this value. A positive context produced by traits like *happy, warm, kind* will produce a positive impression that will make the scale value of *fun-loving* more positive. Similarly, in the context of *unhappy, cold, cruel* the negative overall impression will reduce the scale value of *fun-loving*. This has been called a *halo explanation* as context has a halo effect (see Chapter 7), with the individual traits responsive to the 'halo' of the overall impression.

The halo explanation does not really imply a meaning change of the sort Asch (1946) had proposed but simply a change to a trait's value on a single dimension. In the meaning-change explanation the overall impression is essentially categorical or schematic in that it provides an interpretative framework for the traits. For example, a list of traits leading to an overall impression that we might loosely label 'a trickster' would lead to the meaning of the constituent trait *clever* being viewed as 'the ability to con others'. In the context of 'scientist', *clever* might be seen as meaning 'the ability to understand the complexities of the world'. To Asch the trait *strong* changed in meaning from *fearless* and *helpful* to *ruthless* and *hard* when the context changed from *cruel* to *kind*, in line with the Gestalt of the overall impression, whereas the halo explanation simply sees *strong* as becoming more or less *likeable*, along the *dislike–like* dimension.

An interesting attempt to test the change of meaning and halo explanations came from Wyer and Watson (1969). They pointed out that some traits are more 'ambiguous' than others: that is, they have a large number of possible meanings whereas others have few. A trait like *proud* can range from *noble* and *self-respecting* to *conceited* and *self-important* whereas *dogmatic* has a narrower range. They argued that the meaning-change hypothesis would predict a greater effect of context on the ambiguous traits compared to the less ambiguous traits. Kaplan (1971, 1974) argued that the halo explanation would predict no difference. Using different methods, Wyer and Watson (1969) found some evidence of a difference, Kaplan (1971) found no difference and Wyer (1974) found a much larger difference than Wyer and Watson (1969). Disappointingly, none of these results can be seen as conclusive, as Ostrom (1977) argued that either explanation can be made to account for them.

A second line of investigation considered the response scale rather than the stimulus traits. Hamilton and Zanna (1974) demonstrated the usual context effect but then asked subjects to rate the stimulus trait on a response scale derived from a positive and negative synonym of the trait. For example, with the stimulus trait *proud* they used the scale *confident–conceited*. They argued that if different contexts lead to different ratings on this scale then the meaning of the trait *proud* had changed. Their results supported this hypothesis: a positive context led subjects to rate the trait *proud* more towards the positive (*confident*) end of the scale and a negative context resulted in a more *conceited* rating.

This would have been extremely strong support for the meaning-change hypothesis, had Kaplan (1975) not found that trait values changed with the context on *unrelated* scales as well as on the *synonymous* scales, so the value of the trait *daring* showed a context effect on *witty–cynical* (unrelated) as well as on *courageous–reckless* (related). This is not predicted by the meaning-change explanation, whereas the halo explanation implies that the context changes the scale value of the trait equally for any scale, related or unrelated. Even so, Kaplan (1975) and Zanna and Hamilton (1977) found that the context effect was greater on related scales compared to unrelated scales, once again supportive of the meaning-change hypothesis.

The problems of this debate were even further complicated by Watkins and Peynircioğlu (1984) who argued that the methods used by experimenters may not be the appropriate ones for finding meaning change even if it exists!

Single and multidimensional evaluation

A number of debates in psychology between seemingly conflicting theories are not firmly resolved in favour of one theory over the other for a range of reasons: the theories may be based on different assumptions, they might be considering different aspects of the same question, there might not be a critical test to compare them. This debate was one that produced no winner. Ostrom (1977) noted that the averaging model and the meaning-change model could both explain the available data and therefore it was not very fruitful attempting to reject one in favour of the other. Indeed, the theories focused on different aspects of impression formation: 'whereas the averaging model focuses exclusively on how people respond to stimuli on unidimensional psychological continua, the meaning shift approach focuses on the multiplicity of thoughts people have when considering a stimulus person's characteristics prior to making a judgement' (Ostrom, 1977, p.501).

The averaging model has its strength, therefore, in explaining how we combine information along a single dimension, such as *like–dislike*. Indeed, Anderson (1974, 1981) has developed *information integration theory* that can be used to explain information integration in a range of social judgements (see Shanteau and Nagy, 1984, for examples of its application). However, given a wider range of dimensions on which to register an impression, the complexity of meaning change of the individual traits might emerge. Measuring the impression on the *like–dislike* dimension might not fully reflect the change in impression. Whilst the averaging model could explain changes along a single dimension, the meaning-change hypothesis might be able to explain changes across many dimensions.

A number of studies have looked at multidimensional judgements. Cohen (1971) argued that the impression formed by trait combinations may not be reflected along a single dimension, such as *dislike–like*. In this study subjects rated their impression of traits on thirty-six dimensions. Cohen found that consistent trait combinations were found to vary along pretty much the same dimensions as the traits in isolation. However, when inconsistent traits were combined, the dimensions that varied were different from those for the individual trait. It appears, therefore, that, to make sense of inconsistent combinations of traits, subjects might switch the dimensions on which they form their impression. An interesting finding was that the subjects agreed (to a considerable extent) on the dimensions to switch to with inconsistent trait combinations. This aspect of the research was supported by the study of Asch and Zukier (1984) who presented subjects with apparently conflicting traits like *brilliant* and *foolish*, *sociable* and *lonely* or *generous* and *vindictive*. These appear to be opposites on a single dimension and hence incompatible, yet the subjects were able to make sense of them and form an impression. For example, *brilliant* and *foolish* on the single dimension *intelligent–unintelligent* are at opposite ends yet the subjects saw the combination as indicating someone who is, say, academically *brilliant* but *foolish* in terms of lacking common sense. The 'absent-minded professor' comes to mind as an example. Here we see that the trait combination leads to an evaluation along dimensions such as *intellectual–unintellectual* and *worldly–unworldly*. The *sociable* and *lonely* person was seen as sociable but 'lonely inside', the sociability merely disguising an inner loneliness. Similarly, the *generous* and *vindictive* person is only generous for ulterior motives, it is a veneer to hide the vindictive scheming. Here we can see that in producing an explanation one of the traits is viewed as indicating a 'deeper' aspect of personality and the other becomes more superficial.

It is not difficult to make sense of apparently conflicting information if combined in this way. Consider someone who is *happy* and *sad*. I can imagine a person who is happy 'inside' but sad on the surface, say, due to a tragic event. Interestingly, it is not difficult to combine it the other way round and imagine someone who is sad inside, maybe due to a loss they have never got over, yet happy on the surface, in their dealings with others. This effect was shown by Gergen *et al.* (1986) who found that subjects could combine two traits into an impression regardless of which one was presented as the deeper *source trait* and which as the *surface trait*.

Casselden and Hampson (1990) studied the ease with which pairs of traits could be imagined as belonging to the same person. They found that, although inconsistent traits could be combined in an impression, subjects did find it more difficult to combine inconsistent than consistent trait pairs, with the semantic similarity of the two traits aiding the subjects' capacity to imagine their combination in a person. Interestingly, they found that an inconsistent pair of traits was easier to imagine in combination when they were presented with the word 'but' rather than 'and', so *scornful but tactful* was easier to imagine in combination than *scornful and tactful*. The reverse was found for consistent pairs. Further evidence for the difference in trait combinations for consistent and inconsistent pairs came from the descriptions subjects gave concerning how the trait pair 'go together in a person'. For consistent pairs the subjects provided integrated descriptions relating the traits together whereas, for inconsistent pairs, aggregated descriptions were forthcoming where the traits were not related together. It looks as though consistent pairs of traits are combined quite easily by relating them together in the impression of a person. It is not difficult to imagine someone who is *warm and kind*, these can be seen as complementary aspects of a personality. However, with inconsistent traits they are combined, not by their similarity in meaning or evaluation, but as two different aspects of personality that have to be put together in the same person in some way, possibly by viewing one as an 'inner' and the other as an 'outer' trait. It is harder to imagine someone who is *cruel and kind* than someone who is *cruel but kind*, possibly because the latter helps us to deal with the inconsistency: 'This person is cruel BUT they might appear kind.'

These studies show that people can form an impression from apparently conflicting information and this may not be detected on a single dimension but only by looking at a number of different dimensions. Thus the two models, meaning change and weighted average, both have their strengths. If we are concerned with integrating information along a single dimension, then the weighted average model provides a framework for that integration. However, if we are combining conflicting information in an impression of a single person the meaning-change model provides a framework for explanation: some traits change their meaning to fit into an organized impression and some are even seen as more indicative of the 'inner' person than others to create an overall Gestalt of the person. These changes may be detected only across a number of dimensions.

THE WEIGHTING OF INFORMATION IN IMPRESSIONS

As we have seen, both the Asch and the Anderson models of impression formation allow some traits to be more influential in the overall impression that others. In this section we shall be considering why two kinds of trait information are given more weight that others: negative and extreme information.

An equal weighted averaging model predicts that if a positive trait such as *happy*, with a value of +6 on a +10 to −10 *like-dislike* scale, is combined with a negative trait like *unkind*, with a value of −6, then the impression of the combination should be neutral, with a value of zero. However, in a large number of studies (see Skowronski and Carlson, 1989) it has been found that the impression tends to be negative, say −2. It appeared that people were biased in their impressions by negative information: negative traits have greater weight in the averaging process than positive traits.

There are a number of explanations for this (Skowronski and Carlson, 1989; Coovert and Reeder, 1990). One, the frequency-weight explanation, proposes that we give greater weight in a judgement to unexpected or less frequent information (see Fiske, 1980). (We shall see the importance of unexpected information to judgements again in Chapter 8.) It is not unreasonable to assume that we learn of more positive information than negative information about people or expect people to have positive traits rather than negative ones. Politeness in descriptions and a general expectation that people have positive characteristics could lead to this assumption. On being told that Jack is kind and dishonest, it is not his kindness that we find unusual or unexpected but his dishonesty.

An alternative explanation is that negative information is less ambiguous and hence more informative than positive information. Explanations of this sort have been called range theories (Skowronski and Carlson, 1989) or dispositional-overlap theories (Coovert and Reeder, 1990). Here it is assumed that, whilst a positive trait like *kind* has a value of, say, +6, it has a degree of ambiguity in that its value can vary, from, say, +4 to +8. Negative traits are seen to be less ambiguous, so *dishonest* is not going to vary much from -6. The assumption is that *kind* can vary in its implications from *quite kind* to *very kind* whereas *dishonest* is simply *dishonest*. Combining traits of these types will result in greater weight given in the overall impression to the trait with the narrower range.

A third explanation is based on the idea of expectancy-contrast (e.g. Helson, 1964). Here it is assumed that there is a psychological anchor or reference point from which information is contrasted. In impression formation we assume that people might expect, from their experiences, that personal characteristics are generally positive, leading to an expectation of a trait value that is moderately positive, say +3. When a positive trait occurs such as *kind* with a value of +6 or *generous* with a value of +4, then there is little contrast between the anchor and the trait value (3 and 1 respectively). However, a negative trait like *dishonest* with a value of -6 contrasts strongly with the anchor, as the difference is 9. This contrast, with its large deviation from an expected value, leads to the negative trait being given more weight in the impression.

Skowronski and Carlson (1989) argue that all three of the above explanations are limited either by their logic or in terms of their experimental support and suggest a fourth explanation. In this, the diagnostic approach, they propose that information, like trait information, is used by perceivers to categorize an individual. The diagnosticity of a piece of information is its ability to distinguish between person categories. The person category can be seen in terms of a prototype (Cantor and Mischel, 1979a) or a schema (Reeder and Brewer, 1979). It is assumed that some information given about an individual can be more diagnostic than other information in impression formation, and is more useful in fitting someone to a category. Negative information is seen as more diagnostic than positive information when we are deciding where someone fits on the *good–bad* dimension. Skowronski and Carlson (1989) argue that both a good person and a bad person could perform both good and bad acts: there are circumstances where an honest person might steal and unpleasant people sometimes do good deeds. However, we generally expect a good person to perform good acts, so if someone is performing both good and bad acts we are more likely to infer that they are bad rather than good. Hence the combination of a positive and a negative trait leads to greater weight being placed on the negative trait and the overall impression tends to be negative.

Coovert and Reeder (1990) follow the same logic as Skowronski and Carlson (1989) in their explanation of the negativity effect, graphically illustrating the assumption of consistency in the behaviour of good people over bad people by the following example. We are not surprised by a mafia godfather giving money to charity but we would be very surprised to learn that the Pope was dealing in illegal drugs. Thus, moral acts could be expected from both moral and immoral people whereas immoral acts are indicative of an immoral person. Hence the immoral act is more diagnostic.

Coovert and Reeder (1990) argue that, if schemata underlie the negativity effect, then it will have its strongest effect when the positive and negative information refer to the same person. Even if the two pieces of information concern different people but those people come from a meaningfully related group (such as friends) then schematic expectations will also occur as the perceiver might see members of the group as behaving in a similar way. However, if the information concerns two unrelated people, forming an impression of the aggregate of the two pieces of information might not lead to a negativity effect as the behaviour is not necessarily seen as part of an organized unit of behaviour we would expect from a schema. Without schematic expectations the perceiver might simply combine the two pieces of information in a piecemeal way (see also Fiske and Pavelchak, 1986, later in this chapter), giving equal weight to each. The alternative explanations, listed above, predict a similar negativity effect in all three cases.

In an experimental test of this Coovert and Reeder provided subjects with two pieces of behaviour, such as 'saved a family from a burning house' and 'sold diseased meat'. In one condition the subjects were told to form an impression of a person described by the behaviours, after which they had to rate the person on the *immoral–moral* dimension. In a second condition the subjects were asked to form an impression of two friends, the first behaviour performed by one and the second behaviour by the other. In the third condition the subjects were asked to form an impression, as in the second condition, but it was stressed that the two people were unrelated (chosen at random from the phone book).

The results, in support of their predictions, showed the largest negativity effect in the single person condition, a significant negativity effect in the meaningful group condition (related persons) and no evidence of a negativity effect in the aggregate condition (unrelated persons).

The explanations of Skowronski and Carlson (1989) and Coovert and Reeder (1990) both propose that we are trying to fit the information we receive about a person into a person category (a schema or a prototype) and hence information that helps us in this process receives more weight than information that does not. In many cases negative information serves that function better than positive information but it need not. If some positive information is particularly useful in making a categorization it will receive greater weight than less diagnostic information. Indeed, Skowronski and Carlson (1987) found a positivity effect when the impressions were based on a combination of behaviours concerning ability and a negativity effect when the behaviours were concerned with morality.

This leads us to the extremity effect: extreme information is given greater weight in an impression. Skowronski and Carlson (1989) argued that the extremity effect can be explained by the same theories as the negativity effect (above) but that, once again, the diagnosticity explanation is superior to the others. According to this explanation, more extreme information is more useful to our categorization than moderate information. Knowing that someone is *quiet* or 'does the shopping' can both be viewed as moderately positive characteristics. However, they might not be very diagnostic. Quiet people might be both very pleasant or very unpleasant and similarly most people do the shopping. However, being told that someone is *evil-tempered* or *adorable* locates a person quite specifically on the *dislike–like* dimension.

The above effects demonstrate that impressions are not always based on the averaging of traits with equal weights but that these weights can vary, as both the Asch and Anderson models allow. According to Skowronski and Carlson (1989), the weight of a trait is based on its diagnosticity, that is, its usefulness in categorizing a person during impression formation. Central traits can be explained in this way: the reason why a trait is central is because it is very useful in forming the overall Gestalt, by evoking a particular schema. Certain highly diagnostic traits might be sufficient information to make a categorization regardless of the other traits accompanying them, and that is why they contribute such a large weight to the impression.

THE CONTINUUM MODEL OF IMPRESSION FORMATION

Further evidence that the Asch and Anderson models of impression formation are not conflicting but complementary comes from a study by Pavelchak (1989). In the first part of this research student subjects were asked to rate fifty personality traits and thirty-five academic majors (such as engineering, history, art) on likeability. These ratings served as comparisons for the second part of the experiment. A few days later the subjects took part in an apparently unrelated experiment where they were asked to evaluate the likeability of a person described by four personality traits (for example, *bright, studious, precise, methodical*). They were also asked to guess the person's academic major. A popular guess for the above trait list was 'engineering'. In a clever experimental manipulation one group of subjects, the category group, were asked to guess the academic major of the person before making their evaluation whereas a second group, the piecemeal group, made their guess of the person's major after their evaluation.

Pavelchak then compared the likeability of the person with the likeability ratings made in the first part of the study. If the subjects were forming categorical impressions (as we would predict from Asch's work) then the likeability of the person would match the likeability of the academic major. If the subjects were making 'piecemeal' judgements (as we would predict from Anderson's work) then the person evaluation should match the average likeability of the four traits in the description. The results indicated that the category group were forming categorical impressions and the piecemeal group were making piecemeal judgements.

Just by changing the instructions, Pavelchak (1989) had demonstrated that two different modes of impression formation were operating in his experiment. As further evidence of this, Pavelchak looked at persons seen as taking the same academic major as the subject. The results showed that the person was liked more in the category condition than in the piecemeal condition. In explanation, it looked as though subjects in the piecemeal condition were making their judgements on the basis of the traits, whereas the students in the category condition were possibly thinking: 'My guess is that this person is studying the same academic major as me so must be OK.'

A similar study based on categories and traits was undertaken by Fiske *et al.* (1987). In this study subjects were given an occupation as a category label and a list of five personality traits. There were four conditions in the experiment that varied the relationship between the category label and the personality traits. In the consistent condition the traits were those expected from a person in the occupation: a 'loan shark' with the traits of *opportunistic, shady, greedy, shrewd* and *heartless*. In the inconsistent condition the traits associated with one occupation were put with another, so 'doctor' was presented with the 'hotel maid' traits of *bored, obedient, unenterprising, uneducated* and *efficient*. The label-focus condition had a category label (such as 'artist') but with uninformative traits such as *adult, medium height, employed, television viewer* and *brown-haired*. Finally, the fourth condition, attribute-focus had the uninformative category label 'person' with a set of five traits such as *practical, educated, scientific, skilful* and *observant* (otherwise associated with 'doctor'). The subjects had to evaluate the likeability of the person, the typicality of the person in this occupation and the possibility that the person could be in this occupation. These ratings were then compared to independent ratings of the occupations and trait sets.

As in Pavelchak's results, two different processes of impression formation appeared to be in operation, with the consistent and label-focus conditions based more on category judgements and the attribute-focus and inconsistent conditions based more on piecemeal judgements. The study also showed that results in the consistent condition were relatively more category-based than those in the label-focus condition, indicating that the two modes of processing might be at two ends of a continuum with intermediate positions combining the two modes to varying degrees.

Fiske and her colleagues (e.g. Fiske and Pavelchak, 1986; Fiske and Neuberg, 1990) have developed the continuum model of impression formation to explain these and other data. According to this model, we make a *rapid initial categorization* of an individual on the basis of some piece of information we have learnt about them. It might be their skin-colour, occupation or some other attribute that leads us to this categorization. If the person is of little relevance or interest to us we may not consider them further than this snap judgement. For example, in glancing at a stranger passing in the street we might gain an impression of a 'punk' or an 'officious-sort-of-person' and leave it at that.

When the person is of greater relevance to us, such as when we are going to interact with them in some way, we pay more attention to the information we have about them, first of all to check that our initial categorization was appropriate. If the information is consistent with our classification then *category confirmation* takes place: the woman initially seen as an introvert is actually quiet with a preference for her own company. However, if the information is clearly inconsistent with the category label then we seek an alternative category for the person in a process called *recategorization*. If we classified the woman as introverted simply on the basis of her looks but the other information about her leads us to an impression of extroversion we change our categorization. Finally, if there are no categories that spring to mind after considering the information we have about the person then we are likely to base our impression of them on a *piecemeal integration* of the various attributes that we have learnt they possess.

The processes of category confirmation, recategorization and piecemeal integration lie on a continuum of impression formation processes from category-based processes to piecemeal-based processes. Fiske and Neuberg (1990) argue that category-based processes are likely to have priority, that is, in most cases we try to fit a person into a particular category. However, the amount of attention paid to the information about the person and the motive for forming an impression will strongly influence how far along the continuum the perceiver goes. When there is little time or inclination to attend to the information about a person the perceiver relies more on the category-based processes. The amount of attention paid to the person is important as piecemeal-based processes require attention to combine sometimes disparate pieces of information. Also the motive for forming an impression will influence the processes used. A job interviewer looking for an 'enthusiastic graduate' type of person may use category-based processes. However, a conscientious interviewer seeking accuracy of judgement may adopt a more piecemeal-based approach in an attempt to assess each candidate as an individual.

The continuum model helps to explain how different impression formation processes are used in different situations. The amount of attention paid to the information about a person and our motives for forming an impression will determine whether we form an overall, Asch-type, category-based impression or a more individuated, Anderson type, piecemeal-based impression. When time is restricted and information can be attended to only briefly, impressions tend to be more stereotypical, even at the expense of inconsistent individuating information (Pratto and Bargh, 1991). Indeed, as these authors point out, restrictions on the time we have to process information is typical of life outside the psychology experiment. Hence the use of stereotypical categories is likely to be more prevalent in everyday life than is reflected in the confines of the psychological laboratory, where there are often highly attentive and motivated subjects.

Chapter 6

Implicit personality theory

At MT Design the short-listed candidates had been called for interview and at the end of the day the interview panel of Mary, Peter and Susan were discussing their performance. [To simplify matters we will assume that there were only three candidates, Alan, Brenda and Colin; although in reality there might be more.]

Mary, who was chairing the meeting, opened up the discussion.

'Colin was a very good candidate, certainly the best of the three.'

Susan looked up, surprised, 'Why?'

'He certainly had the drive and enthusiasm we are looking for,' answered Mary. *'I also thought he understood the needs of the post in a very intelligent way.'*

'Hum,' replied Susan unconvinced. *'I thought his answers came out rather too pat. He seemed rather too smart for his own good. I'm not sure he'll fit in.'*

'Oh, I don't know,' said Peter, *'he had done his homework, which shows he is interested in working here. I agree with Mary that he is intelligent but I don't think he showed the same ability as Brenda.'*

'But he had the enthusiasm and intelligence to make up for that,' interrupted Mary.

'I didn't see that. Brenda was much more knowledgeable about the industry. She had some really good ideas. I think she'd get on well here,' said Peter.

'She was pleasant enough,' said Susan unconvinced.

'She came over better than Alan,' said Mary. *'He had some novel but rather strange ideas and I didn't think he would get on well with our clients.'*

'Well,' said Susan, *'there was originality there.'*

Peter agreed. 'Yes, I saw him as quite creative, but I didn't like his approach and that could tell with our clients.'

We do not always agree on what other people are like. Consider the many conversations we have about a third party: 'Did you find that comedian funny on television last night?' 'What do you think about Maria's new boyfriend?' 'How are you getting on with Michael working on the new project?' We can usually provide an answer, but what if opinions differ? I think that the comedian was funny and you do not. We both agree that Maria's boyfriend is a nice guy but you cannot stand to work with Michael and I find it no problem at all. To me Michael is *hard-working* and *innovative* but to you he is *confusing* and *easily sidetracked*.

One way to tackle this question is to consider whether one of us is right and the other is wrong and we shall do this in the next chapter, but here we shall be looking at the question from a different position, not of right or wrong but of *individual differences*. Given that two people have observed the same third party, what is it about the way those two people judge others that leads them to arrive at different judgements? In answer to this question it has been suggested that we each hold a set of assumptions about personality traits. This set of assumptions has been called an *implicit theory of personality*. I might believe that *intelligent* people are also *friendly* and that *honest* people are also *kind*. If I believe Richard to be *intelligent*, I'll also see him as *friendly* as well. However, if you do not hold this belief, or indeed hold a different one such as 'intelligent people are snobbish', then we might well differ on our views of Richard's friendliness despite him behaving in an identical manner to us both. In this chapter we shall see how implicit personality theories arise and also how idiosyncratic they are.

INDIVIDUAL DIFFERENCES IN PERSONALITY JUDGEMENT

Bruner and Tagiuri (1954) were the first to introduce the idea of 'implicit personality theory' when they asked the question: 'what kinds of naive, implicit "theories" of personality do people work with when they form impressions of others?' (p. 649). They were particularly interested in the general inferences that people make about personality rather than individual differences as such, but the term implicit personality theory has come to mean an individual's assumptions about personality characteristics. The implicit assumptions, or theory, of personality that one has could be very idiosyncratic, or alternatively they might be shared with others. To Cronbach (1958) it is as though each of us wears different 'spectacles' with which to view the world: we may perceive people somewhat differently from others and so our judgements will differ.

INDIVIDUAL DIFFERENCES IN THE PERCEPTION OF TRAIT RELATIONSHIPS

Consider two personality traits, *friendliness* and *intelligence*. We take any two people, say Sally and Winston, and ask each to list all their family, friends, enemies, colleagues, old school teachers, indeed anyone they can think of from their lives and write the names down. When both have a large number of names, say 100 or so, we ask them to rate each of the people on their list in terms of friendliness and intelligence. To allow them to be very discerning we give them a broad rating scale from –100 to +100, with –100 indicating the extreme of *unfriendliness* or *unintelligence* and +100 as the extreme of *friendliness* or *intelligence*. Sally and Winston each end up with a list of 100 names, with two ratings next to each name.

We now plot everyone on Sally's list on a graph with *friendliness* and *intelligence* as the two axes. If she has, say, mother on her list with +80 for *friendliness* and +70 for *intelligence* we find the position corresponding to +80,+70 on the graph. We do this for every name on her list. When we have plotted all the people on the graph we draw a boundary line round the points so that they all lie inside it. The graph with the boundary line is shown in Figure 6.1. We also produce another graph for the people on Winston's list in the same way and that too is shown in Figure 6.1

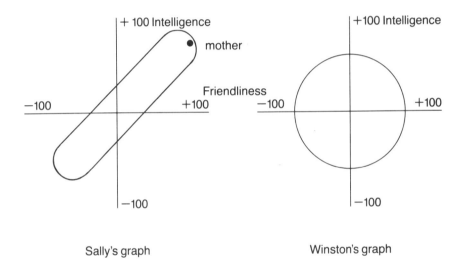

Sally's graph   Winston's graph

Figure 6.1 The perceived relationship between intelligence and friendliness

It is interesting to look at the pattern of points on the graphs as shown by the area marked by the boundary line. For Sally, all the people lie in a narrow area of the graph. If someone is judged to be high in *intelligence*, they are also judged high in *friendliness*. If they are judged to be low in *intelligence* they are also judged to be low in *friendliness*. In Sally's perception of personality traits *friendliness* and *intelligence* are *not independent*, they are related, because if we are told that she finds a person *intelligent* we can predict she also sees them as *friendly*.

The relationship between *friendliness* and *intelligence* is very different to Winston. The people are scattered all over his graph. There is no predictable relationship between the two traits in Winston's judgements. Therefore they are *independent* characteristics to him.

Cronbach (1958) calls these graphs a map of a person's *perceptual space*, in that they show how that person perceives these personality characteristics. The most interesting feature of this kind of information is that it shows how different people view the same personality traits in very different ways.

It is important to know about someone's perceptual space when we consider a situation like an interview. Cronbach (1958) analysed a study where two industrial interviewers rated the same candidate on a number of characteristics. The first interviewer saw *intelligence* and *cooperation* as the two important factors in the assessment. These factors were independent of each other and the decision to hire a candidate was based on a combination of the two. The trait *creative* was not important to this interviewer. For the second interviewer, using the same rating scales, a combination of *expression* and *intelligence* formed one key factor in the decision to hire a candidate. The second important factor for this interviewer was a combination of *inquiring mind* and *creative*. However, being creative with an inquiring mind was seen negatively by the first interviewer: it actually weighed *against* a candidate in the decision to hire. The characteristic of *cooperative* was not important to this second interviewer's decision, with *drive* and *interest* also playing a very minor role. As Cronbach (1958) points out the importance of this finding is that even when interviewers are using the same carefully worked out rating scales, they are still judging others very differently.

Personal construct theory

An explanation of implicit personality theory comes from George Kelly (1955) in his *theory of personal constructs*. He argues that experience shapes the way in which we view the world and different experiences can lead to different perceptions. If I'm brought up in a city and you are brought up in the country then our ideas about what we regard as *peaceful* or *exciting*, for example, could be very different. Kelly also says that the way we view the world goes on to affect the way we experience new events. If I view city life as interesting and exciting and you find it noisy and irritating, a day in the city will be a different experience for each of us. Thus, there is a cycle operating from experience leading to understanding and understanding influencing our interpretation of new experiences.

The key aspect of Kelly's theory is that we want to be able to predict future events. This sounds a little like clairvoyance but it isn't, and can be explained in a very down to earth way. Imagine you had never been to a supermarket before. When you go there you do not know what to expect. It is a completely new experience. What do you do with the trolleys and check-outs? You soon learn that you put your food in a basket or trolley, where the food gets weighed, how to pay at the check-out and so on. Next time you go, the experience is not so strange because you know what to expect. There may be the odd surprise but gradually you develop an understanding that makes shopping in the local supermarket almost completely predictable.

Kelly arrived at his theory through his work as a counsellor. He saw his clients' problems arising out of their unsuccessful attempts to make sense of their own experiences. In certain cases this led clients to hold unrealistic expectations about people and events and their anxiety often led them to seek help. However, he realized, the underlying process of trying to understand experiences in a way that will help to predict future events was no different from the way he went about his own work as a therapist. His clients may have been unsuccessful for one reason or another but the process was the same.

To Kelly we are all 'scientists', because everyone, in their daily lives, attempts to make sense of the world in the same way that scientists gain new knowledge. Scientists predict that something will happen in a certain situation based on their understanding of events (their theory). They then see what really happens. If events turn out as expected, they are more confident that their theory is a good way of viewing the situation. However, if events turn out to be unexpected, the scientists go back and change their theory and set up new predictions. To Kelly this is also the way all of us operate in our everyday lives (Bannister and Fransella, 1971).

Consider an example. I need some help with a college assignment so I decide to ask my friend Susanna to help, as she has always done in the past. If she does help it reinforces my view of her. However, if she refuses then it might make me reconsider my view. Is she really a friend after all? Am I demanding too much of her? The questions I ask myself are attempts to understand my new experience. Until I come up with an answer Susanna is no longer as predictable as I believed her to be. (See also Chapter 8.)

The personal construct

Experience helps us to label and differentiate the world (Kelly, 1955). In calling some people 'friends' I am differentiating them from other people who are 'not friends'. As Shotter (1975) points out, Kelly's theory is a theory of knowledge. We develop *personal constructs* like *friends* in order to categorize people and events. Without constructs we cannot make sense of anything, we cannot predict what will happen. I cannot understand a group of people until I construe them in some way, say in terms of friends and non-friends, men and women, or conservative and liberal. I then have expectations about how they will behave. Thus, a construct is both a description and knowledge of an event.

According to Kelly, each of us, through our own experiences, develops a set of personal constructs, which we use to predict future events. These constructs and the relationships between them form our *construct system*. An individual's construct system is like (in Cronbach's analogy) the pair of spectacles we put on to make sense of the world.

Kelly goes on to say that each construct has two 'poles'. When we use the word *friendly* we are contrasting it with something else, say *unfriendly*, so *friendly* and *unfriendly* are the two poles of a construct. We construe people or events by applying one pole of a construct to them. But constructs are not simply linguistic labels. We might have a number of constructs with the same word *good* representing one pole and yet they are different constructs, *good–evil*, *good–poor*, *good–bad*, used to make sense of different things. A saintly person is seen as *good* as opposed to *evil*, a piece of work is seen as *good* as opposed to *poor* and a piece of food is seen as *good* as opposed to *bad*.

Constructs are not always represented by a single word, indeed it may be hard to put into words at all. Sometimes it is difficult to describe an event that we understand. There might be people that you quite like, but you wouldn't call them friends although they are more than acquaintances. You do not have a word to describe them but you still have a construct for this type of person none the less. Forced to find an expression to describe the construct you might choose the words *second-class friends* or some such phrase although it does not fully capture the meaning you wish to express. Furthermore, we should not assume that, just because two people use the same descriptive term, they are using the same construct. Consider the words *good music*, for example. Even amongst friends the dispute about what constitutes good music is endless.

Being able to construe people and events in terms of one of only two poles appears to imply that we see things in a very polarized way, only in terms of right and wrong, black and white. This is not true. There is room in the system for constructs that refer to less radical differences, for example, we can have a constructs of *dark grey–light grey*. Also, the construct of *friend–enemy* can be seen as a more extreme contrast than *friend–nonfriend* or *first-class friend–second-class friend*, and they would be used in different circumstances.

Clearly a construct cannot be used for every object or event. The *range of convenience* of a construct is the range of objects or events that you would apply it to. The construct of *friend–nonfriend* usually includes only people and, possibly, animals, although some people might construe their car as a *friend*. However, for most people tables and chairs would not be perceived in terms of this construct, they lie outside its range of convenience.

The construct system

So far we have been discussing personal constructs only individually. But they are not independent of each other, they are linked and organized into a system, with some constructs higher up a hierarchy than others. My construct of *friend* might be subsumed by my construct of *nice*. Thus, I regard all my *friends* as *nice* (although not all *nice* things are *friends*).

An important feature of the organization of a person's construct system is that constructs high up in the hierarchy characterize the way someone views the world in general terms. A very sexist view of the world would have the construct *man–woman* high in the hierarchy with constructs like *good–bad* and *intelligent–unintelligent* subsumed by them. This person sees goodness and intelligence in terms of one of the sexes and badness and unintelligence in terms of the other. A non-sexist system would not have this relationship between the constructs. Our construct system is therefore our idiosyncratic way of looking at the world, and as such can be seen as the embodiment of our personality.

The important ways we look at the world will be built up over time and experience. Not surprisingly, we do not radically change our entire system every time we try to make sense of a new event. However, with a new experience people often look at it in a number of different ways, by using subsystems of their construct system. These subsystems are not necessarily linked by any logical connection. Thrown into a novel situation a person construes the world in a variety of ways in an attempt to anticipate and understand it, without it threatening their characteristic view of the world. This can be explained by an example. There is a party game where people pass round a pair of scissors and either say 'open' or 'closed' before passing the scissors to the next person. Everyone playing the game knows what is going on except one person who has to guess the rule of the game. The scissors, of course, have nothing to do with it. The rule is: if you have crossed your legs say 'closed', if not say 'open'. The person soon realises that the scissors are not the key to the game but comes up with a series of bizarre rules (especially if the people are behaving in other strange ways!). The situation is constructed anew as each guess is rejected. However, taking part in the game and reconstruing the event in a number of ways is not actually changing the way in which the person views the world in general. Similarly, in other aspects of life our construction of events may vary quite often, even though we are likely to have a broader, more general view of the world which changes more slowly with our experiences.

Differences in construct systems

Notice that my experience is going to be different from that of other people and this can lead to the development of different construct systems. Even though people use the same word, such as *party*, or *friend*, or indeed any descriptive word, these words could have a different meaning for them. What I understand by *politeness* or *appropriate behaviour* may be very different from your view if we have been brought up in different cultures, for example. Yet, if our construct systems are different from each other, how is it that we can understand other people? How can we discuss the 'same' things if we see them differently? First, we should not underestimate the similarity of many human experiences. Furthermore, we may think similarly to other people about certain things because we have understood them in the same way. Consider a conversation between two people of the same political persuasion. There is likely to be a lot of agreement in their assessment of the political situation and ways to manage it. They think alike or, to put it in Kelly's terms, construe alike. Now consider a discussion between two people of opposing political points of view. There are likely to be fundamental disagreements about the state of the political situation as well as what should be done to manage it. In this case they are clearly construing the world very differently. However, it is not seeing things in the same way that leads to a successful relationship between people, according to Kelly, it is being able to understand the other person's point of view. Successful therapy can be seen as the therapist gaining an understanding of the client's construction of the world and helping to develop and change it.

Construing events

When my friends invite me to a party I expect there to be lots of people, food and drink, dancing and music. According to Kelly (1955), I know what to expect of a party due to my experience of the previous parties I have been to. Over the years I have been to events called parties and gradually from this experience I have built up an idea of what I understand and expect a party to be. Now I go to a party and it is not quite what I expect. There's no dancing and the music is soft, but it is enjoyable none the less. How do I construe this event? Do I call it a *bad party* because the music is not what I expected or do I call it a *good party* because I'm enjoying it? Kelly says that we choose the construct pole that helps to develop our experiences and improves our future expectations. I decide to call it a *good party* and gradually change my idea of what a *good party* is: it does not necessarily have to have dancing.

Consider the first day at a new job or college. The experience is new and we do not know what to expect so we construe the events in ways that we believe will help to develop our understanding. We might decide to treat the people as *friendly* rather than *unfriendly* and see if that works. As we behave in a friendly way to them, the other people might be helpful and we settle in. If, however, we chose the other pole of the construct and treat people as *unfriendly* we might find the place unpleasant and decide to leave very soon.

A person's constructs are not necessarily fixed like definitions inscribed in a dictionary but can be open to change through new experiences. As we have seen above, they will change and develop in ways that help us to better predict future events. However, we are not all always open to the development of our construct systems. Some people have a very fixed view of certain things. Consider the construct *art–not art*. On experiencing new forms of artistic expression some people are willing to extend the range of convenience of their construct to include them as *art*. However, other people might dismiss them as *not art* and keep their fixed view of what *art* is.

Problems can arise if our constructs are not open to change. We will have a very fixed view of the world that does not develop with experience, our mind will be closed to new experiences. There are also problems if constructs are too open to change, we can be too 'open-minded', finding it hard to make sense of things with any degree of certainty. Even a trip to the supermarket becomes confusing.

The repertory grid test

So far we have only considered the theoretical aspects of Kelly's explanation of individual differences in judgement, yet if we cannot actually determine a person's personal construct system then, despite the excellence of the theory, it remains just that – a theory, without practical use. One of the major successes of Kelly's work is the development of a method for revealing a person's constructs. Kelly (1955) calls this the *role construct repertory test*. This has been shortened to the *rep grid test*. With this test the theory has been applied to a whole range of practical situations from clinical therapy (Kelly's own work) to performance assessment in the US Army (Borman, 1987) and even to studying the predictions of financial analysts (Hunter and Coggin, 1988).

The rep test operates in the following manner. The person administering the test, whom I'll call the tester, works with the person whose construct system is to be studied – the subject. First, the tester presents the subject with a number of roles like *mother, father, brother, sister, colleague, old school friend, disliked teacher, someone pitied, an old boy/girlfriend, a successful person*. About a dozen or so roles are usually enough. The subject then thinks of a real person who fits each role. If the subject doesn't know a person to fit a role then another role is chosen. It does not really matter which roles are used, as long as they generate people from the subject's life. The aim of this part of the process is simply to produce a range of people that the subject has known, rather than just friends or family. This way there is more chance of getting a good selection of the subject's constructs.

In the next stage of the test, the tester gives the subject a group of three people from the list: for example, *mother, disliked teacher* and *successful person*. The subject must then think of a way in which two of these people are similar to each other but different from the third. For example, the subject might say that *mother* and *successful person* are both *well organized* and the disliked teacher was *badly organized*. The subject is given another group of three people and asked for a reason for two being similar and the other dissimilar. Another construct is elicited, say *optimistic–pessimistic*. This is undertaken about twenty to thirty times, using combinations of three people from the list to obtain a set of constructs.

The tester now draws up a grid to represent the information produced in the test, with the roles as the rows and the constructs as the columns. In the grid the tester fills in a + for one pole of the construct and – for the other pole.

Under the column *well organized–badly organized* a + is put in the box for *mother* and *successful person* and a – for *disliked teacher*. This is done for each of the constructs elicited.

The tester then completes the grid by taking each construct in turn and asking the subject to go though the people and fill in gaps by saying whether the construct relates to them and, if so, which pole. For example, with the *well organized–badly organized* construct, if *father* is seen as *well organized* then a + is put in the grid in the appropriate place. If the subject doesn't view a person, say *old school friend*, in terms of this construct then the tester puts a 0 in the box.

The rep grid can now be analysed to provide an insight into the subject's construct system. The number and similarity of constructs can be considered. One subject might have generated lots of constructs whereas another may have used the same construct more than once. Also if the pattern of +, – and 0 for a particular construct is similar to that of another construct then the subject might be using these constructs in a similar, if not identical, way. If the pattern for *intelligent–unintelligent* matches that of *friendly–unfriendly* then these traits are related. Further, more complex analyses can be also performed.

There are many variants on the rep test (Fransella, 1981). For example, the person themselves can be included in the roles. Rather than simply having +, – and 0, the roles can be rated on each construct along a scale, say 0–10. However the test is performed, its basic purpose is satisfied if the person's constructs are revealed.

Cognitive complexity

One area of research has considered the relationship between the number of constructs that a person employs and the accuracy of their personality judgements. Bieri (1955) found that *cognitively complex* people, those who had a large number of constructs, were better able to predict the behaviour of others than *cognitively simple* people. Many studies have been undertaken since, and the general finding is that cognitive complexity aids the accurate assessment of others. Crockett (1965) found that cognitively simple people used more polarized descriptions than the cognitively complex. They tended to describe others as good or bad, or strong or weak, rather than giving a more complex description of the good and bad points of an individual. Adams-Webber (1969) gave a number of subjects a rep grid test to find out how many constructs they used. Three weeks later he put them into pairs and asked them to discuss their ideal holiday. This was to give them some experience of their discussion partner, whom they were to assess. The subjects were then given a number of constructs, half of which were from their partner's rep grid and half not. They were asked to select the constructs from the list that their partner used. Adams-Webber found that the cognitively complex people were much better than the cognitively simple at identifying the correct constructs.

Why is it that the number of constructs is related to ability to assess others? If we assume that subtle differences in behaviour indicate subtle differences in personality then we need a suitably complex construct system to be able to appreciate these differences. If we see others in a relatively un-differentiated way – they are only good or bad in the extreme case – then we cannot perceive degrees of, say, goodness or badness. The cognitively simple person, therefore, sees others in a rather stereotyped way because their limited number of constructs must be used to incorporate all the differences in people.

The implicit personality theory of an author

An interesting alternative method for studying implicit personality theory was developed by Rosenberg and Jones (1972). They investigated the implicit personality theory of the American novelist Theodore Dreiser by analysing one of his books called *A Gallery of Women*. This book is a series of fifteen short stories, each one a character sketch of the heroine. This was particularly useful for Rosenberg and Jones as it contained many more personality descriptions than most novels, so there was a rich source of information on the descriptive terms used by Dreiser.

First, they compiled a list of the descriptive terms in the book and then categorized them as character traits. Some were easy to categorize as they were single words like *lovely* or *tall*. Others were more difficult, such as *enjoyed a rich and wasteful life*. When this was done, they calculated how often traits occurred together in the descriptions. For example, when the word *artistic* was used by Dreiser they worked out how often another trait such as *unhappy* was used in the same description. With these measures of trait co-occurrence they then performed a cluster analysis. This is a statistical technique to find out which character descriptions cluster together, so, for example, *indifferent, hard* and *restless* were all closely related in Dreiser's descriptions and so were *emotional, playful* and *sympathetic*. Rosenberg and Jones plotted, on a graph, the ninety-nine most frequently used traits, the 'distance' between them being how often they occurred together in Dreiser's descriptions. They also performed multidimensional scaling, another statistical technique, on these data to find the key dimensions that underlay Dreiser's descriptions. Even though someone uses a range of descriptive terms they might all lie on a key dimension, like *good–bad*, so that all the terms imply a degree of goodness or badness when used. Rosenberg and Jones found three key dimensions for Dreiser: *hard–soft, male–female* and *conforms–does not conform*. The first two dimensions were very closely related with a strong relationship of *hard* to *male* and *soft* to *female* in Dreiser's implicit personality theory. The *conformity* dimension was independent of the other two. As Rosenberg and Jones note, these dimensions match up well with biographical data about Dreiser's life, showing that sex and conformity were important themes in his life, evidence that the analysis was revealing his implicit personality theory, particularly with respect to women.

A similar method was used by Swede and Tetlock (1986) in their analysis of the book *The White House Years*, written by the former US Secretary of State Henry Kissinger. Whereas Dreiser's *A Gallery of Women* had a wealth of descriptions relating to women, Kissinger's book had a large number of descriptions of the political leaders he had met during his time in the US administration. Indeed, Swede and Tetlock extracted 3,759 trait descriptions of thirty-eight important political leaders from the book.

Again, the important aspect of the analysis was to map out Kissinger's 'perceptual space'. This was done by selecting the 106 most frequently used traits in Kissinger's descriptions and finding out how often the various traits occurred together. Swede and Tetlock analysed the co-occurrences in three different ways to minimize the potential bias of a single method. As it turned out, the results of the three methods were very consistent. Swede and Tetlock chose to call the resulting clusters of traits *personality themes* rather than assuming that they were part of personality dimensions as Rosenberg and Jones had done. Five personality themes emerged in Kissinger's descriptions of political leaders: *professional anguish, ambitious patriotism, revolutionary greatness, intellectual sophistication* and *realistic friendship*.

Each of the politicians that Kissinger had described were then characterized in terms of these five themes. Differences emerged, with some leaders scoring high on one theme whilst others scored much lower. Swede and Tetlock then looked at these differences and found, by cluster analysis, that Kissinger was perceiving the leaders in terms of nine different personality types. Kissinger himself, the French statesman Georges Pompidou and the Chinese leader Chou En-lai, each was a type in himself. Leonid Brezhnev and Mao Tse-tung were of the same type, labelled the 'Revolutionary' type by Swede and Tetlock. Richard Nixon was the 'Patriot' type, the former British Prime Minister Edward Heath a 'Personal Friend' and Charles de Gaulle a 'Professional Friend'. The final two types characterized opponents: the 'Able Adversary' and the 'Professional Competitor'.

Employing this method, Swede and Tetlock had reduced well over three thousand descriptions of a significant number of people down to five themes and nine types in their analysis of Kissinger's implicit theory of personality with respect to the political leaders he had met. As with the Rosenberg and Jones study, the findings of this study compared quite well with other biographical data on Kissinger.

This method indicates that it is possible to determine aspects of a person's implicit personality theory by analysing what they write. There are obvious limitations to using only literary sources, in that these focus on a certain aspect of the author's life, such as the political world in Kissinger's book. Also, there is the question of whether public descriptions are the same as private descriptions. However, these should not be seen as major limitations given the interesting outcome of the analysis and the correspondence of the results to other sources of information, such as the biographical data. As with the rep grid, the success of the method is in its ability to reveal the way in which a person perceives others.

IMPLICIT IDEAS HELD BY GROUPS

Some studies, like the ones in the previous section, have looked at the implicit personality theory of an individual. Other studies have aggregated the data from a number of individuals and looked for common implicit personality descriptions across the group. In these studies the following question can be asked: do the people in the group use the same important dimensions of personality in their judgements?

The *good–bad* construct in implicit personality theory

An interesting study in this area is that of Rosenberg *et al.* (1968). They gave college students a set of sixty traits, such as *dominating, artistic, happy.* The students then had to put the traits into piles, each pile representing a person they knew. These piles were seen as sets of trait combinations, that is, personality characteristics that went together. From these data the researchers calculated the 'distance' between traits (in terms of how often they were put together in a pile) and plotted the findings on a graph of the combined students' perceptual space. Analysing these results they found that the students' judgements could be interpreted in terms of two main dimensions of personality. These were *good–bad intellectual* and *good–bad social.* Intelligence was seen as good and unintelligence as bad. On the social dimension, *helpful, sincere* and *popular* were all seen positively whilst *unhappy, vain, unpopular* and *unsociable* were seen negatively.

Here we have a case of a whole group having an implicit personality theory. Whilst there are likely to be individual differences between the students in their beliefs about the relationships between personality characteristics, the finding showed that there was a general tendency in this group to evaluate people, that is to see them as good or bad, and for this evaluation to take place on the intellectual and social dimensions.

In the Rosenberg *et al.* (1968) study the experimenters had provided the students with the trait names to use. Yet, there is no guarantee that these are the descriptive terms that students would normally use. The results could have been influenced by the descriptions the experimenters chose. In order to look at students' own descriptions, Rosenberg and Sedlak (1972) asked each student to describe ten people, half of whom they knew well and the others whom they knew by reputation only. The students were asked for at least five adjectives per description and not to include physical features. The eighty most frequently used traits were selected for analysis. Rosenberg and Sedlak found that a number of dimensions emerged from the analysis, with *good–bad, social good–bad* and *hard–soft* appearing as the most important. *Intellectual good–bad* was not as important in the students' own descriptions as in the Rosenberg *et al.* (1968) experiment, but *good–bad* again came out very strongly as a key dimension in their personality judgement.

Rosenberg (1977) undertook a very detailed study of the implicit personality theories of a number of his students. Each of them was asked to list 100 people from their lives and to include people they did not like as well as ones they did. Initially the students protested that they couldn't think of 100 people! However, they ended up providing more, about 125 per student. They were then asked to provide descriptions of these people, both traits and feelings. The difference between these was that even though someone might be described as *happy* (a trait) that person might not make the student feel happy, they might make them feel *dumb* (a feeling). Each student ended up providing about 150 traits and feelings.

An individual student's descriptions were analysed for clusters of traits and feelings as well as for key dimensions of personality. Some interesting clusters were found, such as *red hair, dumb* and *never in trouble*. It is possible that these clusters tell us about certain unique aspects of the individual's implicit personality theory. It is worth noting that in this example hair colour is included in a cluster. It could be that knowing someone with a particular physical characteristic leads us to perceive other people with that characteristic as having the same personality traits (see Chapter 2; also Secord, 1958). It looks as though each of us is searching for important groups of characteristics by which to categorize other people.

As well as the intriguing individual findings, Rosenberg (1977) again noted that an evaluative dimension (*good–bad*) was an important factor to all the students in his study. But it is not just American students who use *good–bad* in their descriptions. Trzebinski (1985) also found evidence for the importance of evaluation in his study of Polish undergraduates and Nystedt and Smari (1987) with Swedish students.

Models of trait relationships

Clearly, from the above studies, evaluation is an important dimension in personality judgements, at least for students. Are there others? Rosenberg and Sedlak (1972) looked at the semantic differential model of Osgood (Osgood *et al.*, 1957; Osgood, 1962). Originally this was used as a method of finding the meaning of concepts by asking people to rate words on a number of scales (such as *strong–weak*). From these ratings three key factors emerged: that is, despite the number of scales used, it looked as though there were three main dimensions to the meaning of words. These were evaluation (*good–bad, pleasant–unpleasant*), potency (*strong–weak, hard–soft*) and activity (*fast–slow*, *lively–lethargic*). These could also be the basic dimensions underlying implicit personality theory.

Rosenberg *et al.* (1968) found that their results could be expressed reasonably well in terms of these three dimensions (as an alternative to the *good–bad intellectual* and *good–bad social*). Also a number of other studies, where the experimenters have provided the traits, support these three dimensions (see Kim and Rosenberg, 1980). However, Rosenberg and Sedlak (1972) found evidence for evaluation and potency in their study only where the students provided their own descriptions rather than using the ones given by the experimenters. It is possible that the experimental support for the semantic differential model comes from experiments where the trait terms chosen by the experiments are related to evaluation, potency and activity; therefore it is hardly surprising that these dimensions emerge. It may not be that these three dimensions underlie personality descriptions, merely that experimenters like to pick these terms for use in their studies!

Kim and Rosenberg (1980) set out to test the semantic differential model as the basis for implicit personality theory. They contrasted it with their own model, the evaluative model, in which evaluation is assumed to be the only common dimension across individuals. In their experiment Kim and Rosenberg asked students to generate at least 100 people from their lives (following the procedure from Rosenberg (1977)). Students either generated their own traits for these people, rated them using 119 common traits found in the Rosenberg study or rated them on scales related to the dimensions of evaluation, potency and activity.

When the data from the individual students were analysed, evaluation was found to be important for all of them but potency and activity had a much smaller influence, occurring together for fewer than half the subjects. It was only when the results of all the subjects were aggregated that evaluation, potency and activity emerged. Kim and Rosenberg (1980) point out that only evaluation really underlies implicit personality theory as an important dimension for all. Potency and activity emerge as a consequence of aggregation. They are popular dimensions but certainly not with all the students.

Nystedt and Smari (1987) also found support for the evaluation model in their own study, with evaluation emerging as important to all individuals. They found a number of individual differences in their data, and argued that aggregated data should be considered only after the individual differences had been analysed. Otherwise a false account of the findings might emerge from the combined results.

These experiments are fairly conclusive in showing the importance of evaluation as a key aspect of the implicit personality theory of students. No other dimensions emerge as strongly from the research. Although some researchers combine the data from individuals to find a general implicit personality theory of the group they must be careful when interpreting their findings, as not all members of the group will necessarily share the general view.

Cultural differences in implicit personality theories

Norman (1963) and Passini and Norman (1966) found that when they looked at the pattern of personality judgements of a large number of people certain important personality characteristics emerged. Despite the many different terms used, it appeared that there were five key dimensions underlying judgements of personality: *extroversion* (or *surgency*), *agreeableness, conscientiousness, emotional stability* and *culture.*

These five dimensions have been termed the 'Big Five' as they have been found with a range of different subjects (Goldberg, 1981). But, as many of these studies have been with English speakers from the United States, there is the question of whether the American Big Five reflect universal descriptive dimensions of personality or whether there are differences across cultures (Yang and Bond, 1990). Bond and Forgas (1984) looked at this, comparing Australians with Hong Kong Chinese on the dimensions studied by Norman. They found some interesting differences across the cultures with *conscientiousness* being more important to the Chinese and *extroversion* being more important to the Australians. Whilst Yang and Bond (1990) found a Big Five for Taiwanese by using Chinese descriptive terms, there was not a one-to-one correspondence between these and the American Big Five dimensions. The American factors could explain four out of five of the Chinese factors but only in a multifactor way, with only one or possibly two factors indicating a direct one-to-one relationship. And the fifth Chinese factor *optimism–neuroticism* appeared relatively unrelated to the American factors. Thus, it appears that different cultures use different dimensions in their descriptions of others.

PERCEIVED TRAIT RELATIONSHIPS: REAL OR ILLUSORY?

Do we really know what people are like, with our implicit ideas based on solid experience? When I judge you to be both *friendly* and *intelligent*, is that because you *really are* both *friendly* and *intelligent?* Or are implicit personality theories merely fictions, illusions, with little to do with the real relationships of personality traits? I might believe that you are both *friendly* and *intelligent* but is my judgement unrelated to your actual characteristics (whatever they are)?

A number of studies have attempted to answer these questions. Researchers in this area have concentrated on people's beliefs concerning trait relationships and, rather than studying individuals, most of the work has been concerned with aggregated data, looking at the general consensus about the relationship between traits. The basic method for studying this topic has been to ask people about the likelihood of two traits occurring together in the same person. Subjects of the experiments have been asked: if a person agrees with one statement about their personality will they agree with a second statement about their personality. For example, if a person answers 'true' to the statement 'I like to play a lot of sports', will they also answer 'true' to 'I do not like to spend time studying in a library'?

In a study by Lay and Jackson (1969) subjects completed a questionnaire made up of these types of statements. The responses were compared to give a measure of the actual relationship between statements. They then asked a second group of subjects to decide if a person answering one statement as true would also answer a second statement as true. The findings showed that the inferred relationships between traits, the implicit theories of the second group, were a good match of the actual relationships discovered from the first group. They saw this as evidence for implicit personality theories being based on the true relationships that had been learnt through experience.

Further studies (Lay *et al.*, 1973; Stricker *et al.*, 1974) supported these findings. Stricker *et al.* argued that, as there is a broad agreement as to the association between personality traits, this indicates a common experience of the true relationship between traits rather than any individual, idio-syncratic influences on implicit personality theories. That is, we are all pretty good at picking up which personality traits go together.

Essentially what these studies showed was that people are good at inferring the co-occurrence or correlation of traits in others (Jackson *et al.*, 1979). If people answered pairs of statements indicating that they were both *friendly* and *sociable*, then it was found that the subjects in their turn selected the statements indicating that the traits *friendly* and *sociable* went together. However, Mirels (1976), using a different technique, found a much greater difference between the subjects' inferred relationships between personality traits and their actual co-occurrence when he looked at conditional prob-abilities rather than correlations.

Let's digress for a moment to consider what conditional probabilities are. Consider an example. There are one hundred people in a room, sixty men and forty women. Thirty of the men and ten of the women are doctors. A conditional probability is the probability of something happening given that something else has already occurred. We can ask, what is the conditional probability of some-one in the room being a doctor given that they are a man. There are sixty men in the room and thirty of these are doctors, so the conditional probability is thirty out of sixty, half the men are doctors. However, if we ask the question the other way round, what is the conditional probability of someone in the room being a man given that they are a doctor, then we get a different answer. Forty people are doctors and of these thirty are men, therefore the conditional probability is thirty out of forty, or three-quarters.

What has this to do with implicit personality theory? Well the above experimental set up, with the two statements, can be seen in terms of condition probabilities: given that a person has agreed with the first state-ment, what is the probability of them agreeing with the second? This is different from asking them simply which statements correlate, which, as we saw above, people are good at. Mirels (1976) asked for actual conditional probability values. For example, a judge would have to say what percentage of people who had agreed with, say, 'I like working with other people' would also agree with 'I enjoy solving difficult problems'. They were not very good at this.

He also found that people saw conditional probabilities as symmetrical. They judged the conditional probability of a person agreeing to statement B given agreement to statement A as the same as the conditional probability of a person agreeing to statement A given agreement to statement B. In our example we can see that conditional probabilities are often asymmetric: the probability of a person being a doctor given that they are a man (a half) is not the same as the probability of a person being a man given that they are a doctor (three-quarters).

There was much debate as to which method was the better one (Mirels, 1982; Tzeng and Tzeng, 1982; Jackson and Stricker, 1982; Tzeng, 1982) with a number of disputes about statistical and other methodological questions. Mirels maintained that implicit personality theories were illusory whilst Jackson and Stricker maintained that they were accurate assessments of real trait relationships.

A study by Borkenau and Ostendorf (1987) offered a solution to the debate. They found that people can judge accurately which traits go together (correlate), in agreement with Jackson *et al.* (1979). They also found that people were not good at judging the actual values of the conditional probabilities, in agreement with Mirels (1976). In order to compute the conditional probabilities the subject needs to know the 'base-rate' information. In our example, this was how many men there were, how many doctors there were and how many men were doctors. Borkenau and Ostendorf found that the subjects in their experiment did know this information but did not appear to use it in their estimation of conditional probability. They suggested the subjects were using a 'representativeness heuristic' in estimating conditional probability, essentially making a strategic guess. We don't bother to work out statistical values when asked this sort of question, we use our idea of what a, say, *sociable* person is like. If that idea includes the characteristic *friendly* then we conclude that a *sociable* person is also *friendly* (Tversky and Kahneman, 1974; and see Chapter 9).

From these results it looks as though people do know which personality characteristics go together and, as Borkenau and Ostendorf point out, in this correlational sense implicit personality theory is accurate. However, implicit personality theory is poor when an estimation of conditional probabilities is required. Borkenau and Ostendorf argue that this latter aspect of implicit personality is not important when we are judging others. Even though we may not be very good at assessing the conditional probability that a sociable person is also *friendly*, we do know whether *sociable* and *friendly* usually go together or not.

PERCEIVED TRAIT RELATIONSHIPS: LANGUAGE OR EXPERIENCE?

Do we assume that people who are *generous* are also *kind* because we have observed that these characteristics often occur together in the same person? Or do we simply look at the meaning of the two terms and judge their similarity? If my definition of *generous* has a number of features in common with *kind*, then I might say *generous* people are also *kind*, not because of my knowledge of people but on the basis of my knowledge of language.

Shweder (1975,1977) and D'Andrade (1965, 1974) performed a number of studies where subjects were asked questions about the behaviour of people they had observed, such as: 'Did the people who laughed a lot also smile a lot?' The results indicated that the subjects relied on the similarity of meaning between the terms *laughed* and *smiled*, rather than on an accurate memory of the co-occurrence of laughing and smiling in their observations of behaviour.

The experimental set up for this research has three parts to it. One, the subjects observe a person, a film of a person or read about a person's behaviour. They then have to categorize the person's behaviour. For example, is the person behaving in a *dominant* way or an *extrovert* way? Each new piece of behaviour is categorized. From this first source of information the researchers can work out how frequently certain behaviours go together, the actual trait co-occurrence. Two, after the subjects have finished observing the behaviour, they are asked to assess the co-occurrence of traits in the people they have seen or read about. We can see that in the second part the subjects are being asked to remember what they have seen or read and make decisions about it. This gives a measure of their implicit personality theories. Third, and finally, the judges are asked to rate the similarity in meaning between the traits being considered.

Shweder and D'Andrade (1979) argued that, if the *accurate reflection* hypothesis is true and people learnt the co-occurrence of traits through the observation of the behaviour, then the first two sources of information would match each other. The subjects' ratings of trait co-occurrence would match the actual trait co-occurrence. The third source of information might, or might not, match them, it didn't really matter to the hypothesis. However, if the *systematic distortion* hypothesis is true, and people are not using their memory for the actual co-occurrence of behaviours in their personality judgements but are relying on the similarity of meaning of the trait terms, then the second and third sources of information should match and the first would be different.

Shweder and D'Andrade found support for the systematic distortion hypothesis and argued that our implicit personality theories can be in-accurate as 'memory for events contains a systematic bias, in that things that are conceptually similar are recalled as if they covaried' (Shweder and D'Andrade, 1979, p. 1076), implying that implicit personality theory is based on linguistic relationships and not on the actual co-occurrence of traits.

The systematic distortion hypothesis has not gone uncriticized. Block *et al.* (1979) argued that there are problems in Shweder and D'Andrade's conclusions. How behaviours are defined in part one of the method and how similarity is assessed in part three might both influence the correspondence between the three sources of information. We also need to consider what we mean by 'similarity of meaning' and how similarity judgements are made. Different ways of assessing behaviour or similarity might lead to different conclusions. They argued that the way Shweder and D'Andrade measured the actual behaviour, by adding up the occurrences of instances of behaviour in various categories, was too simple. Indeed, Block *et al.* opposing Shweder and D'Andrade, argued that the perceived co-occurrence of traits does reflect the real relationship between them.

Gara and Rosenberg (1981) took up this question of similarity judgements. If similarity judgements reflected only similarity of meaning then the systematic distortion hypothesis does have support from these studies. However, similarity judgements could also arise from an individual's experience of actual trait relationships, in that we might see traits as similar in meaning because we have observed them occur together in the same people. If the latter is the case, then it is not surprising that similarity judgements match trait ratings, as implicit personality theory is influencing both. In this case the comparison of these two sources of information is not really telling us anything about the accuracy of implicit personality theory at all.

Gara and Rosenberg (1981) found that when people are judging the co-occurrence of trait terms they may well base their decision on similarity of meaning, particularly if they have a difficult memory task. But the similarity of meaning judgements are themselves influenced by people's beliefs. When I am judging whether *generous* and *kind* mean similar things, my answer is not solely based on linguistic similarity but also on my belief about whether *generous* and *kind* go together. Whilst they do not offer an answer to the question of the accuracy of perceived co-occurrence of traits, Gara and Rosenberg (1981) argue that both similarity ratings of traits and trait ratings reflect aspects of implicit personality theory. Trait ratings should not therefore be dismissed as simply reflecting linguistic relationships.

Shweder and D'Andrade (1979) measured the actual occurrence of behaviour in terms of an 'identification coding scheme'. The subjects simply identified behaviour according to given categories and worked out the frequency of the occurrence of the behaviour in these categories. Block *et al.* (1979) saw this as rather too simple a measure. Romer and Revelle (1984) went further and argued that this method actually distorted the match between the first and second sources of information, as, they claimed, the first source of information was not being calculated appropriately.

Romer and Revelle used both an identification scheme and a rating scheme in their measurement of behaviour. In the identification scheme a piece of behaviour was classified as an instance of, say, *dominant* behaviour, and not of the other types of behaviour (*extrovert, warm, unassuming, submissive, introverted, cold* or *arrogant*). In the rating scheme it was rated on all categories, say +2 for *dominant*, +1 for *extroverted*, 0 for *warm*, −1 for *unassuming*, −2 for *submissive*, −2 for *introverted*, 0 for *cold* and 1 for *arrogant*.

Romer and Revelle found similar results to Shweder and D'Andrade with identification coding, relatively low correlation between the first two sources of information and a higher correlation between two and three. With the rating scheme they found a much better correspondence between the first and second sources of information and therefore argued that the 'systematic distortion' found by Shweder and D'Andrade was caused by the coding scheme used by the researchers rather than a semantic bias in the subjects. They concluded that people do judge trait relationships on the basis of their observation of the actual trait relationships.

A further criticism of the systematic distortion hypothesis comes from Semin and Greenslade (1985). They distinguished between what they called *immediate* and *mediate* terms. An immediate term is a verb or form of behaviour like the word *smiling*, as in the sentence: 'The man is smiling.' A mediate term is an adjective or a trait term like happy as in: 'The man is happy.' If a subject sees an example of behaviour and has to judge an immediate term then, according to Semin and Greenslade, the memory demands are to do with checking whether something occurred and how often: 'Did the man smile?' However, with an mediate term the judge is required to make inferences: 'Was the man happy?' In this case the subject has to decide if the behaviours observed can be classified as *happy*. They postulated that immediate and mediate terms serve different functions: immediate terms are used to discriminate between acts and events (*smiling* is a distinguishable act, separate from other acts like *frowning* or *crying*) whereas mediate terms have an interpretative function (deciding whether someone is *happy* will involve inferences based in part on semantic information, i.e. what *happy* means).

Semin and Greenslade noted that the systematic distortion hypothesis makes no distinction between immediate and mediate terms. It assumes that both will produce semantic distortion. However, the results of studies using only mediate terms may not be applicable to immediate terms. Indeed, they found that systematic distortion occurred with mediate terms but not with immediate terms. From this Semin and Greenslade argued that the systematic distortion effect need not be explained by arguing that people have a general tendency to use semantic relatedness in making their co-occurrence judgements rather than experience of actual co-occurrence. When immediate terms are used (as in a study of their own that Semin and Greenslade cite) judgements of trait co-occurrence matched the actual co-occurrence but not with similarity of meaning: people do know which behaviours go together. As systematic distortion does not occur with immediate terms Semin and Greenslade conclude that it does not imply a general cognitive tendency in the way we judge the co-occurrence of behaviours but has more to do with the functions of immediate and mediate terms.

In conclusion this work indicates that, with a difficult memory task and mediate terms, people use the similarity of meaning to judge the co-occurrence of traits, rather than the actual observed co-occurrence of traits resulting in the systematic distortion bias. Thus an interviewer, after interviewing a number of candidates, might judge one seen as *friendly* to be *enthusiastic* as well due to the common semantic features of *enthusiastic* and *friendly* rather than due to a recollection of the candidate's actual enthusiasm. However, the problems with the definition of similarity (Gara and Rosenberg, 1981; Semin and Greenslade, 1985) and the coding of observed behaviour (Romer and Revelle, 1984; Semin and Greenslade, 1985) have called into question the systematic distortion effect as a general bias in judgement. People can be accurate in judging the co-occurrence of traits and behaviour as long as they have coded (i.e. understood) the behaviour appropriately in the first place. Also people are better judges of the co-occurrence of immediate terms (observable pieces of behaviour, like *smiling* and *nodding*) than of mediate terms (more general characteristics, like *happy* and *friendly*).

Chapter 7

Accuracy in person perception

The discussion was not clearly favouring one candidate.

'OK,' said Mary, 'let's look at our rating forms.'

Previously, she had drawn up a list of characteristics she believed were important to the job: alert, bright, creative, dynamic, enthusiastic and friendly. She constructed a rating form, shown below, and the three panel members had filled one in for each of the candidates.

Ratings for candidate:

Inattentive	*−3−2−1 0 1 2 3*	*Alert*
Dull	*−3−2−1 0 1 2 3*	*Bright*
Unoriginal	*−3−2−1 0 1 2 3*	*Creative*
Undynamic	*−3−2−1 0 1 2 3*	*Dynamic*
Uninterested	*−3−2−1 0 1 2 3*	*Enthusiastic*
Unsociable	*−3−2−1 0 1 2 3*	*Friendly*

[There are a number of questions you can ask yourself here. Did Mary select the most appropriate characteristics? Will the panel be able to judge these characteristics successfully from the interview? Is this an appropriate way of selecting the successful candidate?]

Mary, Peter and Susan took out their rating forms for the three candidates, Alan, Brenda and Colin. [These are shown on p. 125.]

'We've all chosen a different candidate!' exclaimed Peter, looking at the results.

'Well, at least one of us must be right,' said Susan.

At this point in the book we are faced with the practical question: can we judge other people accurately? A range of occupations dealing with people apparently demand an accuracy of person perception: personnel, medical practitioners, teachers, social workers, the police. If any of these misjudge a person the consequences can be serious. This leads on to the further question of whether some people are better than others as judges of people? If so, what makes a good judge of people?

In the earlier chapters we have looked at the various influences upon a judgement that should make us rather suspicious of the possibility of accuracy in judgement at all, given that we are influenced by a person's attractiveness, stereotypes and our own implicit personality theory. However, the practical necessity of judgement remains: who will be accepted on a course? who will be given the job? who should be promoted?

In this chapter we shall be considering how this question might be dealt with. There are two parts to the chapter. The first will focus on the work performed in the first half of this century that investigated the factors influencing the accuracy of a judgement. This work came to a halt when problems arose as to the definition and measurement of accuracy. The second part of the chapter will consider the more recent work on accuracy that attempts to overcome some of the seemingly insurmountable problems that were illustrated in the early work.

A MEASURE OF ACCURACY

As an example throughout this chapter we shall be using the judgements of the interview panel at MT Design and considering which of them is the most accurate. The results of the ratings are shown in Table 7.1. Is Mary a better judge of personality than Peter or Susan? Is one of them more accurate in assessing the candidates?

The key to knowing whether people are accurate or not in their judgements is having a *criterion score*. This is taken to be the 'true' or accurate assessment. The performance of the judge is then compared with the criterion score and the difference between the two is taken to be the error in the judge's rating. Most of the experiments in this area have involved a procedure where criterion scores are compared to the scores given by the subjects.

Let us assume that we really do know what the three candidates are like on the six personality characteristics chosen by Mary. The criterion scores are given in Table 7.2. You can look back at the ratings the panel gave and decide who you think is the most accurate judge of the candidates on the rating scales. As we go through this chapter we shall consider these ratings to see what we can say about the accuracy of the panel.

THE EARLY WORK ON ACCURACY

From the 1920s to the 1950s there was a period of great enthusiasm for studying the accuracy of person perception. We shall see why the number of studies was much less after the mid-1950s but first it is worth looking at the findings of the earlier research.

Much of this research considered the question of what makes one person a better judge than another. The main concern was to tease out the factors that led to better judgements. There were good practical reasons for this

Table 7.1 Rating scores for the three candidates

			Characteristic				
	Alert	Bright	Creative	Dynamic	Enthusiastic	Friendly	Total
Mary's ratings:							
Alan	1	1	2	2	1	−2	5
Brenda	1	2	0	0	1	3	7
Colin	1	3	2	2	3	1	12
Total	3	6	4	4	5	2	24
Peter's ratings:							
Alan	1	0	2	0	1	−1	3
Brenda	3	2	3	1	2	3	14
Colin	1	2	1	1	2	1	8
Total	5	4	6	2	5	3	25
Susan's ratings:							
Alan	1	1	2	2	0	−1	5
Brenda	0	1	1	−1	1	1	3
Colin	−1	1	−1	0	1	−2	−2
Total	0	3	2	1	2	−2	6

Table 7.2 Criterion scores for the three candidates

			Characteristic				
	Alert	Bright	Creative	Dynamic	Enthusiastic	Friendly	Total
Alan	1	1	2	1	1	0	6
Brenda	2	1	2	0	1	2	8
Colin	1	2	2	1	3	1	10
Total	4	4	6	2	5	3	24

approach. Much of occupational psychology is concerned with how people are assessed in all aspects of employment, be it during the selection process or the evaluation of performance in post. In their review paper, Bruner and Tagiuri (1954) cite three important effects discovered during this time that influenced the accuracy of personality judgement.

The first of these is the *halo effect* named by Thorndike (1920). It was found that if a person judges someone highly on one personality characteristic, usually the *good–bad* dimension, then this can result in them rating the same person highly on a range of characteristics. It is as though they have a general impression of a person with positive characteristics and this 'halo' influences their judgement of additional characteristics: an interviewer who finds certain candidates very likeable is likely to judge them high on friendliness too. The interviewer might also go on to rate them high on a number of other factors such as intelligence, creativity, motivation, for example, which are not directly linked to the *good–bad* dimension of personality. The 'halo' effect can work both ways. Someone disliked by the interviewer might also be seen as low on a number of other characteristics. It could be that when we are uncertain of how to rate people on character traits, such as when we have met them only briefly, we might use our general impression of them being a 'good sort', or 'a nasty piece of work' as a guide for our assessment of a range of personality characteristics. Comparing Peter's rating of Brenda with the criterion, he is consistently rating her higher than she actually is. His comments suggested he saw her as a very knowledgeable person and this judgement may have influenced his assessment of her other characteristics.

The second effect is termed the *logical error* (Guilford, 1936). Here a person assumes that certain characteristics go together. For example, someone might believe that intelligent people are honest. A candidate for an interview who is judged as high in intelligence will also (illogically) be judged as high on honesty. We can link this now to implicit personality theory: we have acquired a belief that these personality traits go together. The reason for this could be due to past experience, that the people known to be intelligent have also been honest. However, this does not mean that other intelligent people we meet will necessarily be honest.

The third judgemental effect is called the *leniency effect*. This is the tendency to rate all people positively on a number of characteristics. It is like having an optimistic or positive view of the world: 'rose-coloured spectacles'. An interviewer might see a number of candidates and rate them all highly on a range of character traits. It might be true that their qualities really are all good but if other judges are more discriminating, then the first is showing leniency. Without much information about the other people we are asked to judge, it may be tempting to assume that they have positive characteristics. It is also a tactful approach when we don't want to upset anyone. On some TV talent shows the judges say how wonderful everyone is, including the out-of-tune singer, and score everyone highly. It isn't very accurate but it makes everyone happy.

As well as these three effects, there were lots of studies that found factors that influenced the accuracy of judgement. Basically, these studies separated judges into groups according to a certain factor, such as intelligence (high and low) or sex (men and women). Then the people were asked to make personality judgements and the researchers looked at which group was the most accurate. Bruner and Tagiuri (1954) concluded that there were five general findings from the vast amount of information produced by these studies.

First, the similarity of the judge to the person being judged improved the accuracy of judgement, regardless of whether the similarity was due to sex, age, background or a range of other factors, the implication being that we are better at judging others who are like us rather than those who are unlike us.

Second, people were found to be better at judging others on traits that can be observed through a person's behaviour. It is easier to judge someone on politeness than creativity. Within a society there are set rules of politeness that can be clearly seen in behaviour such as getting up to greet someone, shaking hands or opening a door for someone. It is not quite so easy with creativity. There are no set rules of behaviour to indicate creativity. Someone might act like Albert Einstein or Pablo Picasso and we might still decide they are not creative. We must make more of an inference in our judgement of creativity compared to politeness.

Third, much of the inaccuracy of judgement occurs due to systematic errors (such as the halo, logical error or leniency effects listed above).

Fourth, people who can detach themselves from their judgements rather than being emotionally involved appear to make better judges. In certain circumstances intelligence and being socially skilled were also found to aid judgement. These seem to be the skills that professional assessors, like personnel officers, are encouraged to acquire: the ability to deal with people in interviews in a socially skilled way (putting the candidates at their ease, encouraging them to talk about themselves and so forth) and then to make a rational assessment of their character traits rather than an emotional or gut reaction.

Finally, an empathy between the judge and the judged improved accuracy. Being able to see things from the other person's point of view, being able to comprehend their experiences all appear to increase the accuracy of person perception.

A lot of research had been undertaken up to the 1950s but, despite the findings mentioned above, it was not clear whether accuracy of personality judgement was a general ability or whether it depended on the circumstances and the characteristics being judged. Were there people who were good at judging the whole range of personality traits? Was a good judge of *business drive* also a good judge of *theatrical flair*? Taft (1955) reviewed over fifty studies and came to the conclusion that there wasn't a general ability of personality judgement but that in certain circumstances some people were better than others at assessing certain personality characteristics.

PROBLEMS FOR ACCURACY RESEARCH

In the mid-1950s a number of problems were highlighted in the area of accuracy research. These problems had a rather devastating effect on the research and the number of studies in the area dropped markedly. What caused this virtual abandonment of the field?

Is accuracy being measured?

It may sound like a truism but one interesting finding was that judges who assumed that others were like themselves were able to assess another person accurately when the other person was genuinely like them (Cook, 1984). If someone asks me how my friend Tom would behave in a certain situation, I might consider what I would do in that situation and assume that Tom would act in the same way. If Tom does behave in this way then it appears that I am an accurate judge of him. However, it is my assumption of similarity, that Tom and I behave in the same way, that is producing the accurate assessment, not my judging ability. Not surprisingly, if similarity is incorrectly assumed then the judgement is not good (Cook, 1984).

Researchers, therefore, had a methodological problem in that they might find accuracy of assessment in their experiments but these results might be due not to a genuine ability to judge accurately but to other factors, such as assumed similarity.

What kind of accuracy?

The situation for the researchers was made considerably more difficult when Cronbach (1955) claimed that there was not a single measure of accuracy but that accuracy scores could be subdivided into four components: *elevation, differential elevation, stereotyped accuracy* and *differential accuracy*. As previous researchers had not broken their results down into these four components it was not clear what aspect of accuracy they were looking at.

Elevation is like the leniency effect. Here a person judges all others on all traits consistently higher (or consistently lower) than the criterion scores. There are two possible reasons for this inaccuracy (Cook, 1984). The judge may have a genuine leniency bias and view others more positively than they really are. Alternatively, the person might not understand the rating system properly, and, although they perceive people quite accurately, score everyone too high (or too low).

If we look at Susan's ratings in our example, she is scoring much lower than the criterion scores. Adding up all her ratings gives a total of 6 compared to the total of the criterion scores of 24. It could be that she is giving a rating of 1 or 2 when she believes someone to be very high on a trait. She hasn't scored a 3 anywhere. She might not understand the rating system properly.

Whatever the cause, she is rating everyone below criterion. Adding 1 to all of her ratings would bring the general level of her scores more in line with the criterion scores.

Differential elevation is a measure of the variation of the judge's scores across the people being judged. Accuracy on differential elevation implies that the judge is distinguishing appropriately between them. Is Mary a good judge of Alan, Brenda and Colin? We can add up Mary's ratings for Alan across the various traits. We can also do this for her ratings of Brenda and Colin as well. Comparing these values with the ratings total for Alan, Brenda and Colin on the criterion scores gives an assessment of Mary's differential elevation. Looking at the figures, Mary's ratings totals of 5, 7 and 12 compare quite well with the criterion totals of 6, 8 and 10. Unlike Peter and Susan, Mary's totals give the same relative order as the criterion scores: she has accurately identified the best and worst candidates. Clearly differential elevation is an important measure of accuracy for interviewers. Mary's greater experience in her profession may have given her that greater accuracy on differential elevation. But then again she also drew up the rating form!

The third of Cronbach's components is stereotyped accuracy. This is the judge's assessment of the characteristics observed. It is like differential elevation but is concerned with the traits rather than the people. Is the judge good at judging the characteristics of the group of people being judged? The criterion scores might show that the people are generally high in *intelligence* and low on *creativity*. A judge who rates them as lower in *intelligence* and higher on *creativity* than the criterion scores has not made a very accurate assessment of the characteristics of the group.

We can see why it is called stereotyped accuracy if we consider an example. A person is rating a group of accountants on a range of characteristics. One might expect (from our stereotype) that a group of accountants will score higher on *conscientiousness* than *avant-garde nature*. If the stereotype has a basis in truth, then the criterion scores will show the difference in these traits. If the judge's score on the traits reflects this difference then the judge is good at assessing the personality characteristics of accountants as a group rather than any particular individual.

If we look at Peter's trait totals and compare these with the criterion trait totals, they are remarkably similar. This indicates that overall Peter has an accurate idea of the characteristics of a general candidate for the job, high on creativity and enthusiasm, lower on dynamism and friendliness.

Finally, we come to differential accuracy, which is the ability of the judge to rate an individual accurately on a particular trait. For example, whilst accountants in general might rate high in *conscientiousness* and the judge can pick this up (stereotyped accuracy), can the judge accurately rate the accountant who is not very conscientious? Differential accuracy is the closest of the components to being a true measure of accuracy in judging each person on each personality trait.

We can compare each of Mary's ratings with each of the criterion scores and work out the difference. Adding up the differences we get a value of 10. Peter's difference total is 11 and Susan's 20. On this rough and ready calculation of differential accuracy, Mary is marginally better than Peter with Susan much worse. We might decide to correct for elevation on Susan's ratings and add 1 to each of her scores before calculating differential elevation, but she doesn't do much better, her difference total is still 14.

After Cronbach (1955) had shown that there wasn't a single type of accuracy, researchers had to be more careful when they claimed that people were accurate or inaccurate in their judgements. Were they testing the ability to judge a group (stereotyped accuracy) or individuals (differential elevation) or the specific traits of an individual (differential accuracy)? Cronbach (1955) argued that differential elevation and differential accuracy were the two components that reflected true accuracy. We can see this in our example. Being able to put the candidates in order was very important, as well as being able to judge each person on each characteristic. Peter's ability on stereotyped accuracy wasn't very useful in this case, but there are instances where being able to judge the general characteristics of a group of people might be quite useful, say, to a politician wanting to influence a particular section of society (Cook, 1984).

The problem of selecting a criterion

A further problem for accuracy researchers lay in the selection of criterion scores. In our example I said let's assume these are the real values for Alan, Brenda and Colin, presenting the figures like rabbits being pulled out of a hat. Unfortunately, in real situations we cannot magically conjure up real values for personality characteristics. Selecting criterion scores can be a serious problem.

Let us consider an example of a standard accuracy test. Margaret is asked to rate four friends in terms of *running ability*. She makes her judgement, which is then compared with the criterion scores. If her judgement matches the scores then we say that she is a good judge of running ability. If they don't match we say she is not a good judge. But what criterion do I choose? What is an appropriate criterion for running ability? Clearly I would not take high-jump performance. This seems fairly obvious but in personality assessment there are occasions when people use seemingly unrelated criteria to measure personality characteristics. Is a certain pattern of handwriting related to one's *sociability*? Or should we be looking at evidence that the person likes to socialize? A number of employers use personality tests in selecting their personnel. Is the test measuring the personality traits relevant to the job?

Let us assume that we use the time to run 100 metres on the racetrack as our criterion score for running ability. If Margaret's ratings don't match the criterion scores we can say she is inaccurate. But she might claim she is accurately assessing distance running ability. Indeed, had we asked the people to run 1500 metres, 5000 metres or even a marathon the criterion scores might have been different. One difficulty is making sure that the judge and the criterion are measuring the same characteristic. How we measure intelligence (say, a paper and pencil test) might not be the same as how the judge assesses intelligence (say, the ability to talk competently on a topic). Clearly the criterion score and the judge need to be assessing the same thing; otherwise differences between them may be due to factors other than a lack of accuracy in judgement.

In the case of running ability we can be more specific in our instructions to the person doing the judging. We could ask Margaret for her judgement of how well her friends would do in the 100 metres race. We should then be measuring the same thing. We can time a race and use the times as the criterion scores. The good thing about running ability is that it is measured by a clock. And clocks are very good at measuring time and your clock measures time in the same way mine does. However, consider a personality variable like *friendliness*. If a person is asked to rate four friends on *friendliness*, what criterion should be used? We might choose a set of behaviours to measure (smiles, talks in a certain tone of voice, spends time with others and so on) but these might not be the ones Margaret or other researchers might choose. We cannot find a machine, like a clock, that accurately measures *friendliness*. Indeed, it is quite difficult to decide on a clear definition of what friendliness is, let alone try to measure it. Without a machine like a timer to measure personality characteristics, what can we use? A number of different criteria have been chosen by different researchers (Cook, 1971).

The first possibility is to ask people to rate themselves on traits like *friendliness*, on the assumption that they know themselves better than anyone else, and use this value as our criterion score. But there are problems. We may not be very good judges of our own personalities. Also, in cases like applying for a good job or to a dating agency, we might pretend we have a personality different from our own. There is no certainty that a person's own assessment is any more accurate than that of someone else.

The second possibility is to ask a specialist or 'expert', who should have a good knowledge of an individual's personality. These experts might simply be friends, family or colleagues although they could be people with professional skills that are assumed to give them expert knowledge, like teachers or personnel officers. Lots of employers ask for references when people are applying for jobs. However, ratings by other people may well be influenced by factors such as the context in which the person knows us, the length of time that they have known us and their own implicit ideas about people. Also, in naming a referee in a job application we try and find someone who we hope is going to present us in a positive light. Yet we should not underestimate expert opinion. If personality perception is something that one can become better at with practice then experienced people in the field, such as personnel officers, may well have developed an expertise.

Due to the problems with the above criteria, psychologists have endeavoured to develop personality tests, in an attempt to produce the objective 'machine' that gives a true assessment of personality characteristics. These tests have been found to be valuable in certain situations but have themselves been criticized. First, they may assume that we actually have enduring character traits that can be measured. If the test indicates that you are friendly, the assumption is that you will be consistently friendly. Second, it is possible that people can fill them in to present themselves as they wish to be seen rather than how they actually are. Finally, each test is developed from a theoretical and methodological stance that is open to criticism from other researchers.

At times personality tests are subject to much criticism. However, one can see the logic of trying to develop them when one appreciates that many people, such as employers, require some way of assessing people, who may become their future employees. Other methods have been employed in an attempt to find a measure of the true 'hidden' personality, often without questioning the validity of these methods and the assumptions underlying them. An example of this type of assessment is that of hand-writing analysis (graphology). Many psychologists would dispute that there is a fixed set of personality traits waiting to be revealed (see Mischel, 1968) but this cannot deny the wish of employers to measure them!

The difficulty is that we have no absolute measure of personality to act as a criterion for accuracy judgements. This appears to be an insurmountable problem but many practical situations demand an assessment and employers, even those that appreciate this problem, still want to interview candidates for jobs and still want to know if their procedure is selecting the right people. They want to know who on their staff is a good judge of future employees. In our example Mary would find it very helpful to know that she's better than Peter and Susan in finding the best candidate for the job. Often, in many cases like this, a pragmatic approach has been adopted. We may never know the degree of friendliness someone *actually* has. We may even reject the existence of a fixed value. However, we can, for practical purposes, find a value, knowing that it will not be perfect. Indeed people often take a range of values: self-reports, references and other information and compare all of these with the interviewer's assessment, in the hope that some general pattern will emerge. Confidence in the accuracy of a judgement is then based on its agreement with other assessments.

THE END OF ACCURACY?

With the demise of accuracy studies, researchers during the 1960s and 1970s began to look into the underlying process of social judgement, rather than its accuracy, and made comparisons between human reasoning and norma-tive models of judgement, such as logical reasoning or statistical inference, in attempts to model this process (see Chapters 8 and 9). The dominant finding has been that people's judgements do not match up to the pre-dictions of the normative models. Thus, the human perceiver has been seen as biased and error-prone in making judgements. Much of this period was spent in revealing the range and variety of these biases and errors. Now, as Kruglanski (1989) points out, the emphasis has shifted away from directly investigating the judgement process as such, to focus on the study of human inaccuracy as represented by these errors and biases.

THE RETURN TO ACCURACY OF JUDGEMENT

Errors and mistakes

It is tempting to argue that accuracy of judgement is something that can never be achieved. First, there may not be a 'real' personality to compare our judgements with (Cook, 1984). Second, Cronbach's criticisms tell us there is more than one type of accuracy. Third, the studies of implicit personality theory have emphasized that we have our individual ways of perceiving the world, and when we agree on a judgement with others that consensus is likely to correspond to our common implicit ideas rather than accuracy *per se*. Finally, more recent work on social perception has revealed a whole series of errors and biases in judgement.

It is not surprising, given the points made above, that the study of accuracy was almost abandoned. However, a number of researchers have rekindled interest in the question of accuracy by looking again at what it means to be accurate or inaccurate. Foremost in this field is the work of Funder (1987). He has argued that the lack of work on accuracy in the 1960s and 1970s has given a false picture of person perception. During this time much of the work has been concerned with our biases and errors. However, as Kenny and Albright (1987) point out, even though a person makes errors, it does not mean that they are unskilled or even inaccurate. Even the greatest tennis players in the world make errors yet still perform brilliantly accurate shots. If we studied only a player's double faults then we would have a totally false picture of their tennis-playing ability. Similarly, the findings in the laboratory that we have biases and make errors in judgement may well hide the fact that we really are quite good in our everyday judgements.

Funder (1987) questioned our understanding of 'errors'. He distinguishes them from mistakes. In a formal sense an error is merely a deviation from a expected position. The expected position is one that is predicted by a theoretical model. There might be a theory that the perfect tennis shot is made from the centre of the racket. According to this theory, I am making an error when I hit the ball off centre, but it may still be a good shot and win the point. A mistake occurs when a real-world situation is judged incorrectly. The ball bounces over the net and I aim to hit it with my racket. A complete miss is a mistake. I have totally misjudged the situation. No one wins tennis matches by missing the ball. Without this distinction between error and mistake it is tempting to assume that they are the same thing. However, errors are not mistakes and may serve a useful purpose in developing judgemental skills. Our individual experiences and idiosyncrasies might actually help us to predict events in our own lives very well (Kelly, 1955). As Funder (1987) points out, theories of judgement should not be seen as standards which prescribe the way people should behave. The top tennis players are often said to be 'rewriting the rule-book' or 'making up new shots' when they hit brilliant winners. These shots, according to the theory, are errors!

Similarly, in social judgement the massive amount of work on errors should not necessarily be taken as evidence for human inaccuracy. Indeed, it is worth considering whether they have an adaptive usefulness rather than emphasizing their deviation from some hypothetical position. In the psychological laboratory we may observe a whole range of biases from our normative model of correct performance. However, outside the laboratory these may not be errors at all if they serve a practical function. As Funder (1987) notes, studies of visual perception in the laboratory have shown that people are susceptible to a whole range of visual illusions and other errors of perception. However, the psychological processes that produce these errors are seen as important adaptive processes that help us understand the visual world in our daily lives. Funder argues that the accuracy of personality judgement should be studied in real world situations, rather than in the laboratory, where accuracy may be seen in the context of the situation in which people are making judgements to do with their own lives. The 'errors' of judgement found in the laboratory might lead to accuracy in the real world.

As an aside, it is worth considering Kelly's view here. He is willing to accept that each of us develops our own individual construct system with its own biases and errors. However, the reason we develop this system is to help us to predict and understand our world. As with the attributional errors we shall be looking at in Chapter 8, it may be that the errors and biases assist us in successfully perceiving the world in the context of our own lives and experience. Is it so surprising that student judgements focus on the intellectual and social dimensions (as we saw in Chapter 6) when we consider the importance of intellectual and social activities to student life?

The interpersonal context of accuracy judgements

Swann (1984) has also rejected the argument that accuracy in person perception is not possible due to bias and error. However, his argument is that, in the past, judging people has been considered by analogy with judging objects, like judging how heavy a ball is. There is a difference, he argues, in that, unlike a person judging the weight of a ball, person perception involves a social interaction between perceiver and perceived. It is only in the context of this interaction that we can really consider the question of the accuracy of personality judgement. A judgement of personality is 'negotiated'. Mary's assessment of Colin in the job interview involves a series of 'behavioural transactions': Mary greets him, Colin responds; Colin asks a question, Mary answers and so on. How these encounters are negotiated between the individuals will influence Mary's perception of Colin.

It is not surprising, according to Swann, that people negotiate different personalities in different situations. How a mother perceives her adult son may be very different to how the same man is perceived by his boss. The personalities have been negotiated in different contexts. Swann sees two kinds of accuracy, *circumscribed accuracy* and *global accuracy*. Circumscribed accuracy is the perceiver's accuracy in a limited context, say of the mother judging her son in the home environment. She might be very good at this. Global accuracy involves being able to judge a person across a range of contexts (situations and people). There has to be a criterion for accuracy but that too results from the negotiated personalities. The mother perceives her son to be kind and that is confirmed by his behaviour in her presence. However, her definition of what *kindness* is in this context is based on the mother–son relationship that they have developed. She might see him as kind because he does her shopping, buys flowers on her birthday or telephones her regularly. Other mothers might not see these behaviours as relevant to their judgement of whether their children are kind or not.

Kenny and Albright (1987) also emphasize the interpersonal context in which accuracy must be considered. Like Cronbach (1955), they break down a person's judgement into four components but the components are different as they consider the judgement to involve a social relationship. Two of their components, *individual accuracy* and *dyadic accuracy*, correspond to Swann's global accuracy and circumscribed accuracy. So the modern researchers are looking for the appropriate component of accuracy, as Cronbach (1955) recommended, but they are also attempting to unravel the important contextual influences upon our accuracy judgements.

Much of the early work on accuracy concerned global accuracy without a specific context or relationship. But, as Swann argues, the goals of the people in an interaction are likely to have a bearing on their judgemental accuracy. Mary's assessment of Colin is taking place in the context of her goal of employing a new member of staff. His goal might be to get the job. However, his goal might simply be a free trip into town and he's attending the interview just to get the expenses money. Mary's judgement of Colin's *enthusiasm*, for example, will be influenced by her own goals. She's only interested in his enthusiasm with respect to the job, not as a potential friend or tennis partner. His goals may well affect his behaviour and hence her perception of him. He's unlikely to want to spend much time in the interview if his goal is to see the town rather than get the job. If this is the case, she may judge him as *unenthusiastic*. This could be accurate in terms of circumscribed accuracy: he is unenthusiastic in this context, with Mary, as he doesn't want the job. But it could be inaccurate in terms of global accuracy: Colin could be a very *enthusiastic* person in general.

Again we have the argument for looking at the purpose of the judgement in order to assess its accuracy. It may well be that the specific real life situations that people find themselves in when judging others involve a degree of accuracy that is absent in the decontextualized global assessments of many research studies.

ACCURACY IN JUDGEMENT

As Funder (1987) points out, in real life situations 'accuracy' usually implies two things. First, agreement and, second, prediction. If an interview panel agree on the characteristics of a candidate, then they are likely to believe themselves to be accurate. If they disagree, there is usually discussion to try and understand the reasons for the different judgements. Why does Peter see Brenda as more *creative* than does Mary or Susan? Their discussions might reveal how he defines creativity and also how his view differs from the others. Also, the panel might consider Brenda's behaviour to determine what Peter used as evidence for her creativity.

Viewing accuracy as agreement does not necessarily conflict with the definition of accuracy as a deviation from a criterion (Kruglanski, 1989). We can see disagreement as one person not matching the criterion of the other person's judgement. In psychology experiments the subject's judgement does not agree with the psychologist's answer (Hastie and Rasinsky, 1988). Often when there is a dispute, such as in an interview, people discuss the reasons for their decisions and one person might change an opinion when presented with arguments from another. Similarly, subjects usually accept the psychologist's arguments for the appropriateness of the criterion, possibly because these are well thought out (Hastie and Rasinsky, 1988). Yet it is possible that in some circumstances the subject might convince the psychologist of the accuracy of a judgement. Thus, agreement can be seen as indicating that people are accepting a common standard of judgement.

As well as coming to an agreement, an interview panel wants to be able to predict the future behaviour of the candidates. Will the appointed person perform well in the job? Their decision has a practical outcome. They need to be accurate enough to appoint someone who can do the job successfully. But this is a pragmatic accuracy. One never knows whether unsuccessful candidates could do the job better because they don't get the chance to try. From the panel's point of view that does not really matter if they have done their job as well as they need to.

Finally, in the experiences of our daily lives, the implicit ideas we have may help us in judging others, as Kelly would expect in a successful construct system. Rothstein and Jackson (1984) found that professional employment interviewers had a very clear idea of the sort of personality of people in various occupations. This can be seen as a stereotyped accuracy. The interviewers saw advertising people as *thrill-seeking, impulsive, changeable, attention-seeking* and *fun-loving,* with accountants as *meek, seeking definiteness* and *orderly.* If these are the characteristics needed for the relevant jobs (and the research indicates that they could well be) then the interviewers know what to look for in the candidates. Rothstein and Jackson also found that, despite the limited amount of candidate behaviour the interviewers saw, they were actually quite good at assessing the personality characteristics of the candidates. All in all, this research adds to the view that personality judgement can be accurate in a real life context in which we have developed expectations based on experience.

Returning to the ratings with which we began the chapter, there are a number of points we can now consider. There was a broad agreement on a number of characteristics, shown by the ratings and the discussion (at the beginning of Chapter 6). Brenda was seen by all the panellists as the most *friendly.* Colin had *intelligence* and *enthusiasm* although they were not seen positively by Susan. Alan was seen as *creative* but with *unusual ideas* linked to a *difficult approach.* The panel might be quite accurate in these assessments. Despite differences in their judgements they could well perform their function successfully and select a suitable candidate for the job.

Chapter 8

Attribution theory

Mary decided she wanted to discuss the candidates further and work out the reasons for their applications.

'I just don't think Colin would be suitable,' said Susan. 'He sounded very pat in many of his answers. Our clients would be put off if he's too slick.'

'It could have been because he was nervous,' suggested Peter. 'He might be very different in the job.'

'Well,' said Mary who had Colin's CV in front of her, 'don't forget he has worked for H & D for a number of years. He must be pretty good with the clients.'

'So why is he leaving now?' said Susan unconvinced. 'Maybe they are trying to get rid of him.'

'He said he wanted a new challenge,' answered Mary. 'And we would be paying him more than at H & D.'

'It could be, I suppose,' said Susan slowly.

'What about the others?' asked Mary.

'I was quite impressed by Brenda,' said Peter.

Now it was Mary's turn to be unconvinced. 'I didn't find her very dynamic. Also she's earning the same money as we're offering already. And she would be working longer hours with us.'

'It could mean that she's really interested,' suggested Peter.

'Or that she's got some other reason. Isn't her company going through a rough patch? She could be trying to get out while the going is good.'

'Possibly,' answered Peter, 'I've heard the rumours. But that shouldn't put us off her.'

'It could mean she's just looking for anything to get out,' said Susan.

'And Alan?' asked Mary.

'It is a natural progression from his current job,' said Peter. 'And he's been there a few years. It is the right time for him to move on.'

'But he didn't seem to have a natural friendliness,' interrupted Mary. 'He hardly looked at me and sounded rather abrupt.' The others nodded in agreement.

When we make judgements of other people we often look to their behaviour as a clue to their personality. We decide a man talking loudly in a restaurant is an extrovert or a show-off. However, this is not the only possible reason for his behaviour. He might have a hearing problem and not realize how loudly he is speaking. Alternatively, he might be talking to a hard-of-hearing fellow diner. There may well be a range of other explanations that could be offered. On many occasions in our social lives we cannot or do not check whether our explanation is correct or not: the shop assistant we see as an unpleasant person may have just been insulted or even mistaken us for someone else. The interesting question here, therefore, is not just whether we are right or wrong in our decision but also how we arrive at that particular cause: what process of reasoning do we adopt in our attributions? There are important consequences of our attributional decisions: the doctor who attributes a patient's complaints to malingering may undertake fewer tests than the doctor who judges the patient to have a genuine illness. The teacher's response to a child's naughtiness might be different if it is seen as arising from family problems rather than the child's nature.

It is interesting to note that in the examples I have given so far the explanations can be placed in two broad categories: *internal* or *external* attributions. An internal attribution places the cause of the behaviour within the person, such as seeing a person who trips over as clumsy. An external attribution places the cause of the behaviour outside the person, attributing the fall to a slippery floor. Making an internal attribution as opposed to an external attribution can have very different consequences and therefore how we arrive at one as opposed to the other is an interesting research question that we shall be investigating in this chapter.

HEIDER'S WORK

Heider (1958) argued that, in our everyday lives, we wish to make sense of the world in order to be able to predict and control it. This is important in our social interactions. If we can decide *why* someone has done something it will help in deciding our own behaviour towards them as well as being able to predict what they will do. To Heider we are therefore biased towards *intentionality*: we look for causes in the events around us. A simple example of our perception of intentionality comes from an experiment by Heider and Simmel (1944). Subjects observed an animated cartoon film of shapes moving about the screen. In one sequence a small triangle and small circle moved along a similar trajectory about the screen. A large triangle moved along the same trajectory but a moment after the small shapes. The trajectory of the two small shapes took them inside a square. The large triangle stopped at the edge of the square. Subjects were asked what happened. They didn't describe events as I have done but said things like: the large triangle *chased* the small shapes. Other descriptions included words like *fight* or *escape*.

These words imply intentionality. The motion of the different shapes is not seen as unrelated. Shapes that moved first were seen as initiating the sequence of events. A shape following the same trajectory as another was chasing it. This type of description is also shorter. It sums up and gives sense to the action quite simply, in a way that a description of complex trajectories does not.

To Heider we can be viewed as 'naive scientists' in our everyday lives, looking for evidence for the causes of events. It is worth noting the similarity here between George Kelly's view of people in his theory of personal constructs and that of Heider. Whilst Kelly looked at the structure of our knowledge, Heider concentrated on how we attribute causes to events. As he pointed out, the attributions we make are an important influence on our own behaviour. If we decide that the stick that has just hit us has been thrown by an enemy we are likely to act very differently from when we decide it has fallen from a rotten tree (Heider, 1958). In the former case we attribute the cause to a person, in the latter case to a environmental factor. Heider also considered the distinction between *intentional* and *accidental* behaviour. Again, we will act differently if we decide that the person threw the stick intentionally to hit us compared to accidentally hitting us while throwing it for a dog. In deciding the cause of an event Heider proposed that we logically consider two questions. Was it caused by a person or a situation? If we believe it was caused by a person, did they intend it to happen or not?

Heider (1958) also argued that the behaviour of people is more salient than environmental factors to the perceiver, implying that in our attribution of causes we are biased in favour of personal causation. So, if we see someone fall over, there is a tendency to focus on the person (and attribute the fall to clumsiness) rather than, say, the less obvious unevenness of the ground. We shall be discussing this 'fundamental attributional error' later in the chapter.

THE THEORY OF CORRESPONDENT INFERENCES

Heider's ideas concerning the attribution of causes were developed by Jones and Davis (1965) in their theory of correspondent inferences. Essentially, the attribution of a cause to behaviour is an *inference*, and Jones and Davis were particularly interested in discovering the circumstances under which people make a *correspondent inference*, that is, the inference that a particular act corresponds to the disposition of the person. An example of this is attributing John's examination pass to his intelligence or ability rather than to luck or help from others.

The Jones and Davis theory concerns acts that are assumed to be freely chosen by the person performing the behaviour (the actor). Clearly, a correspondent inference is inappropriate if the actor has no choice in what to do. I am unlikely to infer that you are a generous person if I see you giving money to a stranger with a knife at your throat! Furthermore, Jones and Davis agree with Heider that we are essentially concerned with inferring the causes of acts that we believe are intended by the actor. In deciding whether an act is intentional or not we look at the ability and knowledge of the actor. The very inexperienced driver who presses too hard on the accelerator and drives into a neighbour's car is likely to be seen as lacking the ability to have intended that act. Correspondent inference theory is about attributing causes to acts that are viewed as intentional.

Jones and Davis (1965) note that any act is likely to have more than one effect. If I go into a shop and buy a bar of chocolate, this simple act has many effects: I have less money, I have a chocolate bar, I spoke to the assistant, the shop has one less chocolate bar, it might even be sold out. The problem for the person making the attribution (the observer) is in deciding which of these effects I intended: did I do it because I was hungry? did I want an excuse to talk to the assistant? Jones and Davis suggest that we consider two important factors in making attributions: the commonality and the desirability of effects.

A friend, Linda, always goes to France for a holiday. However, this year she visits Paris rather than the Riviera. Why? In both places she will be able to enjoy French food and wine, sit outside cafés and watch the people go by and have a lively time. These effects are common to both choices. However, the Riviera offers a holiday with sand, sea and watersports, whereas Paris offers the theatres, museums and architecture of a famous city. These are effects not common to both choices, they are the *noncommon effects*. Jones and Davis argue that a consideration of the noncommon effects influences our inferred reason for why she went to Paris. The fewer non-common effects there are the easier it is to infer what was intended.

The second determinant is the desirability of the effects. The effects of Linda going on holiday might be that she has a good time, sees some beautiful works of art, wears out a pair of shoes and goes into debt to pay for it. We assume that people usually intend a desirable effect, that Linda didn't go on holiday just to get into debt but rather that it was worth going into debt for the enjoyment of seeing Paris. Interestingly, Jones and Davis argue that, because of this assumption, the more noncommon negative effects of an action there are, the more likely we are to make a correspondent inference. If we assume that we all like to do desirable things then we are more likely to believe that someone really wanted to do something the more undesirable the outcomes become. If Alice goes to visit her friend Paul despite the high cost of the trip, the fact that she will miss a good party and might even lose her job for being away, then we are likely to infer that she really wanted to see him.

A further influence upon our decision concerning the causes of behaviour is the *role* of the actor. There are certain actions that are expected in certain roles. Nurses are required to care for patients as part of their job, it is in-role behaviour, so we are unlikely to see a caring act by a nurse as sufficient evidence of a caring nature. However, when people act out of role, then a correspondent inference is more likely. The nurse acting unkindly is more likely to be seen as an unkind person. This effect was demonstrated in an experiment by Jones *et al.* (1961). Subjects listened to two fictitious job interviews, one group hearing interviews for a submariner and another group for an astronaut. At the beginning of the interview the submariner subjects heard the 'ideal submariner' described as obedient, cooperative, friendly, gregarious; very much involved with other people, so 'other directed'. In one interview the submariner candidate's statements were also other directed, in the other the submariner interviewee responded with 'inner-directed' statements, showing inner resources. The astronaut subjects heard that the ideal astronaut was inner directed and one candidate made inner-directed statements while the other responded in an other-directed way. The subjects then had to decide what the candidates were really like by rating the candidates on a number of traits and indicating how confident they were of the ratings.

The results were as follows. Where the candidates had behaved in role they were rated as moderately affiliative and independent but the subjects were not very confident of these ratings. Where the candidates had behaved out-of-role the subjects were very confident of their ratings, seeing the submariner candidate as independent and non-affiliative and the astronaut candidate as very conforming and affiliative.

In-role behaviour is seen by Jones and Davis (1965) as having multiple effects (the job gets done, people treat you appropriately) and as being socially desirable (we are expected to behave this way, we get paid if we do the job properly, we might even get promoted). Therefore it is not very informative. In contrast, out of role behaviour is much less common and socially undesirable, and is more likely to lead to a correspondent inference. The shop assistant who responds to our polite request for a price check with a scowl and a curt response is likely to be seen as an unpleasant individual.

Up to now it appears that the 'naive scientist' is very logical in arriving at a correspondent inference. However, Jones and Davis argue that a perceiver is more likely to make a correspondent inference when the act has a direct impact on him or her (hedonistic relevance) or when the act is seen as intending to benefit or harm him or her (personalism). The act of a politician proposing new legislation on truck safety is more hedonistically relevant to the truck driver than to the car driver. The trucker whose vehicle has to be modified is most likely to view the proposal as characteristic of the politician, an example of personalism.

Jones and Davis acknowledge that past information can help our decisions: information on previous choices that other people have made and expectations we have about their behaviour from past experience will both influence our inferences. These expectations about behaviour were explicitly introduced into the theory by Jones and McGillis (1976). They point out that what had been described in the theory as 'social desirability' was better termed 'expectation' as it was both more general and more accurate. Usually, the socially desirable act is the one we expect someone to perform. However, a socially desirable act might be the unexpected, for example, when someone takes a homeless vagrant to live in their own home. It is not the socially undesirable act as such that is informative about a person's character but one that goes against our expectations. Similarly, we expect people to behave according to their roles, hence out-of-role behaviour is more informative and unexpected than in-role behaviour.

Jones and McGillis (1976) argue that there are two types of expectation: category-based expectations and target-based expectations. Category-based expectations concern the expectations we have about a group of people, such as expecting Americans to be open and friendly and the English to be reserved. In the extreme case these reflect the stereotypes we have of the group. The second type of expectation is the target-based expectation, an expectation about an individual's behaviour based on the knowledge we have of them. These expectations tap the perceiver's implicit personality theory that we discussed in Chapter 6. If I believe that chess players are unfriendly and I learn that you are a chess player I will expect you to be unfriendly. If people behave contrary to our expectations, whether category-based or target-based, then we are more likely to make a correspondent inference.

The pattern of inferences predicted by the theory is shown in Table 8.1.

In conclusion, correspondent inference theory suggests that the unexpected act, with few effects, is likely to be seen as intended by the actor and 'in character'.

THE WORK OF KELLEY: THE COVARIATION MODEL

The theory of Jones and Davis essentially focused on the attribution of internal causation from a single act. However, there will be cases where we have knowledge about the behaviour of a person on a number of occasions. A theory that has been developed to take account of this information in our attributions is that of Kelley (1967).

Kelley's theory of attribution also derived from the work of Heider and, like the work of Jones and Davis (1965), was concerned with the information used to guide a perceiver's attribution of causation to an act. As Kelley (1967) considered behaviour over time, the present act could be analysed in terms of other acts performed by the same person or others. Kelley's work endeavoured to show what this analysis involved and hence how an attribution to a particular cause was produced.

If we consider examples of behaviour, such as 'Juan lent money to Marie', 'Norman bought a new car', 'Robert went to see Michael', there are a number of sources of information that we can use to help us make an attribution. First, we have *persons*, the actors performing the behaviour. We also have

Table 8.1 Expectation and noncommon effects in correspondent inferences

| | | Expectation of the behaviour | |
		High	Low
	High	There are lots of reasons for this choice and it was expected, so we cannot make an inference between the act and the person's disposition.	There are lots of reasons for this choice so we cannot make a correspondent inference, yet it is intriguing why this act was performed given that it was not expected.
Number of noncommon effects	*Low*	It is clear what was intended as the effects are few but we cannot make an inference about the person's disposition as we expected the person to behave in this way and it gives us no new information about them.	It was clear what was intended as the effects are few. Also it was unexpected so we assume that the act corresponds to the person's disposition: we make a *correspondent inference*.

Source: adapted from Jones and McGillis (1976, p. 392).

what Kelley refers to as *entities* which are essentially the objects of the action. And finally we have time: what has happened on other occasions? Kelley's theory looks at the variability of behaviour across these three sources of information: persons, entities and time. In attributing a cause to an act we ask the following questions.

1. Do other people do the same in the same circumstances?

Here we need to know about 'persons'. We want to know whether the behaviour of the actor is unusual or whether other people behave in the same way in this situation. Essentially we want to know the variation in the behaviour of 'persons'. This information is called *consensus* information as we are looking at whether different actors do the same thing or not. Taking our first example: do other people lend money to Marie?

2. Does the same person do the same thing in other circumstances?

This time we are concerned about 'entities'. We want to know whether the person behaves in a similar way with other entities or whether this behaviour is rare. This is information about the *distinctiveness* of the action by the person. For example, does Juan lend money to other people?

3. Does the same thing happen at other times?

Now we must consider the *consistency* of this act over time. We want to know whether the person always does the same thing in the same circumstances or whether they behave differently. Does Juan always lend money to Marie?

Social scientists analysing the relationship between factors often use a statistical technique called 'the analysis of variance'. In an experiment on the mathematical skill of children we might analyse their performance in terms of two factors, the school they attend and the amount of time they spend learning mathematics. The analysis of variance tells us how much the performance of the children varies on these two factors. If there is no difference between the performance of children at one school compared to another (low variance on this factor), then we will not conclude that mathematical skill is due to the school they attend. If we find that the performance varies with the amount of time studying mathematics (high variance on this factor) then we are more likely to conclude that mathematical skill is related to the time spent in learning. Thus, in the experiment, analysing where the variability occurs tells us something about the relationships between the performance and the factors. In Kelley's attribution theory, the 'naive scientist' performs a mental analysis analogous to the analysis of variance, with 'persons', 'entities' and 'time' as the three factors in the analysis. Consensus, distinctiveness and consistency are measures of the variability of the three factors. From the result of the analysis the perceiver makes an attribution of the cause of the actor's behaviour. Kelley's theory is also called a *covariation model* as the perceiver is seen to be looking for the factors that co-vary with the behaviour: when one changes then so does the other. If different people do different things in the same situation then 'persons' and behaviour co-vary.

From this model we can predict the attributions perceivers will make. If Juan is the only person who lends money to Marie (large variation of the behaviour across 'persons') then the consensus is low. If he lends money to other people as well as Marie (little variation in the behaviour across entities), then distinctiveness is low. Finally, if he has lent money to Marie on other occasions (little variation in the behaviour over time), then consistency is high. As the variation is occurring only across persons we attribute the cause of the behaviour to the person, Juan. Thus we have made an internal attribution: Juan is a generous man or a soft touch.

If consensus is high (everyone lends money to Marie), distinctiveness is high (Juan doesn't usually lend money to people) and consistency is high (Juan always lends money to Marie), then the attribution will be to the entity (as this is where the variation is occurring). There is something about Marie that is causing the behaviour. She knows how to get money out of people!

McArthur (1972) undertook an experimental test of Kelley's theory. She presented subjects with descriptions of behaviours that gave information indicating whether consensus, distinctiveness and consistency were high or low. An example is as follows. 'John laughs at the comedian. Hardly anyone who hears the comedian laughs at him. John also laughs at almost every other comedian. In the past John has almost always laughed at the same comedian.' She then asked the subjects to attribute a cause to the behaviour: to the person, the stimulus (entity), the circumstances or some combination of the three. She predicted, from Kelley's theory, that a person attribution would occur when consensus and distinctiveness were low and consistency was high and a stimulus attribution when all three were high. Her results supported Kelley's theory, showing that people did make attributions along the lines predicted by his model.

In a development of the above work, Hewstone and Jaspers (1987) proposed an attribution model for all the various patterns of information available to the perceiver. They argued that subjects could look for necessary and sufficient conditions for the behaviour to occur. A condition is necessary if the behaviour does not occur when it is absent. A condition is sufficient if the behaviour occurs when it is present. If the behaviour occurs only when it is present but not when it is absent, then the condition is necessary and sufficient and a causal attribution can be made. This model is consistent with Kelley's view that subjects make causal attributions by analysing covariation. Hewstone and Jaspers call this the *logical model* and were able to make a causal prediction for each of the combinations of high and low consensus, distinctiveness and consistency.

The model can be made clear by an example. Try and decide why Juan lent Marie money when consensus is low (no one else lends her money), distinctiveness is high (he doesn't lend other people money) and consistency is high (he always lends her money).

The logical model operates as follows. Juan (the person) is a necessary condition because without him no money is lent. Marie (the stimulus) is also a necessary condition, as is Juan *and* Marie. Sufficient conditions are Juan *and* Marie, and Juan *and* Marie *and* the circumstances. Therefore Juan and Marie form the only necessary and sufficient conditions and the model predicts that the cause of the behaviour is due to the relationship of Juan and Marie. The same process of logic can be used for any other example.

Hewstone and Jaspers (1987) concluded that the logical model was able to predict subject's responses in the McArthur-type experiment better than other models but also acknowledge that the attributions people make do not always follow its predictions, suggesting that people are not always logical in their attributions, as we shall see later.

THE WORK OF KELLEY: CAUSAL SCHEMATA

Kelley acknowledges that a perceiver, in making an attribution, may not be able to go through the detailed analysis that is implied in his covariation model:

The attribution process implied by the analysis of variance model is undoubtably somewhat on the idealized side. It would be foolish to suggest that anything like a large data matrix is filled out with effect observations before a causal inference is made. The framework should be regarded as simply the context within which some limited and small sample of observations is interpreted. Beyond that, it is obvious that the individual is often lacking the time and the motivation necessary to make multiple observations.

(Kelley, 1973, p. 113)

When there is only a single observation the perceiver is not entirely in the dark. As Kelley (1973) points out, the perceiver's own experience or belief about the causes of events will assist in an attribution. In thinking about a piece of behaviour the perceiver will consider potential causes. If there is only one then this is likely to be the attribution. However, Kelley argues, a cause will be discounted (i.e. seen as less likely) if other plausible causes are present. This is termed the *discounting principle*. If you see me fall over then you might attribute this to clumsiness. However, if it has been snowing and the road is icy then the first cause will be discounted because another, plausible, potential cause is present. The degree of discounting appears to depend on the importance we give to the alternative causes (Hull and West, 1982). If an actor appearing in an advert is paid a lot of money we are unlikely to discount 'he did it for the money' in favour of 'he had nothing better to do on that day'.

Kelley (1971) also proposes *the augmentation principle* that operates during this process. Some causes facilitate behaviour and others are inhibitory. Where there are both facilitatory and inhibitory causes present, the facilitatory cause will be augmented (seen as more likely). For example, a friend, Margaret, goes to medical school. A facilitatory cause is that she wants to be a doctor. However, it takes years of difficult study to qualify. This is an inhibitory cause, as it is likely to discourage people from going to medical school. Given that your friend has already gone, the presence of the inhibitory cause makes you more likely to believe that she *really* wants to be a doctor.

In employing the discounting or augmentation principles to make an attribution, we are considering and comparing possible causes of an event that has occurred. For Kelley these single observational attributions arise out of *causal schemata*, that is, 'general conceptions about how certain kinds of causes interact to produce a specific kind of effect' (Kelley, 1972, p. 151). Through our experience of events in the world we have certain beliefs and assumptions about what causes produce what kinds of effects and these are organized into schemata which we then employ in our attributions. The discounting and augmenting principles imply causal schemata in that they present ways of considering plausible causes in the light of an event that has occurred.

In Kelley's causal schemata we can see themes common to other theories considered in this book. We have already considered, in Chapter 4, other forms of schemata in which information and experience are organized and related. There are links also with personal constructs and implicit personality theory in that causal schemata guide our understanding of events. Armed with our repertoire of causal schemata we make sense of the behaviour of others when the available information is limited.

COMPARISON OF MODELS

We can consider whether the theories of Jones and Davis and Kelley are complementary or conflicting. Both theories offer an account of the logic with which a perceiver attempts to attribute causality to an act. They also both argue that the perceiver uses knowledge of other acts to guide their attributions. In the correspondent inference theory, this information is used to develop expectations about behaviour, whereas, in Kelley's covariation model, the consensus, consistency and distinctiveness information is used more directly. This does lead to an apparent conflict between the theories (Jones and McGillis, 1976). For example, the unpleasant shop assistant is seen as an unpleasant person by behaving out-of-role and against our expectations, according to the correspondent inference theory. However, there might have been a particularly obnoxious customer who annoyed the usually pleasant assistant. If we had a chance to observe the assistant with a range of different customers we might find that unpleasant behaviour is rare and hence modify our view and decide that the behaviour is out of character, as Kelley's theory predicts.

How can we account for this difference? One answer lies in the explicitness of the knowledge we hold about a person (Jones and McGillis, 1976). With specific knowledge of this person's behaviour our attribution can follow Kelley's prediction. However, without such detailed knowledge of the person, we must rely on our expectations about the behaviour of shop assistants in general, which is by its nature less specific with respect to this person. The majority of cases of shop assistants behaving pleasantly to customers leads us to expect pleasant behaviour in a shop assistant, so that one who behaves unpleasantly would be viewed as behaving in character, as correspondent inference theory predicts.

Unexpected behaviour cries out for explanation (Semin and Manstead, 1983) and the question we must answer is whether this unexpected behaviour indicates a disposition or a temporary aberration due to situational factors. Different levels of knowledge might lead to different attributions. When a shop assistant behaves rudely we will simply walk away, thinking what an unpleasant person. We are unlikely to remain in the shop to observe their behaviour further. However, if a friend behaves unexpectedly badly we are likely to consider it as uncharacteristic (being distinctive and inconsistent) given our knowledge of them. Thus, rather than pitting the theories against each other we can consider the situations in which they are more appropriately applied.

ATTRIBUTION THEORY AND ATTRIBUTION RESEARCH

The theories considered here present a picture of attributions being made by logical, rational beings, taking into account alternative explanations and arriving at the most likely cause. However, much of the research into the attributions that people actually make show these to be subject to a range of irrational biases (Nisbett and Ross, 1980). What then is the relationship between attribution theory and attribution research? Jones and McGillis provide an answer:

> Correspondent inference theory is essentially a rational baseline model. It does not summarize phenomenal experience; it presents a logical calculus in terms of which accurate inferences could be drawn by an alert perceiver. . . . But the role of the theory has been as much to identify attributional bias as to predict precisely the course of the social inference process.
>
> (Jones and McGillis, 1976, p. 404)

According to this justification, attribution theory provides a normative model for comparing actual performance in attribution research. The deviation of performance from the predictions of the theory can be observed and hence identified as a bias. Without this baseline for comparison, this would not be possible.

BIASES IN CAUSAL ATTRIBUTION

A number of biases have been discovered in the attribution research, where a greater emphasis has been placed on a causal factor than predicted by a normative model.

'People are the causes of their own behaviour'

There is tendency for perceivers to attribute causes to the individual rather than the situation. This has been termed *the fundamental attribution error* (Ross, 1977). Compared to a normative model, people are biased by their over-attribution to internal causes. Even when people are constrained in their behaviour, it may still be taken to indicate an underlying disposition. For example, Jones and Harris (1967) presented subjects with essays favouring or opposing the government of Fidel Castro in Cuba. The subjects were asked to decide how favourable the essay writer was towards Castro. Even when the subjects were told that the essay writers had no choice in the type of essay they wrote (whether favourable or unfavourable), the subjects still attributed more favourable attitudes towards Castro to the writers of the favourable essays.

Heider (1958) noted that the behaviour of an individual tended to dominate the observer's perception of an event and it may be that the fundamental attribution error arises out of the greater attention paid to the actor compared to the situation (Fiske and Taylor, 1984). In support of this view, it has been shown that if attention is directed from the person to the situation then, in certain cases, the reverse occurs (Quattrone, 1982), producing a bias toward external attribution.

'From where I see it. . .'

A second bias in attribution was studied by Jones and Nisbett (1971). They found that subjects giving reasons for their own actions and those of other people tended to attribute internal causes to the behaviour of others (as we would expect from the fundamental attribution error) but external causes to their own behaviour. This they termed *the actor–observer effect*. For example, if you arrive at a party on the wrong day I am likely to see you as forgetful or disorganized, but if I do it, it is because someone gave me the wrong information or the date was badly written on the invitation.

One explanation of this effect follows on from that of the fundamental attribution error. Given that the observer attends to the behaviour of the actor then it is possible that the actor's behaviour is more *salient* than the observer's own and leads to an internal attribution. This was supported by an experiment by Storms (1973) who found that people's attributions altered when they were given a different perspective on an event by observing themselves on videotape. A second explanation concerns the greater amount of information available to observers about their own behaviour compared to that of an actor: we are more aware of the situational causes influencing our own behaviour. It is possible that both explanations are contributing to the effect (Fiske and Taylor, 1984).

'I did well in the circumstances'

An intriguing attribution bias is the *self-serving bias* (Miller and Ross, 1975). This is the tendency to attribute our own successes to internal factors but our failures to external factors. The reason I passed one examination is because I am clever but I failed another because I was distracted in the examination room, the questions were confusing and I was poorly advised on my revision topics! Whilst cognitive factors, such as the expectations we have of our own success, may be involved in this bias, motivational factors may also contribute as this bias helps us to maintain a positive view of ourselves (Fiske and Taylor, 1984).

'I'm sure anyone would do the same'

A second bias that might originate from either cognitive or motivational influences is the *false consensus effect*: the assumption that others would behave as we do (Ross *et al.*, 1977). In the experiment by Ross *et al.* students were asked if they would carry a sandwich board around campus with 'Eat at Joe's' written on it. Irrespective of their response, they were asked what percentage of students would do the same. Those who responded 'yes' predicted that 62 per cent of students would do the same as them and those who said 'no' predicted a 67 per cent agreement with their own choice. False consensus is like assumed similarity, discussed in Chapter 7 (see also Cook, 1984), in that they both show that we assume others to be like us and do what we would do.

This effect could be explained as a cognitive phenomenon reflecting limited knowledge of people: the people we know about most are our friends who usually have similar views to our own. So we overestimate the number of people who would agree with us. An alternative explanation is that we are motivated to see ourselves as normal, behaving appropriately according to the situation. Attempts have been made to decide between these explanations (e.g. Sherman *et al.*, 1984) although it remains unresolved.

Even when genuine consensus information is available we tend not to use it (Kahneman and Tversky, 1973), contrary to the covariation model, relying more on the information that readily comes to mind (see Chapter 9).

ATTRIBUTION BIASES IN PERSPECTIVE

It is tempting to see these and other attributional biases (see Nisbett and Ross, 1980) as indicating that people are poor in their attribution of causation. Indeed, there is a further temptation to see these 'naive psychologists' as not matching up to the 'real psychologists' who can produce the rational theory (Howitt *et al.*, 1989). But we must be careful: attributing 'failure' to the ordinary perceiver may be itself be biased. Essentially 'failure' in this case is an indication that people do not match up to the normative model of reasoning as implied by attribution theory. Recall from Chapter 7 that an error is not necessarily the same as a mistake. Thus, human judgement is only a failing if we see the normative model as a better, more successful method of attributing causation than that actually used by individuals. Unfortunately, as Semin (1980) argues, the model of the human attributer contained in attribution theory does contain this prescriptive element, implying that attribution theory provides a model of 'right thinking'. However, it may be useful to look, not at the limitations of human thought for an explanation of these 'failings', but to the limitations of attribution theory itself in being able to take into account the various factors that lead to our everyday explanations.

The first point to consider is the question of being 'wrong' or 'right' in an attribution. As we have seen, certain of the biases might be due to motivational factors. A person may not be 'right' in attributing their success to a guiding spirit rather than their own hard work but how important is correctness to them? If being biased leads to a more contented life, happy in our view of the world and successful in our social interactions, then it is functionally superior to being logically correct.

One limitation of attribution theory is that it does not take account of the social context and the culture in which the behaviour occurs (Semin, 1980). These provide us with 'rules' of meaningful behaviour. The behaviour of a row of people standing in line pushing wire trolleys full of food makes sense because of our knowledge of shopping. A stranger unfamiliar with this behaviour is not going to find the cause of it by analysing covariation, they need to learn the 'rules' of shopping. If a man hands me a drink you are unlikely to ask why he did it if we are in a café and he is the waiter. As Semin (1980) points out, the underlying social 'rules' provide explanations in themselves: waiters serve drinks. I'm even likely to think you odd if you do ask, wondering why you asked such a silly question, unless you come from a different culture which doesn't have cafés or you are a young child. However, when 'rules' are broken, asking why becomes relevant (Semin, 1980). The waiter gives me a drink *before* I've ordered one. That does not usually happen. Why did he do it? Is there a promotion of a new drink product? Does everyone get a free drink? Is there a friend sitting at another table who sent it across? Everyday explanations are, therefore, usually contained within the meaningful social context of the behaviour and we are required to go through a process of causal attribution only when something unexpected happens. We do not have to make sense of all behaviour afresh.

The normative models may also be limited in their presentation of the attribution process as a kind of naive scientific investigation of potential causes and effects (Billig, 1987). In looking for answers to questions in everyday life we are not simply interested in who, if anyone, caused something to occur but also whether it was right or wrong, whether it should or ought to have been done, whether the person should be rewarded or punished for the deed and so forth. Consider the example of an adult looking after a young child. If the child dashes across the road onlookers might attribute more blame to the adult when the child is knocked down by a car than when the child arrives safely at the far kerb. The cause of the child's act (say, the child seeing a friend and the adult's lack of supervision) is unrelated to the outcome of the act (either injury or no effect). Hence the different attributions of responsibility are 'biased' according to the normative model: the attribution should be independent of the outcome. But, as Howitt *et al.* (1989) point out, the wider moral considerations are ignored by the normative model in the logic of determining causal factors. But people may be making moral judgements (such as arguing that it is the duty of the adult to protect the safety of the child) in their attributions. When the child is unharmed we may be more forgiving in our attributions of responsibility ('You need eyes in the back of your head with children these days') than when harm is done ('You *should* have been watching the child'). (See Shaver (1985) for a detailed analysis of the attribution of responsibility.)

ATTRIBUTION OF SUCCESS AND FAILURE

One interesting area of study in the field of attribution has been concerned with how we attributed causes to success or failure. The attribution of a cause for performance on a task can have an important effect both on our feelings about success or failure and our expectations about future success or failure (Weiner, 1979). The reason for this is that the attribution will provide us with the degree of personal responsibility we accept for this success or failure. If we believe that we failed a test due to luck rather than ability we are less likely to feel shameful about the performance and more likely to try again (when we might not be so unlucky). Weiner (1979) argues that there are three important factors in our attributions of success and failure: locus of causality (either internal or external), stability (stable or unstable over time) and controllability (controllable or uncontrollable). The various combinations of these factors provide the possible causes we attribute to our performance.

Our expectations of future success depend, according to Weiner, on whether we attribute our present success or failure to stable or unstable factors. If success is attributed to stable factors and failure to unstable factors, then expectations of future success on the task are increased. If the reverse is true, with success attributed to unstable factors and failure to stable factors, then our expectation of future success is decreased.

Table 8.2 Attribution of causes of success or failure

		Internal	*External*
Stable	*Controllable*	Usual effort exerted	External bias, e.g. culture bias
	Uncontrollable	Ability	Task difficulty
Unstable	*Controllable*	Effort on this task, e.g. might try particularly hard	Help from others, such as special coaching
	Uncontrollable	Temporary effects, e.g. illness, mood	Luck

Source: after Weiner (1979).

How we feel about success or failure depends on whether we attribute the cause of our success or failure to internal or external factors and controllable or uncontrollable factors. We are less likely to take pride in our performance if it was a very simple task or we attributed it to luck. Likewise, failure in an extremely difficult task or, again, due to luck is unlikely to be seen as a cause for shame. However, if our success or failure is seen as due to internal causes, then we also feel it is the occasion for pride or shame. As we saw earlier, the self-serving bias might help to ameliorate some of the consequences of failure.

One interesting finding in the area of success and failure is that different causes may be attributed to men and women for the same level of achievement (Deaux, 1976). In certain cases, success has been attributed to ability in a man but hard work or luck in a woman. Failure also is attributed to different causes: bad luck or lack of effort in a man but lack of ability in a woman (Deaux, 1976). Why should this be, given the same level of male and female success? It appears that the perceiver is making attributions in accordance with stereotypes of the sexes. The causal attributions, rather than seeking a logical explanation for the success or failure, actually reinforce a pre-existing stereotypical view of men and women (Fiske and Taylor, 1984). Thus, the successful performance of a woman, apparently denying a stereotype of lower female ability, can be 'explained' without threatening the stereotype, if her success is attributed to luck or effort. In this way, regardless of the behaviour (success or failure), attributions can be made to support and reinforce a view of men and women. As we saw in Chapter 4, Billig (1985) argued that particularization is important in stereotyping. We can see how this is important to our attributions as well, especially when we maintain a distinction along a particular dimension such as gender, rather than using other categories, such as education level, in our attributions of success and failure. As Fiske and Taylor (1984) note, attributions may be employed to support other stereotypes as well as those for sex roles. Consider a discussion in a bar or across the dinner table. Two people may choose to explain the same event, say the election of politician, in different ways: one claiming the electorate was duped by a trickster and the other arguing that the politician won by a combination of expertise and experience. In analysing the arguments they use to support their explanations of events we can attempt to uncover the beliefs that they are endeavouring to maintain (see Billig, 1987).

CONCLUSION

Attribution theory has uncovered how we can rationally decide on the cause of a certain action. Yet attribution research has shown that our attributions are often biased according to the normative models. This may be for a number of functional reasons, such as helping to maintain our view of the world (for example, all young men drive too fast, there is a young man in a car crash, therefore it must have been due to his driving too fast) or to support a positive view of ourselves (I was unlucky to fail the examination, I revised for the wrong questions). Moral considerations might also influence our attributions. The so-called failure of the perceiver to attribute 'correctly' might be due to a limited view of what is 'correct' and hence, in understanding people's attributions, it is worth considering the rich source of information that people offer in explanation and justification of their attributions: that is, the arguments they put forward.

Chapter 9

Strategies of social judgement

The discussion of the candidates was getting rather bogged down. Peter decided it was his turn to say something.

'I must say that I preferred Brenda but neither of you agree. Mary favours Colin and I'm willing to go along with that. He may not be the best possible candidate there is for the job but he has been at H&D for quite a while. I just don't think we can go wrong with an H&D person. They train them well and have good client liaison.'

Mary nodded: 'They have high quality staff there.'

Susan interjected with some feeling. 'You cannot choose him just because he works for H&D!'

'Why not?' answered Peter calmly. 'I haven't heard a better argument yet.'

Many of our social judgements concern predictions: will John make a good accountant? will Brian and Michael get on together? what will Mary do when she finds out about Stephen's failed examination? It is interesting to consider how we make these judgements: what reasoning processes do we engage in to produce a decision? Consider the example of Louise who is asked by her friend Helen whether she should stay in her flat-share with Linda, whom she doesn't always get on with, or move in with another friend Lesley, with whom she has not shared before. Louise could attempt to weigh up all the advantages and disadvantages for Helen in staying or moving and select the choice with the greatest chance of happiness for Helen. But she might not. We have seen in previous chapters that learnt expectations influence our judgements, such as stereotypes or implicit ideas about personality. Louise might offer advice in terms of a maxim or proverb, such as 'better the devil you know': stay with Linda because Lesley could be worse. The key thing about proverbs is that they provide us with a 'supposed truth', a received wisdom that can be applied in many situations. The advantage of a proverb over the weighing up of evidence is that it can be applied without having to go through a detailed and difficult process of analytical thought. It is much simpler for Louise to come out with her proverb. But she could be wrong: Helen might be much happier with Lesley.

In this chapter we shall be looking at human reasoning, exploring how people make these judgements; considering whether they engage in a detailed reasoning process or rely on 'shortcuts', like proverbs and other 'received wisdom', when called upon to make such a decision.

THE PROBLEMS OF SOCIAL JUDGEMENT

Understanding the question

In the previous chapter we saw that the attribution biases indicated that people were not always logical in providing a cause for behaviour, and that this could be taken to indicate that human reasoning is somehow 'flawed'. We also saw that there were a number of explanations for these biases that place the perceiver in a better light. Both Chapter 7 and Chapter 8 showed us that an 'error' of judgement is not necessarily a mistake if it provides the perceiver with a functionally useful decision. A further point to examine is whether people understand what is being asked of them. An apparent failure of reasoning may not be so if someone has simply misunderstood the question. Consider the difficulties facing a subject in making a successful judgement in a psychological experiment on attribution. It is possible that the question is more ambiguous in the experimental test than in some real life cases (Kahneman and Miller, 1986). A seemingly simple question such as 'Why did John laugh at the comedian?' can be interpreted in a number of different ways and the person making the judgement has to decide on the focus of the question: what is the questioner getting at. The question appears to contain an underlying accusation with the text: 'explain yourself!' (Howitt *et al.*, 1989). As Kahneman and Miller (1986) point out, the respondent has to decide what the questioner wants to know, what is the surprising aspect of the situation that requires explanation? In conversation the ambiguity is lessened by the stress within the sentence. If the emphasis is on *John* then the question might be understood as asking what was surprising about him, with the expected response to be about John: why did John, *of all people*, laugh at the comedian? Similarly, if the stress is on the word *laugh*, then the question could be interpreted as: why did John laugh, *of all things*, at the comedian? Here the laughter is surprising possibly because John never laughs or no one else laughed. Maybe the comedian had an accident. John's laughter here is unusual and may have been embarrassing or insulting. Thus, in the psychology experiment the subject does not have the same help with the expected focus of the answer that exists in other conversations. And so the form of the reply might be influenced by the interpretation put on the question (Kahneman and Miller, 1986). Therefore, an 'error' of judgement could simply indicate a misunderstanding of what is being asked.

Logic and experience

Much of the work on human reasoning (e.g. Johnson-Laird and Byrne, 1991) has shown that people are apparently not logical in their thinking. In the standard experimental set-up subjects are given a truth statement like 'if the ball rolls to the left then the green light comes on', and then asked what can be concluded if (a) the ball rolled to the left, (b) the ball did not roll to the left, (c) the green light came on and (d) the green light did not come on (Rips and Marcus, 1977). The only logically valid conclusions follow from (a) and (d): with (a) we can conclude that the green light came on and with (d) we can conclude that the ball did not roll to the left. The results show that people do not make the logical choices; for example, a third of them stated that the conclusion from (d) was only sometimes true rather than, logically, always true (Rips and Marcus, 1977).

If people are not reasoning logically, then what are they doing? It appears that one of the reasons why people get the answers 'wrong' when given a logic problem is because they do not follow the rules of logic but rely on their knowledge of the world and apply that to the problem (Cohen, 1983). This was clearly shown by Scribner (1977) in logic tests presented to Mexican farmers. In one problem, they were told a farmer needed a horse and cart to carry corn from his farm and he had a horse but no cart. The question was: could he carry corn from his farm? Logically, the answer is no, both a horse and cart are needed. However, the Mexican farmers answered yes, because they would borrow one. They may have been illogical but they were answering very reasonably. Rather than accepting the rather peculiar constraints of the problem, accepting only the given information, they answered in terms of their practical experience and knowledge of the world (Cohen, 1983): if you have no cart and need to transport corn then you borrow one. The failure to follow the rules of logic here is not so much a failing, as the reply is certainly reasonable, but simply a failure to keep to the constraints of the problem and using one's own knowledge in answering the question.

Consider the statement 'if you loved me then you would have remembered my birthday', familiar to many partners in a relationship! The aggrieved partner is being perfectly logical in concluding that forgetting the birthday indicates a lack of love. However, the illogical partner, in claiming that forgetfulness does not indicate a lack of love, is not accepting the truth of the statement. Knowledge and personal experience direct the reply: I love you despite the fact that I forgot your birthday. (This does not mean an argument will not develop!)

Ill-defined problems

The apparent inability of people, unless specially trained, to reason logically could be interpreted as a failure of the human thinker. One way of understanding this apparent 'failing' of human reasoning is to consider the types of problems we have to face in our daily lives, as opposed to those in the psychology experiment. There are two types of problem. A *well-defined* problem is one where all the information for a solution is given. The game of noughts and crosses is a well-defined problem: at each point there is a limited set of moves and a best move can easily be determined from the available information. A computer can be programmed so that it never loses at this game, as it can calculate every move for every situation. Logic problems are often well defined. An *ill-defined* problem is one where the information for a solution is not given, where the problem has to be defined by the solver (Kahney, 1986). For example, achieving a pass mark in an examination is an ill-defined problem. We can see it as a problem of learning the examination material. Solutions could involve reading everything on the topic in the library, learning the topics that always come up on past examination papers or finding out the examiner's topics of special interest and concentrating on them. However, the unscrupulous candidate might not see it a problem of learning at all, but of merely acquiring the mark, possibly by cheating or bribing the examiner! There is no certain, set way of arriving at a successful solution.

It has been suggested that real life problems are ill defined (Kahney, 1986). If people are used to dealing with ill-defined problems then they are unlikely to attempt to consider every possibility as these could be enormous. A further difficulty is that limitations of human memory might make it impossible for people to consider many possibilities together (Kahney, 1986). However, a failure to take account of all possibilities can lead to errors with well-defined problems, such as noughts and crosses. Indeed, studies of logic problems show that people do not take all possibilities into account when arriving at a solution (Johnson-Laird and Byrne, 1991).

It appears that people employ strategies to solve a range of problems (Kahney, 1986). Strategies are useful methods for solving ill-defined problems. The advantage of a strategy is that it eschews the consideration of all possibilities and may well be successful. Throughout our lives we have learnt a range of strategies that guide our actions, either through being taught or through our own experiences. One person might adopt the examination strategy of learning the topics that have come up most frequently on past papers, as this has worked successfully in the past. As with all strategies it might lead to a successful solution (the examination is passed) but it does not guarantee success; this year the questions are on the less popular topics.

STRATEGIES OF SOCIAL JUDGEMENT

A lot of our social judgements concern predictions: will Ronald and William like each other? is Diana trustworthy? will Paul do a good job on the project? There is no guaranteed answer, our decision has to be made under conditions of uncertainty. Yet we are answering questions like this every day and often we can supply a rapid judgement. Consider the question of Diana's trustworthiness. We could check if she has a criminal record. Even if she hasn't she might still be untrustworthy. We could ask her friends and family. Indeed, there are many checks that we could do, such as contacting her former employers. From this we hope to gain the evidence of her past trustworthiness. We still have to make the inference that this is a useful predictor of her future trustworthiness. All of this takes time and effort. It is only in certain circumstances that we might go through this detailed process, such as when employing individuals for responsible jobs. What if we don't have the time or the inclination to do this? One way is to employ an heuristic, a 'rule-of-thumb' strategy, that we have learnt for judging people. We might decide that Diana is trustworthy because she has an 'honest face' (see Chapters 2 and 10 about the face and perceptions of criminality). This certainly saves us the difficulty of finding out more about her and she might actually turn out to be trustworthy. However, as many sufferers of confidence tricksters realize to their cost, 'looking honest' can turn out to be a poor indicator of trustworthiness.

A statistician making a decision concerning an uncertain course of events, assesses the probabilities of the possible outcomes and chooses the most likely. Imagine that you are playing poker. There is only one person in the game against you, Edward. You could base your decision to play on or not on the probability of Edward having a better hand. To work this out you would need to calculate how many hands out of all possible poker hands beat yours. This figure divided by the total number of possible poker hands gives you the probability of being beaten. Indeed, there are books you can buy on poker odds with these figures printed in them. Then you base your decision on this probability. If the chances are good then you go on. However, more often than not the decision to play on will not be based on probability but thoughts like 'Edward always plays on even when he's got a poor hand' or 'I am a better player than him' or even 'I feel it in my bones I've won this one!' Despite the situation when the probability is against you, an intuition might carry you through to a win but it might also lose you your shirt! In the famous 1965 film about poker, *The Cincinnati Kid*, it was not the man who checked the odds who won. But neither was it the hero, played by Steve McQueen.

It appears from a range of psychological research (Nisbett and Ross, 1980; Tversky and Kahneman, 1974) that when we make social judgements we do not behave like statisticians but make our decisions strategically. That is, we employ certain heuristics like 'smartly dressed people are more competent than those who are slovenly dressed'. Stereotypes can be seen as heuristics (Bodenhausen and Wyer, 1985). Through my own experience I might have acquired the belief (however erroneous) that smartly dressed people are indeed more competent than slovenly dressed individuals and I find that this a very useful way of judging people. The advantage of heuristics is that they can be employed quickly and almost without thought or effort (Fiske and Taylor, 1984); also, heuristics might be useful to us more often than not (Hogarth, 1981).

Much of the work on cognitive heuristics has been undertaken by Daniel Kahneman and Amos Tversky (Kahneman *et al.*, 1982). These two researchers have identified a number of heuristics that people employ in a range of situations where decisions have to be made under conditions of uncertainty. They have also illustrated how the judgements made by the people in their studies differ from the normative model of statistical probability.

Representativeness

The first heuristic we shall consider is *representativeness* (Kahneman and Tversky, 1972). This heuristic indicates that we do not employ probability but use similarity or representativeness in making a decision. An example will illustrate this. Kahneman and Tversky (1973) asked one group of subjects ('the base-rate group') to say what percentage of first-year graduate students in the USA were enrolled in each of nine subject areas. Humanities and education came top (20 per cent), followed by social science and social work (17 per cent), business administration (15 per cent), physical and life sciences (12 per cent), engineering and law were equal fourth on 9 per cent, medicine (8 per cent), computer science (7 per cent) and finally library science (3 per cent). Two further groups of subjects were presented with the following description of Tom W.

> Tom W. is of high intelligence, although lacking in true creativity. He has a need for order and clarity, and for neat and tidy systems in which every detail finds its appropriate place. His writing is rather dull and mechanical, occasionally enlivened by somewhat corny puns and by flashes of imagination of the sci-fi type. He has a strong drive for competence. He seems to have little feel and little sympathy for other people and does not enjoy interacting with others. Self-centred, he nonetheless has a deep moral sense.
>
> (Kahneman and Tversky, 1973, p. 238)

One of the groups of subjects ('the similarity group') was asked to say how similar Tom W. is to a typical graduate student in the nine fields of study. They saw him as most similar to a computer science graduate student and least similar to a social science and social work graduate student. The other group ('the prediction group') was told that the personality sketch was a psychologist's report on Tom in his final year in high school based on projective tests. This group was also told that Tom is now a first-year graduate student and to predict his subject area by ranking the nine areas in order of likelihood of that being his discipline. They saw him most likely to be an graduate student in computer science or engineering and least likely to be a student of social science and social work.

The results indicated that the prediction group were basing their judgements on similarity rather than base-rate probabilities, that is, the probabilities based on the number of graduate students in each field. It is clear from the base-rate group that the subjects knew that it was much more likely for a graduate student to be studying humanities or education than computer science, yet the prediction group saw Tom W. as more likely to be studying the latter. Not surprisingly, the description of Tom W. had influenced their views. What was surprising was that, when asked, the subjects did not think projective tests were very good at predicting a person's choice of graduate study. Despite this, they still used the information from them in making their predictions rather than relying more on the base-rate probabilities as a statistician would do.

It appears therefore that in making decisions of this kind the personality sketch dominated the judgement at the expense of both base-rate probabilities (more students study humanities or education than anything else) and the usefulness of the information (first, whether it should be given any credence and, second, what it tells us: with most students in humanities and education we should expect some of them to have Tom's personality simply because there are more of them). Thus, it appears that the subjects were employing the representativeness heuristic in their judgement of Tom's area of study. To these subjects, who were psychology students, Tom was closest to their idea of a computer science student, and they based their decision on that.

In a further experiment, Kahneman and Tversky (1973) presented subjects with five personality descriptions that were supposedly chosen randomly from a group of thirty engineers and seventy lawyers. The subjects were asked to predict the probability of the person in the description being an engineer or a lawyer. Again the subjects used the representativeness of the description in their judgements rather than the fact that there were more members of one profession than the other in the group. It appears that, when a description fitted the stereotyped image of a member of one of the professions, this guided the decision.

Interestingly, when given completely unhelpful information the subjects still did not use the relative frequency of lawyers over engineers. Subjects were given the following information.

> Dick is a 30-year-old-man. He is married with no children. A man of high ability and high motivation, he promises to be quite successful in his field. He is well liked by his colleagues.
>
> (Kahneman and Tversky, 1973, p. 242)

This information is irrelevant to the engineer or lawyer stereotype: it could fit them both. The subjects estimated that the chances of Dick being an engineer were 50 per cent. This implies that they realized the information didn't help so saw the chances of him being a engineer as opposed to a lawyer as equal and responded 50–50. However, with more lawyers in the group the chances were really 30–70, taking into account the relative numbers of engineers to lawyers. Only when given no personality description at all did the subjects use the base-rate information concerning the number of people in the two professions in the group.

Kahneman and Tversky (1973) also noted that subjects make predictions along the same lines as evaluations, rather than following the statistical knowledge that predictions should be less extreme than evaluations. Given the description that a student is *intelligent, self-confident, well-read, hard-working* and *inquisitive*, subjects' evaluations of the student's academic ability coincided with their predictions of the student's performance. Representativeness appears to be operating here as well: if the student looks good then they are expected to perform well. However, as Kahneman and Tversky point out, an evaluation is an assessment of the information, so it is reasonable to regard an intelligent, hard-working student as very high on ability. But predictions concern what will happen and outcomes depend on a number of factors. Predictions should therefore take into account the possibility that the information may not be correct and that good students do not always perform well. The researchers concluded that subjects were making predictions on the same basis as they would judge similarity or make an evaluation, that is, by selecting the outcome that is most representative of the information given rather than using statistical prediction.

The influence of stereotypical descriptions to guide subjects' predictions was illustrated by a detailed study by Fischhoff and Bar-Hillel (1984). Prior probabilities were taken into account only when the descriptions were ambiguous, and then only to some extent. When the descriptions were stereotypical, the predictions were based solely on representativeness. Thus, we might predict that a neighbour who fits our 'criminal' stereotype will behave like a criminal without due regard for the low probability of criminal acts being committed by someone from our neighbourhood.

This power of stereotypical descriptions to influence decisions rather than statistical probabilities was further demonstrated in a study by Tversky and Kahneman (1982). They presented subjects with person descriptions, set up to be representative of one stereotype but not of another. One was of an accountant but not of someone who plays jazz for a hobby: 'Bill is 34 years old. He is intelligent, but unimaginative, compulsive, and generally lifeless. In school, he was strong in mathematics but weak in social studies and humanities.' After being presented with the person description the subjects were asked to rank eight statements about the person in order of probability. Not surprisingly, the subjects chose the statement 'Bill is an accountant' as the most probable of the eight statements and 'Bill plays jazz for a hobby' as the least probable.

So far the results are hardly unexpected. However, they also included a conjunction statement: 'Bill is an accountant who plays jazz for a hobby.' Now here we come to the interesting point: statistically the probability of being an accountant and an amateur jazz player is less than the probability of being an accountant or the probability of playing jazz as a hobby. We can see this from Figure 9.1

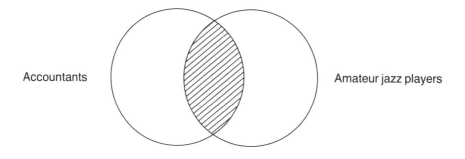

Figure 9.1 People who are both accountants and amateur jazz players

If we look at the circle on the right we can see that not everyone who plays jazz for a hobby is necessarily an accountant so the probability of playing jazz is greater than that of playing jazz and being an accountant. However, over 80 per cent of the subjects placed the conjunction as more probable than the single unrepresentative statement, irrespective of whether the subjects were statistically naïve or sophisticated. This *conjunction effect* shows that subjects were using representativeness rather than statistical rules in their decision making. Thus Bill was seen as more likely to be an accountant who plays jazz for a hobby than simply an amateur jazz player as the former statement was more representative of the description than the latter. This shows the influence of stereotypical information on decision making, even with statistically sophisticated subjects who were graduate students in a business school, all of whom had taken advanced courses in probability and statistics.

The availability heuristic

A second heuristic investigated by Kahneman and Tversky is the *availability* heuristic (Tversky and Kahneman, 1973). When we are asked to judge the likelihood of an event we base our decision on the availability of relevant information to our memories rather than on the base-rate information. For example, if you are asked to predict the reliability of a particular model of car you might think of friends who have one and remember that none has had problems, and you predict a high level of reliability. Alternatively, if you recall that some friends have had breakdown problems then you are likely to predict lower reliability. However, to make a good prediction statistically you should find out how many of this model have had reliability problems relative to the number produced and compare this to the equivalent figure for comparable models by all other manufacturers to give an estimate of the model's reliability.

Tversky and Kahneman (1973) performed an interesting experiment demonstrating this heuristic. Subjects were given lists of well-known people, some of whom were more famous (like Richard Nixon, Elizabeth Taylor) than others (William Fulbright, Lana Turner). A list contained either nineteen famous men and twenty less famous women or nineteen famous women and twenty less famous men. One group of subjects, who were asked to recall all the names in a list, remembered more of the famous people than the less famous names. A second group of subjects were asked to judge whether there were more men or more women in the lists. These subjects judged there to be more men in the list when the men were more famous and more women in the list when the women were more famous, indicating that the judgements were made on availability.

Availability is clearly a quicker strategy than trying to discover countrywide statistics. The weakness of this heuristic is the problem of a *biased sample*. The sample of instances I can recall are not necessarily typical or representative of a wider population. Imagine that someone asks me for an opinion of the police. If my knowledge of the police is from friends who were burgled and through advice on neighbourhood security, availability might lead me to see the police as charming and helpful. However, if my friends and I had been subject to searches and questioning which we believed to be harassment then my opinion might be different. In both cases the judgement is influenced by the availability heuristic, rather than by a consideration of the wide range of contacts between the police and the public.

It is possible that the availability heuristic is operating in a number of our judgements of the social world (Taylor, 1982). Someone who claims that most teachers are on the political left might be making their judgement on the basis of the teachers that come to mind rather than considering the relative number of left-wing to right-wing teachers in the country. As Tversky and Kahneman (1973) point out, we might estimate that the divorce rate is higher if a number of friends have just divorced rather than remaining married.

Tversky and Kahneman (1973) discussed two ways of bringing things to mind where the availability heuristic might be used. The first is *recall* where we attempt to retrieve instances from memory. For example, we claim John is sporty because we can remember the occasions when we have seen him engaging in sporting activities. The second is *construction* where we attempt to infer what would happen from what we know. An example of the latter is the question: will John like Michael? Here the availability heuristic can be used by trying to bring to mind relevant examples of the people John does like and considering how similar to Michael they are.

Taylor (1982) identifies three areas where the use of the availability heuristic could bias social perception. First, distinctive or otherwise salient examples could bias a judgement due to their greater availability. For example, David might cite his friend Philip as clumsier than another friend Brenda because of the unforgettable occasion when Philip knocked over a large pot of red paint. Second, the way information is stored and retrieved can lead to availability biases. For example, each member of a shared household might believe that they do more of the chores than the others, as examples of their own efforts are more readily available to mind. This could be due to the greater amount of attention or concentration paid to their own efforts compared to those of the others. Finally, cognitive structures, such as schemata, can also bias judgements based on the availability heuristic. When recalling information about an engineer acquaintance, one's engineer schema could lead to stereotypic information being more available. Hence the practical qualities of the engineer are better recalled than his or her artistic talents (see also Chapter 4 on recalling schema-consistent information).

Anchoring and adjustment

If we were discussing what percentage of adults were also parents and I suggested a figure of 75 per cent you might think this number high and suggest a lower number, say 60 per cent. What would your estimate have been had I suggested a different figure, say 30 per cent? Tversky and Kahneman (1974) studied this type of probability estimation and found that people did not make their judgement independent of the number they had been given but used this as an *anchor* for their own estimation and made an *adjustment* to a figure they believed to be more likely.

In one of their own experiments, Tversky and Kahneman had subjects guess the number of African countries in the United Nations. However, subjects first saw a wheel of fortune spun and were asked if the number of countries was lower or higher than the number that came up before giving their numerical estimate. Even though the wheel of fortune number was clearly randomly generated the subjects were using it as an anchor and making an adjustment from it. When the anchor was 10 the average estimate was 25 countries and when the anchor was 65 the average estimate was 45. As well as the influence of the anchor, subjects do not make a sufficient adjustment from the anchor in their estimation, further emphasizing its effect on their judgement (Tversky and Kahneman, 1974).

This heuristic could be operating in our social judgements. In deciding how friendly Ray is, I might be influenced by your extolling of his delightful character. I conclude he's not as friendly as that but he is still very friendly. But why, given its obvious bias, would people employ this heuristic in their social judgements, given its reliance on the anchor? One answer comes from

Hogarth (1981), who makes the interesting point that people appear to perform badly in laboratory judgements yet are quite successful in judgements in their everyday lives. Hogarth suggests that this might be due to the different conditions in which the decisions are made, between discrete and continuous environments. In the former, such as in psychology experiments, each decision is a discrete entity, separate from all others, whereas in the latter, such as in our everyday lives, we are continuously making new decisions in the light of previous ones and the feedback we have gained. Anchoring and adjustment might lead to an incorrect decision in a 'one-shot' discrete environment.

> However, in continuous environments, the adjustment and anchoring heuristic provides the basic mode of judgement. Consider, for instance, how one forms impressions of strangers through interaction. That is, in discrete incidents a single (possibly inaccurate) judgement is made. In continuous processing, however, a series of adjustment and anchoring responses, all of which may be relatively inaccurate, takes one progressively to the target.
>
> (Hogarth, 1981, pp. 206–7)

Thus, I meet Barry for the first time and don't find him very friendly. Maybe Barry is having a bad day and that's why he sounds brusque. When I meet him again he turns out to be more friendly but my judgement adjusts only a little from my anchor. I see him as not quite so unfriendly. Gradually over a period of time my judgement of Barry adjusts each time from its previous anchor until I end up with a fairly good judgement of Barry's friendliness.

Conclusion to heuristics

Studies of heuristics in judgement have provided further evidence that we are biased in our reasoning compared to normative models, in this case statistical inference. Yet, as Kahneman (1991) points out, the emphasis on errors and biases has more to do with the way the topic has been investigated than with any generally negative view of human nature. Heuristics, employing our knowledge and experience of the world, might provide us with functional solutions to problems of social judgement. Indeed, employing well-learnt strategies allows a rapid decision, apparently requiring little effort or thought. Furthermore, as Hogarth (1981) points out, in a situation where we can use feedback and review our decisions, heuristics may not be as inaccurate as they appear in the laboratory.

We have to be careful here not to assume that people cannot reason logically or statistically just because they employ heuristics. The psychologists undertaking the studies have clearly learnt logical and statistical methods and they are people too! Indeed, we should be careful not to see the psychologists performing the experiments as logical rational beings and the subjects taking part in the experiments as blindly employing heuristics. Not wishing to make a distinction between psychologists and non-psychologists we must look to the conditions when individuals (be they psychologists or others) engage in different types of thinking, such as the logical reasoning processes in McArthur's (1972) study or employing rapid reasoning strategies (Tversky and Kahneman, 1974).

THE SOCIAL THINKER

Our own experience tells us that we do not give the same attention to every piece of information available to us. We might concentrate on constructing an argument in a difficult essay, marshalling a complicated set of arguments. Yet at other times we appear not to be concentrating at all. As the famous psychologist William James (1890, p. 115) noted, few of us can say which sock or shoe we put on first in the morning, unless we actually go through the process to find out. These two modes of thinking have been termed conscious, or controlled, processing and automatic processing (Posner, 1978; Schneider and Shiffrin, 1977). These researchers have argued that we are limited in our capacity to process information consciously: that is, we can concentrate on only a limited amount of information at once. However, automatic processing requires little or no processing capacity and hence can be undertaken apparently without thought.

A new or complex task requires conscious processing. For a novice, driving a car is extremely difficult: controlling the wheel, the pedals and watching the road requires great concentration and effort. However, after a lot of practice, driving becomes seemingly automatic, with the driver able to attend to other things, such as listening to a radio programme, with only a busy intersection or roadworks requiring the driver to redirect his or her attention back to the control of the car. Whilst the advantage of automatic processes is that they are rapid and require little effort or awareness they tend to be inflexible (Posner, 1978). Driving a new car with controls in different places takes some getting used to.

We can apply this two-process model of thought to social cognition. When do people engage in 'thoughtful' conscious processes and when do they engage in 'thoughtless' automatic processes? One implication of our limited capacity for conscious processing is that we can be viewed as 'cognitive misers' (Fiske and Taylor, 1984). 'The idea is that people are limited in their capacity to process information, so they take shortcuts whenever they can. . . . The capacity-limited thinker searches for rapid adequate solutions, rather than slow accurate solutions' (Fiske and Taylor, 1984, p. 12). The inference here is that a considerable amount of our thinking is based not on thoughtful analysis but on strategies.

Langer (1978) took the conscious–automatic processing distinction into the field of social psychology in her studies of 'mindful' and 'mindless' processing of information. She saw mindlessness as occurring in those 'instances where people believe they had been thinking, but where, in fact, they were behaving according to well-learnt and general scripts, rather than on the basis of new, incoming information' (Langer, 1978, p. 39). She argued that initially conscious attention is required for a task but over time the behaviour becomes over-learnt. We might still believe that we are behaving thoughtfully, as we were required to do so initially, when, in fact, we are actually relying on these over-learnt scripts. A script is an expected sequence of events (Schank and Abelson, 1977). Scripts are similar to schemata in that they contain learnt expectations, although scripts specifically include a sequence within them. For example, a shopping script could entail the following: enter the shop, find the goods we want, pay for them and leave. If asked outside a shop if you had paid for your purchases you might reply yes, not because you can actually remember that you did but because you believe that you must have done.

Langer *et al.* (1978) illustrated mindlessness in an experiment employing the photocopying machine at the Graduate Centre of the City University of New York. An experimenter interrupted a person using the machine and asked to use it first. When the request was small (five pages), as many people complied with the request when the reason given was completely un-informative (because I have to make copies) as when the reason was informative (because I'm in a rush). When no reason was given, compliance was much less. It appeared that the presence of the reason, no matter how uninformative, led to mindless compliance by evoking a script such as: a favour is usually granted when a reason is given. Hence the reason is not examined thoughtfully. When the request was larger, however, the un-informative request led to no more compliance than when no reason was given, and less than for the informative reason. Langer (1978) argued that the effort of complying with the larger request led to the subjects paying atten-tion to the reason and evaluating it mindfully.

The distinction between conscious and automatic processing has been made in a number of areas of social information processing. As we shall see in Chapter 10, Petty and Cacioppo (1985) proposed two processes of per-suasion: being persuaded via the peripheral route ('mindlessly') and through a mindful evaluation of the arguments, via the central route. Devine (1989) has also investigated these two types of processing in the field of stereo-typing. She argued that stereotypes are automatically activated by a member of the stereotype group but that personal beliefs, including our acceptance or rejection of the validity of the stereotype, require conscious attention for their activation. In support of this, she found that both high and low pre-judiced individuals had equal knowledge of a racial stereotype. In one experiment, subjects had stereotype-related words flashed before their eyes under conditions where they were consciously unaware of the content of the words. These word primes were found to influence the subjects' judgements of 'Donald' who was described in a twelve-sentence paragraph as engaging in ambiguously hostile behaviours. The priming words were assumed to activate the racial stereotype automatically which then led to a stereotypical interpretation of Donald's hostile behaviour, regardless of the prejudice level of the subject. Thus, the automatic activation of the stereotype occurred for both high and low prejudiced subjects. In a third experiment, designed to encourage conscious processing, subjects were asked to list their thoughts concerning the racial group anonymously. Low prejudiced subjects wrote more positive than negative thoughts, more belief thoughts (e.g. all people are equal) than trait thoughts (about the characteristics of the group). For the high prejudiced subjects, the situation was reversed. These also included many more hostile themes in their responses.

Devine (1989) argued that the low prejudiced subjects were inhibiting the automatically activated stereotype and negating it, as well as stressing equality in their thoughts. She suggested that this is like breaking a bad habit. We have all learnt the negative stereotype but we can consciously endeavour to overcome it if we choose to do so.

The work on automatic and conscious processing leads to some interesting conclusions. Well-learnt behaviours, be they based on scripts, schemata or heuristics, can lead to responses requiring little time, effort or thought. These may be successful in allowing us to get on with those aspects of our social life we wish to think about without having to spend our time contemplating the complexity, individuality and unpredictability of people and events. However, this does not mean that we are locked inexorably into our learnt expectations, obliged to interpret the social world mindlessly. As Petty and Cacioppo (1985) argue, when elaboration (thoughtful consideration) is encouraged we are less likely to be persuaded by peripheral cues (such as heuristics). Similarly, knowing a stereotype does not imply that we have to accept it (Devine, 1989; Billig, 1985).

Chapter 10

Practical implications of social inference

Mary looked at her watch. It was getting late. She looked up at the other two.

'So it's decided?' she said. 'We'll offer the job to Colin?'

'He's not my choice,' said Susan, 'but I accept what you've said about him.'

Peter nodded. 'I think he'll be OK.'

'Good,' said Mary, 'I'll let him know.'

Social judgements are having practical effects all the time, in both our professional and our private lives. How we are perceived by others and how we perceive them can lead to employment, promotion, discrimination, care and consideration, friendship, animosity. The list is endless. Indeed, unless we were isolated from all other people it is hard to imagine a situation where interpersonal perception would not affect our lives. Even then, being human, we might even perceive personality in the inanimate objects about us: the faithful old car and the friendly teapot!

In the example beginning each chapter, the interview panel have done their job and chosen the new designer. We will never know whether any of the other candidates could do the job better than Colin as they will not get a chance. If Colin 'fits in' and performs the job successfully then Mary is likely to be satisfied with the choice, due to its practical outcome, regardless of whether he was truly the 'best' candidate or not. Only if Mary finds problems with his work, or she believes the process to discriminate unfairly against certain people, will she look closely at the selection procedure.

In this chapter we shall be briefly considering four examples of inter-personal perception to illustrate how important the practical implications can be. The first will be concerned with interpersonal perception by two groups in the criminal justice process: witnesses and jurors. The second example will look at employment selection, an example we have considered in a number of places in the book so far. The third area will be that of intercultural contacts, considering potential misperceptions between people of different cultures. Finally, we shall look at the area of successful communication, considering how and why people are persuasive and persuaded. The inferences we make in each of these four areas can have a major practical effect on people's lives.

THE INTERRELATIONSHIP OF FACTORS

Each of the previous chapters has focused on a particular aspect of person perception. Yet we should not forget that all aspects of interpersonal perception may be operating in a social situation. At a party, for example, a judgement of a person might change throughout the evening as you learn more about them: the woman who looks like an opera singer turns out to be a bank manager. The pleasant-looking man is an incredibly boring conversationalist. As he moves away, a friend regales you with details of his colourful private life, explaining it in terms of his unconventionality. You look back at him in a new light. A woman knocks into you and you think of her as rude. She is charming in her apology and you find yourself suggesting that it wasn't her fault with the room so crowded. You strike up a conversation and learn that she is a doctor. This strengthens your view that she isn't a clumsy person.

At the party you are being presented with information about the other guests all the time, from the way they look, from what they say, from what others say about them. You may also have previously learnt information about them as well as having a range of expectations about people and their behaviour. All this can lead to your responding to them in a particular way based on your inferences about them. We should be aware that a range of factors can influence interpersonal perception and that our perceptions can change with time and additional information.

PRACTICAL EXAMPLES OF INTERPERSONAL PERCEPTION

The witness and the juror

In our society laws are passed by the governing powers and it is up to the police to investigate transgressions of those laws. Individuals accused of criminal acts may go before a jury who must collectively decide on their guilt or innocence after a trial involving witnesses and other evidence analysed by the defence and prosecution lawyers. Finally, the judge passes sentence on those found guilty. The process itself to be just must be fair and correct. Yet this ideal of justice may not be matched by what actually happens. Sometimes the guilty are found innocent and the innocent are punished. As well as looking at the fairness of the legal system, we should not forget the importance of understanding the psychology involved in what are essentially social judgements. For example, the judge, the police, witnesses, jurors and others may hold certain views concerning the type of person who commits a certain type of crime and these expectations can influence their perceptions. In this section we shall be focusing on the witness and the juror and seeing how their interpersonal perceptions can influence the criminal justice process.

You are walking down the street one day thinking about the shopping when someone rushes out of a bank and dashes past you. You catch a brief glimpse of a face and the person is gone. Moments later the hubbub round the bank makes you realize a robbery has occurred and you are a witness.

Given that you saw the escaping thief your testimony could be crucial to the case. However, psychological research has shown that eyewitness reports are not necessarily accurate accounts of the events (e.g. Loftus, 1979; Clifford and Bull, 1978). In one example, a film of a mugging was shown on television followed by a line-up of six suspects (Buckhout, 1980). Viewers were asked to identify the mugger. Of two thousand witnesses only one in seven selected the correct man and a third identified a man of a different race from the white mugger.

Crimes, thank goodness, are actually quite rare events. However, this poses a problem for a witness who was probably not prepared for it, nor attending closely to the action, nor fully aware of what was happening at the time. In making sense of any event we are interpreting information in terms of our own knowledge and experience. Our implicit ideas, be they schemata about people, events or causes, can all lead us to 'go beyond the information given' and produce an explanation that makes sense but may not be accurate. Perceiving or remembering an event as a robbery can lead to recall based on what is expected as well as what is seen or heard. Stereotypical ideas about robbers and how they are expected to behave can influence recall. For example, we might assume that an escaping hooded figure is a man. Also, Loftus (1979) argues that memory is a process of reconstruction and additional information can, under certain circumstances, be included in the reconstructed memory. Thus, you might recall that a robber had brown hair because another witness mentioned it rather than from seeing it yourself.

We saw in Chapter 2 that in the nineteenth century there were attempts to link certain physiognomic characteristics to 'criminal types'. Whilst this has been discredited, it does not mean that we do not hold stereotypical expectations about what criminals look like. Who would you expect to be more likely to commit a drugs offence or, alternatively, a violent assault: a thin-faced young man with straggly long hair or a thick-set bullish man with a crew cut? In a study by Shoemaker et al. (1973) subjects were presented with pictures of faces and asked to judge the likelihood of the man committing a particular type of crime (murder, robbery or treason). Particular faces were linked to the specific crimes, indicating that the subjects had stereotypical ideas about what a murderer or robber looks like. These faces, when attached to accounts of crimes, significantly influenced the judgements of guilt. Unlike Shoemaker et al., Macrae and Shepherd (1989) selected faces of equal attractiveness in their study, as attractiveness can affect judgements of guilt (see below) and this was not controlled in the earlier work. They still found that facial stereotypes influenced the subjects' judgements of guilt. Looking the part might help in the job interview but not in the court room, if that role is of the guilty party. It is not only facial stereotypes that produce these effects, ethnic stereotypes have also been shown to influence juridic judgements (Bodenhausen and Wyer, 1985). In an interesting study, by Bodenhausen (1990), subjects read an account of a (constructed) court case and were asked to estimate the guilt of the defendant on the basis of the evidence. Some of the subjects were given the court's verdict with the case summary, so could make their estimation with the knowledge of hindsight. Bodenhausen found that in most cases there was a hindsight bias, that is, knowing the outcome of the case (either guilty or innocent) led the subjects to see the evidence as more indicative of that outcome than when the judgement took place without the benefit of the verdict. However, there was one exception: when the defendant was stereotypically related to the crime (such as a Hispanic linked to assault), knowledge of a innocent verdict did not produce a hindsight bias in favour of innocence. As Bodenhausen points out, the clear hindsight bias for a guilty verdict with a stereotyped offender was as though the subjects were thinking 'I knew he was guilty' but, when he was found innocent, it was as though the subjects who held the stereotype did not accept the jury's verdict of innocence. These stereotypical expectations, if held by the police, witnesses and jurors, could influence their perceptions of an accused person regardless of their actual guilt or innocence.

Studies have also shown that an attractive defendant is treated more leniently than an unattractive one (Clifford and Bull, 1978). This could be due to the 'attractiveness is good' stereotype influencing the judgement. As we saw in Chapter 3 attractive people are better liked than less attractive individuals as well as being attributed a range of positive characteristics. This finding does, however, depend on the nature of the crime. Sigall and Ostrove (1975) found that for the crime of burglary the attractive female defendant was given a more lenient sentence but for a swindle the sentence was harsher. With burglary the attractiveness of the defendant is unrelated to the crime and so the stereotypical inference of 'goodness' worked to her advantage but with a swindle the defendant could be perceived as having exploited her beauty to commit the crime and hence as particularly 'bad'. Further evidence that facial features can be used to infer characteristics of a defendant comes from Berry and McArthur (1986) who found that for a crime of negligence the babyfaced man was more likely to be convicted than the mature-faced man. With an intentional deception the mature-faced man was more likely to be convicted. Given our inferences concerning faces, Berry and McArthur argue that it is more believable for a youthful-looking person to be negligent and a mature-looking person to act with intent.

It is not only the defendant's attractiveness that can influence a jury but also the attractiveness of the victim. An attractive victim leads in general to greater severity by the jury (Kerr, 1978). However, victim attractiveness has been found to interact with other victim factors such as disfigurement and precautions taken to avoid the crime (Kerr *et al.*, 1985). Generally these results can be explained in terms of the *just world hypothesis* (Lerner, 1980). Lerner suggests that people hold a view that the world is just: bad things happen to bad people and good things happen to good people. This can be a very supportive belief, things do not occur by chance, misfortune does not strike just anyone: I am a good person so bad things will not happen to me. If contrary evidence emerges, such as something bad happening to an apparently good person, an individual can retain the belief in a just world (Lerner and Miller, 1978) by either compensating the victim (to 'make up' for the misfortune), attributing blame to the victim (it was his or her own fault) or derogating the victim (he or she was not such an innocent after all). In this way attributions of guilt or innocence are made to support a belief in the ways of the world rather than on the basis of the evidence. For example, rape is an evil crime regardless of the respectability of the victim. However, experimental juries attribute more blame to victims the less respectable they are (McCaul *et al.*, 1990).

In sum, these psychological studies have shown that juries are not just influenced by the evidence of the crime but also by a range of factors such as their own stereotypical expectations, the attractiveness of the defendant and the victim, as well as the juror's own beliefs about the ways of the world. Regardless of the evidence, perceptions such as 'he looks a nasty piece of work' or 'she looks such a sweet young thing' could be influencing jurors' decisions. Criminal justice involves human beings and, as we have seen in this book, our judgements may be based on heuristics rather than a careful evaluation of evidence. What is necessary, therefore, is that those involved in the criminal justice system are aware of these and other potential biases. Then the system can be developed to maximize the chances of a fair and just outcome and minimize the chances of a miscarriage of justice.

Personnel selection

Personnel selection is often an area where decisions have to be made on limited information, such as a short interview or a brief account of a candidate's career. In a number of studies (e.g. Dipboye *et al.*, 1977) a group of subjects have been asked to make employment decisions from resumés, including a photograph of the candidate. Not unexpectedly, better qualified candidates are preferred over less qualified candidates but more attractive candidates are also preferred over their less attractive counterparts by both students (Dipboye *et al.*, 1977) and personnel officers (Schuler and Berger, 1979).

Attractiveness did not always lead to a candidate being preferred for a post. Heilman and Saruwatari (1979) found that attractive women were preferred over unattractive women for a traditionally female, clerical position but that the less attractive females were preferred for a traditionally male position, a managerial post. This can be explained in terms of stereotypical expectations concerning the characteristics of men and women as well as those required for certain jobs (Cash and Kilcullen, 1985). If attractive men are seen as more masculine than unattractive males and attractive women as more feminine than less attractive women (as considered in Chapter 3) the attractive man will be seen as most suitable for a post requiring stereotypically male characteristics (such as leadership and decisiveness). Cash and Kilcullen point out that for a post emphasizing stereotypically male characteristics an attractive woman might be seen as 'too feminine' for the position and hence judged as less suitable than the less attractive woman. Whilst attractive persons are often preferred over the less attractive candidates in these studies, it is clear than the type of position being offered and the expectations the judges have concerning the appropriate characteristics for the post can also influence their judgements.

It is not just differences in physical attractiveness that can influence employment decisions. Grooming style and the clothing worn during an interview can also affect the judges' decisions (Cash, 1985; Forsythe, 1990). Forsythe presented videotapes of simulated interviews to banking and marketing professionals. The interviews were of a woman applicant for a middle-management position and the judges were asked to rate her on five characteristics (forceful, self-reliant, dynamic, aggressive and decisive). The videos differed in the clothing style worn by the interviewee, with four costumes differing in their masculinity. This dimension was chosen as successful managerial characteristics are stereotypically seen as masculine. The results showed that the woman was rated more highly on these characteristics and was also seen as more likely to be hired when she wore the more masculine clothing, irrespective of whether the judge was male or female. Again we can interpret these data in terms of stereotypical expectations about managers. The woman in the more masculine attire is seen as closer to this stereotype. She is attributed the ('masculine') management characteristics and hence seen as more suitable for the post.

We should be careful here in isolating certain factors such as attractiveness and perceived masculinity. The experimental procedures looking for an effect of one factor will attempt to restrict the influence of other factors. For example, Forsythe (1990) had the sound off on the videoed interviews. In a genuine job interview many factors might all be influencing the interviewer's perceptions in a complex way. As Argyle and McHenry (1971) found, the effect of spectacles on perceptions of intelligence disappeared when the person was listened to for a while. However, these results do demonstrate that a successful candidate is likely to be one that fulfils the interviewer's expectations concerning the characteristics suitable for the position.

Intercultural contacts

Many aspects of human behaviour are learnt within a culture and have a specific meaning for the people of that culture. A polite greeting in one culture might be a bow, in another a kiss on both cheeks and in a third a handshake. Where there are intercultural contacts there are many opportunities for misinterpretation of the meaning of another's behaviour. Cultural differences in nonverbal behaviour can therefore be a source of miscommunication (LaFrance and Mayo, 1978). Also, if someone does not behave in an expected manner then, as we saw in Chapter 8, the perceiver might be tempted to make an internal attribution. In a society where there is limited emotional expression a member of a more expressive culture might be inferred to be 'over-emotional'.

In Britain there is the social convention that everyone makes a neat queue when waiting for a bus. Someone who does not queue is likely to be perceived as antisocial. This can have implications for visitors to Britain. In Oxford, for example, there are a large number of young foreign students attending the many English language schools during the summer. These students, possibly in Britain for the first time and unaware of the queuing convention, are sometimes misperceived as rude by the locals, attributing the behaviour to an antisocial tendency rather than to a cultural difference. Misperceptions of this kind don't always occur. As Argyle (1988) notes, allowances are often made when it is made clear that a person is from a different culture. Thus, unconventional behaviour, which in some cases would be extremely insulting if performed within a culture, is taken as indicative not of a personality disposition but rather of a lack of knowledge of the cultural convention.

The most obvious cause of misperception is behaviour that has very distinct meanings in different cultures. An example of this is the 'thumbs up' gesture (Morris *et al.*, 1979). The meaning of this gesture to indicate 'OK' is more prevalent in northern Europe than in the south. When seen at the roadside coupled with a jerking movement of the hand the gesturer is readily identified as a hitch-hiker seeking a lift, but not in southern Sardinia or northern Greece where it is more commonly used as an obscene insult gesture. As Morris *et al.* note, in these countries it is advisable for the hitch-hiker to seek a lift by a loose wave of the flat hand. The same gesture means two very different things in the different cultures and can have very different effects!

Not all cultural differences are so clearly detected. There are a range of subtle differences that we may be unaware of. These can have important effects not just in the major area of diplomatic negotiations between states but also in the everyday encounters within a multi-cultural society: teachers, police, doctors, interviewers and others working with people from a range of cultures may make judgements of others unaware that the behaviour has a cultural basis that they are misinterpreting. Differences across cultures can exist in factors such as how close it is appropriate to stand in conversation with another person, when and how often you touch another person, the amount and direction of gaze and the behaviour accompanying speech (Argyle, 1988).

Gaze is a good example to consider. There are strong cultural differences in gaze, and cross-cultural interactions may be problematic if the meaning of the gaze is misinterpreted (Argyle, 1988). For some Europeans and North Americans, a person who does not look at them at all in conversation may be seen as inattentive (Kleinke, 1986). However, someone who looks at them during conversation is seen as interested. They are therefore likely to react more positively towards the listener and so, during interaction, gaze can be very reinforcing (Argyle, 1988). A person from another culture might be seen as disrespectful, inattentive or rude due to the different patterns of gaze between the cultures (Argyle, 1988). Along with other differences in non-verbal conventions, this can lead to the inference about the personality of all members of an entire cultural group; that they are aggressive, rude or overly intimate. For example, a teacher might label a child as 'inattentive' or 'un-interested' due to the child's lack of response or gaze whilst the teacher is talking. Yet there are cultural differences that could sometimes better explain the behaviour: black Americans respond less than white Americans when listening (Argyle, 1988). A teacher's misreading of a child's response as inattentive, coupled with factors such as a teacher's stereotypical expectations (and the self-fulfilling nature of them), can have a major influence on a child's learning experiences and the amount of encouragement given by the teacher.

I have focused on the potential misattribution of causation to a particular piece of culturally determined behaviour, but there is also the potential for differences between cultures in the type of attributions they make. Fletcher and Ward (1988) argue that, despite many similarities between cultures in the way attributions are made, the differences are not 'merely cosmetic' (p. 244), with evidence suggesting that aspects such as the fundamental attri-bution error, found with Western cultures, may not be universal and hence not quite as 'fundamental' as previously believed.

We should also be careful in placing too great an emphasis on the differences in behaviour between cultures without acknowledging the simi-larities as well. For example, York et al. (1988) found that the interpretation of eight nonverbal displays was very similar regardless of whether the subjects were American, Arab, Oriental or Latin American students (all studying at an American university). However, it should be noted that all subjects had been in the United States for at least one year.

Studying people within only a single culture tends to focus on the similarities, with the temptation to view these as common to all. The importance of cross-cultural investigations is that they can confirm the universality of certain findings but also indicate where other findings are specific to a culture. With the majority of studies being carried out in the USA, there has been a tendency to emphasize the similarities due to the narrow cultural focus of the research (Zebrowitz-McArthur, 1988). Future cross-cultural studies might reveal the true extent of the similarities and differences in interpersonal perception across cultures.

In conclusion, in the increasingly numerous cross-cultural contacts that occur in the modern world there are many occasions where misperception can occur due to different display rules, different expectations, different implicit personality theories, different attributions and so forth. Awareness of cultural differences may lead to them being taken into account in social judgement but, if they are not or if the many similarities are assumed to indicate cultural identity, then the potential for misinterpretation will remain.

The good communicator

There are many occupations where a person wishes to make a good impression on an audience: politics, the media and advertising, for example. There is practical significance in knowing what makes a good communicator. But first we have to consider what we mean by 'good' here. Often a person wants to appear honest and convincing, so we want to know what leads an audience to attribute these characteristics to a communicator.

Hovland *et al.* (1953) argued that the acceptance of a message by an audience depended to a large extent on the audience's perception of the communicator's *credibility*. A message given by a credible person is more believable and more persuasive than a less credible source. But what makes a person credible? Hovland *et al.* (1953) saw two important components of this rather general characteristic. These are *expertise* and *trustworthiness*. If we perceive individuals as expert in the area they are discussing, then their opinions will be given greater weight than those of the non-expert. On news programmes the expertise of the commentators is often indicated by their introduction: professor at the university, head of the institute. A professor of nutrition is likely to be seen as more credible in offering dietary advice than a hotel manager. Also, someone who is seen as trustworthy will be given greater credence than a less trustworthy individual. People can be seen as more trustworthy if they are not perceived as having deliberately set out to persuade or if they have nothing to gain from the message. Students overhearing 'by chance' graduate students talking in the next room were found to be persuaded to a greater extent by the opinions expressed when the students believed that the graduates were unaware of their presence (Walster and Festinger, 1962). A communicator who might personally lose by their advice is also seen as more trustworthy. For example, a criminal advocating longer prison sentences is seen as more persuasive than a respected public official (Walster *et al.*, 1966a).

A perceiver has to consider two factors when listening to a communication in order to make an attribution of credibility: does the communicator know what she or he is talking about? and, why is the communicator giving this message? This is particularly the case if we have little knowledge of the topic of the message. If we attribute the quality of expertise to the communicator, then we are likely to value their judgement more. But this will be tempered by our attribution of the cause of their utterance. If we attribute the message to self-promotion or financial gain we are less likely to be convinced than if we attribute it to public concern or a desire to preserve the environment.

It has been found that a range of communicator factors influence audience persuasion, such as speed of speech (Apple *et al.*, 1979) or attractiveness (e.g. Mills and Aronson, 1965). Someone who speaks fluently is likely to be perceived as more expert than the person who hesitates, possibly because the latter is inferred to know the subject-matter less well, and, as we saw in Chapter 3 we like to agree with attractive individuals. By manipulating these factors a communicator can be persuasive even before the audience has heard the message. As many politicians now know, if you look convincing you might be convincing. Impression management is now big business for politicians and it is not difficult to see why. As we have seen throughout the book, we have expectations about others and, thus, certain information, such as smart clothes, can lead to inferences of, say, competence. We might have a schema for 'convincing politician' which includes the features 'smartly dressed' and 'personable'. If a politician matches these expectations then the arguments might sound much more convincing than those from one who looks slovenly and unkempt, whom we might see as disorganized in thought as well as in dress.

But surely we do not judge the arguments of politicians by such things as the style of their clothing? It appears that we do, but not always. Petty and Cacioppo (1985) propose in their *elaboration likelihood model* that there are two routes to persuasion. The *central route* is via thoughtful reasoning. Take as an example attending a debate on the environment involving a politician. This is a subject you are interested in and have considered quite a lot. In the hall you listen carefully to both sides of the debate and you are genuinely convinced by the arguments put forward by the politician. Here you have been persuaded by the central route: you have taken the time and effort to consider the matter and have been persuaded by force of argument. Now consider a different situation. You are busy at home with the television on. An attractive, well-dressed politician appears on the screen talking confidently about a new proposal for defence, something you do not know much about. The talk includes statements like 'care of our citizens' and 'protecting our children'. You don't catch it all as the telephone rings in the middle. But at the end you find yourself agreeing with what has been said, despite not remembering the arguments put forward for the policy. Here you would have been persuaded via the *peripheral route*. It is not detailed reasoning that has persuaded you but some peripheral cue such as the persuader's attractiveness or an heuristic like 'we should protect our children' evoked by the speech. The difference between the two routes is due to the amount of 'elaboration' given to the message. Elaboration here refers to the extent to which the information is considered and evaluated. We do not spend our lives mulling over every item of information we receive. As we saw in Chapter 9, it might be impossible or at least effortful to reason out every decision in our lives; so we often rely on heuristics and over-learnt responses. We may continue to shop in a familiar store despite the fact that a better, cheaper one has been built nearby. We make judgements 'without thinking' that sometimes we regret. The washing machine bought for the free toaster might be fine but it could turn out to be totally inappropriate to our needs. Having a friend with you while shopping or saying you will come back later both reduce the possibility of being persuaded into buying something by the peripheral route, as these factors increase the likelihood of elaboration: you get more chance to think about the purchase. Your friend asks if you *really* want it and on reflection outside the shop you decide that you don't really want to pay so much after all.

It's probable that we are more susceptible to persuasion by the peripheral route for trivial issues. For example, Aronson (1976) argues that persuader attractiveness is unlikely to influence us on important issues. However, as we can see from Petty and Cacioppo's model, it is the likelihood of elaboration that is crucial. Not surprisingly, important topics are often ones we consider in detail. Deciding who should run the country can lead people to weigh up the policies of the various opposing politicians carefully. But this does not necessarily mean that people will engage in detailed reasoning in making important decisions. Despite the importance of our vote in an election, being attractive as a politician can certainly help. Furthermore, we have all heard of cases where people have spent their savings on cars, dream holidays and so forth, when hurried and distracted (usually under the pressure of 'if you don't sign now you'll miss this fantastic deal'), only to regret the purchase in the cold light of day.

CONCLUSION

If we learnt nothing from our experiences of people then we would find the world confusing and unpredictable. If we did not make inferences we would not be able to exist in the social world. These inferences help us to make judgements of people in innumerable practical situations. Yet, we may apply them so effortlessly and with so little awareness that they appear to be less the 'supposed truth' than truth itself. However, we are able to consider the views we hold, the assumptions we make about people. We can consider and reconsider them. And if we find them to be inappropriate we can change them.

References

Adams-Webber, J.R. (1969) 'Cognitive complexity and sociality', *British Journal of Social and Clinical Psychology*, 8, 211–16.

Addington, D.W. (1968) 'The relationship of selected vocal characteristics to personality perception', *Speech Monographs*, 35, 492–503.

Addison, W.E. (1989) 'Beardedness as a factor in perceived masculinity', *Perceptual and Motor Skills*, 68, 921–2.

Alicke, M.D., Smith, R.H. and Klotz, M.L. (1986) 'Judgements of physical attractiveness: the role of faces and bodies', *Personality and Social Psychology Bulletin*, 12, 381–9.

Alley, T.R. and Cunningham, M.R. (1991) 'Averaged faces are attractive, but very attractive faces are not average', *Psychological Science*, 2, 123–5.

Allport, G.W. (1937) *Personality: A Psychological Interpretation*, London: Constable.

Allport, G.W. (1958) *The Nature of Prejudice*, Garden City, NY: Anchor Books.

Andersen, S.M. and Klatzky, R.L. (1987) 'Traits and social stereotypes: levels of categorization in person perception', *Journal of Personality and Social Psychology*, 53, 235–46.

Andersen, S.M., Klatzky, R.L. and Murray, J. (1990) 'Traits and social stereotypes: efficiency differences in social information processing', *Journal of Personality and Social Psychology*, 59, 192–201.

Anderson, N.H. (1965) 'Averaging versus adding as a stimulus-combination rule in impression formation', *Journal of Experimental Psychology*, 70, 394–400.

Anderson, N.H. (1966) 'Component ratings in impression formation', *Psychonomic Science*, 6, 179–80.

Anderson, N.H. (1971) 'Two more tests against change of meaning in adjectival combinations', *Journal of Verbal Learning and Verbal Behaviour*, 10, 75–85.

Anderson, N.H. (1974) 'Information integration theory: a brief survey', in D.H. Krantz, R.C. Atkinson, R.D. Luce and P. Suppes (eds) *Contemporary Developments in Mathematical Psychology*, Vol. 2, San Franscisco, Calif.: Freeman.

Anderson, N.H. (1981) *Foundations of Information Integration Theory*, New York: Academic Press.

Anderson, N.H. and Lampel, A.K. (1965) 'Effect of context on ratings of personality traits', *Psychonomic Science*, 3, 433–4.

Apple, W., Streeter, L.A. and Krauss, R.B. (1979) 'Effects of pitch and speech rate on personal attributions', *Journal of Personality and Social Psychology*, 37, 715–27.

Argyle, M. (1988) *Bodily Communication*, 2nd edition, London: Methuen.

Argyle, M. and McHenry, R. (1971) 'Do spectacles really affect judgements of intelligence?' *British Journal of Social and Clinical Psychology*, 10, 27–9.

Aronson, E. (1976) *The Social Animal*, 2nd edition, San Francisco, Calif.: Freeman.

Asch, S.E. (1946) 'Forming impressions of personality', *Journal of Abnormal and Social Psychology*, 41, 258–90.

Asch, S.E. and Zukier, H. (1984) 'Thinking about persons', *Journal of Personality and Social Psychology*, 46, 1230–40.

Bandura, A. (1977) *Social Learning Theory*, Englewood Cliffs, NJ: Prentice-Hall.

Bannister, D. and Fransella, F. (1971) *Inquiring Man: The Theory of Personal Constructs*, Harmondsworth: Penguin.

Bartlett, F.C. (1932) *Remembering*, Cambridge: Cambridge University Press.

Bartolini, T., Kresge, J., McLennan, M., Windham, B., Buhr, T.A. and Pryor, B. (1988) 'Perceptions of personal characteristics of men and women under three conditions of eyewear', *Perceptual and Motor Skills*, 67, 779–82.

Beck, L., McCauley, C., Segal, M., and Hershey, L. (1988) 'Individual differences in prototypicality judgements about trait categories', *Journal of Personality and Social Psychology*, 55, 286–92.

Beck, S.B. (1979) 'Women's somatic preferences', in M. Cook and G. Wilson (eds) *Love and Attraction*, Oxford: Pergamon.

Beck, S.B., Ward-Hull, C.I. and McLear, P.M. (1976) 'Variables related to women's somatic preferences of the male and female body', *Journal of Personality and Social Psychology*, 34, 1200–10.

Berry, D.S. and Brownlow, S. (1989) 'Were the physiognomists right? Personality correlates of facial babyishness', *Personality and Social Psychology Bulletin*, 15, 266–79.

Berry, D.S. and McArthur, L.Z. (1986) 'Perceiving character in faces: the impact of age-related craniofacial changes on social perception', *Psychological Bulletin*, 100, 3–18.

Berscheid, E. (1985) 'Interpersonal attraction', in G. Lindzey and E. Aronson (eds) *Handbook of Social Psychology*, New York: Random House.

Berscheid, E. and Walster, E. (1974) 'Physical attractiveness', in L.Berkowitz (ed.) *Advances in Experimental Social Psychology*, Vol. 7, London: Academic Press.

Berscheid, E. and Walster, E. (1978) *Interpersonal Attraction*, 2nd edition, Reading, Mass.: Addison-Wesley.

Bieri, J. (1955) 'Cognitive complexity – simplicity and predictive behaviour', *Journal of Abnormal and Social Psychology*, 51, 263–8.

Billig, M. (1985) 'Prejudice, categorization and particularization: from a perceptual to a rhetorical approach', *European Journal of Social Psychology*, 15, 79–103.

Billig, M. (1987) *Arguing and Thinking: A Rhetorical Appproach to Social Psychology*, Cambridge: Cambridge University Press.

Block, J., Weiss, D.S. and Thorne, A. (1979) 'How relevant is the semantic similarity interpretation of personality ratings?', *Journal of Personality and Social Psychology*, 37, 1055–74.

Bodenhausen, G.V. (1990) 'Second-guessing the jury: stereotypic and hindsight biases in perceptions of court cases', *Journal of Applied Social Psychology*, 20, 1112–21.

Bodenhausen, G.V. and Wyer, R.S.Jr. (1985) 'Effects of stereotypes on decision making and information-processing strategies', *Journal of Personality and Social Psychology*, 48, 267–82.

Bond, M. and Forgas, J.P. (1984) 'Linking person perception to behaviour intention across cultures', *Journal of Cross-Cultural Psychology*, 15, 337–52.

Borkenau, P. and Ostendorf, F. (1987) 'Fact and fiction in implicit personality theory', *Journal of Personality*, 55, 415–43.

Borman, W.C. (1987) 'Personal constructs, performance schemata, and "folk theories" of subordinate effectiveness: explorations in an army officer sample', *Organizational Behaviour and Human Decision Processes*, 40, 307–22.

Brigham, J.C. (1971) 'Ethnic stereotypes', *Psychological Bulletin*, 76, 15–38.

Brontë, C. (1847) *Jane Eyre*, London: Nelson.

Brown, R. (1965) *Social Psychology*, London: Collier-Macmillan.

Bruner, J.S. and Tagiuri, R. (1954) 'The perception of people', in G. Lindzey (ed.) *Handbook of Social Psychology*, Vol. 2, Cambridge, Mass.: Addison-Wesley.

Bruner, J.S., Shapiro, D. and Tagiuri, R. (1958) 'The meaning of traits in isolation and combination', in R. Tagiuri and L. Petrullo (eds) *Person Perception and Interpersonal Behaviour*, Stanford, Calif.: Stanford University Press.

Brunswik, E. (1956) *Perception and the Representative Design of Psychological Experiments*, 2nd edition, Berkeley, Calif.: University of California Press.

Buckhout, R. (1980) 'Nearly 2,000 witnesses can be wrong', *Bulletin of the Psychonomic Society*, 16, 307–10.

Bull, P. (1987) *Posture and Gesture*, Oxford: Pergamon.

Bull, R. (1979) 'The psychological significance of facial deformity', in M.Cook and G.Wilson (eds) *Love and Attraction*, Oxford: Pergamon.

Buss, D.M. (1987) 'Sex differences in human mate selection criteria: an evolutionary perspective', in C. Crawford, M. Smith and D. Krebs (eds) *Sociobiology and Psychology: Ideas, Issues and Applications*, Hillsdale, NJ.: Erlbaum.

Buss, D.M. and Craik, K.H. (1983) 'The act frequency approach to personality', *Psychological Review*, 90, 105–26.

Byrne, D. (1971) *The Attraction Paradigm*, New York: Academic Press.

Byrne, D. and Clore, G.L. (1970) 'A reinforcement model of evaluative responses', *Personality: An International Journal*, 1, 103–28.

Byrne, D., Clore, G.L. and Smeaton, G. (1986) 'The attraction hypothesis: do similar attitudes affect anything?', *Journal of Personality and Social Psychology*, 51, 1167–70.

Cahoon, D.D. and Edmonds, E.M. (1989) 'Male–female estimates of opposite-sex first impressions concerning females' clothing styles', *Bulletin of the Psychonomic Society*, 27, 280–1.

Calden, G., Lundy, R. and Schlafer, R. (1959) 'Sex differences in body concepts', *Journal of Consulting Psychology*, 23, 378.

Campbell, D.T. (1967) 'Stereotypes and the perception of group differences', *American Psychologist*, 22, 817–29.

Cantor, N. and Mischel, W. (1977) 'Traits as prototypes: effects on recognition memory', *Journal of Personality and Social Psychology*, 35, 38–48.

Cantor, N. and Mischel, W. (1979a) 'Prototypes in person perception', in L.Berkowitz (ed.) *Advances in Experimental Social Psychology*, Vol. 12, New York: Academic Press.

Cantor, N. and Mischel, W. (1979b) 'Prototypicality and personality: effects on free recall and personality impressions', *Journal of Research in Personality*, 13, 187–205.

Cash, T.F. (1985) 'The impact on grooming style on the evaluation of women in management', in M.R. Solomon (ed.) *The Psychology of Fashion*, Lexington: Heath.

Cash, T.F. (1990) 'Losing hair, losing points? The effects of male pattern baldness on social impression formation', *Journal of Applied Social Psychology*, 20, 154–67.

Cash, T.F. and Kilcullen, R.N. (1985) 'The aye of the beholder: susceptibility to sexism and beautyism in the evaluation of managerial applicants', *Journal of Applied Social Psychology*, 15, 591–605.

Cash, T.F., Dawson, K., Davis, P., Bowen, M. and Galumbeck, C. (1989) 'The effects of cosmetic use on the physical attractiveness and body image of college women', *Journal of Social Psychology*, 129, 349–55.

Casselden, P.A. and Hampson, S.E. (1990) 'Forming impressions from incongruent traits', *Journal of Personality and Social Psychology*, 59, 253–362.

Cauthen, N.R., Robinson, I.E. and Krauss, H.H. (1971) 'Stereotypes: a review of the literature 1926–1968', *Journal of Social Psychology*, 84, 103–25.

Chapman, L.J. (1967) 'Illusory correlation in observational report', *Journal of Verbal Learning and Verbal Behaviour*, 6, 151–5.

Christensen, D. and Rosenthal, R. (1982) 'Gender and nonverbal decoding skill as determinants of interpersonal expectancy effects', *Journal of Personality and Social Psychology*, 42, 75–87.

Clifford, B. and Bull, R. (1978) *The Psychology of Person Identification*, London: Routledge & Kegan Paul.

Clifford, M.M. and Walster, E. (1973) 'The effect of physical attractiveness on teacher expectation', *Sociology of Education*, 46, 248–58.

Clore, G.L. and Byrne, D. (1974) 'A reinforcement-affect model of attraction', in T.L. Huston (ed.) *Foundations of Interpersonal Attraction*, New York: Academic Press.

Cohen, G. (1983) *The Psychology of Cognition*, 2nd edition, London: Academic Press.

Cohen, R. (1971) 'An investigation of the diagnostic processing of contradictory information', *European Journal of Social Psychology*, 1, 475–92.

Condon, J.W. and Crano, W.D. (1988) 'Inferred evaluation and the relation between attitude similarity and interpersonal attraction', *Journal of Personality and Social Psychology*, 54, 789–97.

Cook, M. (1971) *Interpersonal Perception*, Baltimore, Md.: Penguin.

Cook, M. (1984) 'The good judge of others' personality: methodological problems and their resolution', in M.Cook (ed.) *Issues in Person Perception*, London: Methuen.

Coovert, M.D. and Reeder, G.D. (1990) 'Negativity effects in impression formation: the role of unit formation and schematic expectations', *Journal of Experimental Social Psychology*, 26, 49–62.

Crockett, W.H. (1965) 'Cognitive complexity and impression formation', in B.A. Maher (ed.) *Progress in Experimental Personality Research*, New York: Academic Press.

Cronbach, L.J. (1955) 'Processes affecting scores on "understanding of others" and "assumed similarity"', *Psychological Bulletin*, 52, 177–93.

Cronbach, L.J. (1958) 'Proposals leading to analytic treatment of social perception scores', in R.Tagiuri and L.Petrullo (eds) *Person Perception and Interpersonal Behaviour*, Stanford, Calif.: Stanford University Press.

Cunningham, M.R. (1986) 'Measuring the physical in physical attractiveness: quasi-experiments on the sociobiology of female facial beauty', *Journal of Personality and Social Psychology*, 50, 925–35.

Cunningham, M.R., Barbee, A.P. and Pike, C.L. (1990) 'What do women want? Facial metric assessment of multiple motives in the perception of male facial physical attractiveness', *Journal of Personality and Social Psychology*, 59, 61–72.

D'Andrade, R.G. (1965) 'Trait psychology and componential analysis', *American Anthropologist*, 67, 215–28.

D'Andrade, R.G. (1974) 'Memory and the assessment of behaviour', in T. Blalock (ed.) *Measurement in the Social Sciences*, Chicago: Aldine-Atherton.

Deaux, K. (1976) *The Behaviour of Men and Women*, Monterey, Calif.: Brooks-Cole.

Deaux, K. (1977) 'Sex differences in social behaviour', in T. Blass (ed.) *Personality Variables in Social Behaviour*, Hillsdale, NJ: Erlbaum.

DeJong, W. (1980) 'The stigma of obesity: the consequences of naive assumptions concerning the causes of physical deviance', *Journal of Health and Social Behaviour*, 21, 75–87.

Deutsch, M. and Gerard, H.B. (1955) 'A study of normative and informational influence upon individual judgement', *Journal of Abnormal and Social Psychology*, 51, 629–36.

Devine, P.G. (1989) 'Stereotypes and prejudice: their automatic and controlled components', *Journal of Personality and Social Psychology*, 56, 5–18.

Dion, K., Berscheid, E. and Walster, E. (1972) 'What is beautiful is good', *Journal of Personality and Social Psychology*, 24, 285–90.

Dipboye, R.L., Arvey, R.D. and Terpstra, D.E. (1977) 'Sex and physical attractiveness of raters and applicants as determinants of resume evaluations', *Journal of Applied Psychology*, 62, 288–94.

Duck, S. (1988) *Relating to Others*, Milton Keynes: Open University Press.

Ekman, P. (1982) *Emotion in the Human Face*, 2nd edition, Cambridge: Cambridge University Press.

Ekman, P., Wallace, V. and Friesen, W. (1969) 'Non-verbal cues to deception', *Psychiatry*, 32, 88–106.

Feinman, S. and Gill, G.W. (1977) 'Females' response to males' beardedness', *Perceptual and Motor Skills*, 44, 533–4.

Feldman, S.D. (1971) 'The presentation of shortness in everyday life – height and heightism in American society: towards a sociology of stature', paper presented before the meetings of the American Sociological Association; cited in E. Berscheid and E. Walster (1974) op. cit.

Festinger, L., Schachter, S. and Back, K. (1950) *Social Pressures in Informal Groups: A Study of Human Factors in Housing*, New York: Harper.

Fischhoff, B. and Bar-Hillel, M. (1984) 'Diagnosticity and the baserate effect', *Memory & Cognition*, 12, 402–10.

Fiske, S.T. (1980) 'Attention and weight in person perception: the impact of negative and extreme behaviour', *Journal of Personality and Social Psychology*, 38, 889–906.

Fiske, S.T. and Neuberg, S.L. (1990) 'A continuum of impression formation, from category-based to individuating processes: influences of information and motivation on attention and interpretation', in M.P. Zanna (ed.) *Advances in Experimental Social Psychology*, Vol. 23, London: Academic Press.

Fiske, S.T. and Pavelchak, M.A. (1986) 'Category-based versus piecemeal-based affective responses: developments in schema-triggered affect', in R.M. Sorrentino and E.T. Higgins (eds) *Handbook of Motivation and Cognition: Foundations of Social Behaviour*, New York: Guilford Press.

Fiske, S.T. and Taylor, S.E. (1984) *Social Cognition*, New York: Random House.

Fiske, S.T., Neuberg, S.L., Beattie, A.E. and Milberg, S.J. (1987) 'Category-based and attribute-based reactions to others: some informational conditions of stereotyping and individuating processes', *Journal of Experimental Social Psychology*, 23, 399–427.

Fletcher, G.J.O. and Ward, C. (1988) 'Attribution theory and processes: a cross-cultural perspective', in M.H. Bond (ed.) *The Cross-Cultural Challenge to Social Psychology*, London: Sage.

Forgas, J.P. (1983) 'The effects of prototypicality and cultural salience on perceptions of people', *Journal of Research in Personality*, 17, 153–73.

Forsythe, S.M. (1990) 'Effect of applicant's clothing on interviewer's decision to hire', *Journal of Applied Social Psychology*, 20, 1579–95.

Fransella, F. (1981) 'Repertory grid technique', in F. Fransella (ed.) *Personality: Theory, Measurement and Research*, London: Methuen.

Funder, D.C. (1987) 'Errors and mistakes: evaluating the accuracy of social judgement', *Psychological Review*, 101, 75–90.

Furnham, A. and Alibbai, N. (1983) 'Cross-cultural differences in the perception of female body shapes', *Psychological Medicine*, 13, 829–37.

Furnham, A. and Radley, S. (1989) 'Sex differences in the perception of male and female body shapes', *Personality and Individual Differences*, 10, 653–62.

Furnham, A., Hester, C. and Weir, C. (1990) 'Sex differences in the preferences for specific female body shapes', *Sex Roles*, 22, 743–54.

Gara, M.A. and Rosenberg, S. (1981) 'Linguistic factors in implicit personality theory', *Journal of Personality and Social Psychology*, 41, 450–7.

Geiselman, R.E., Haight, N.A. and Kimata, L.G. (1984) 'Context effects on the perceived physical attractiveness of faces', *Journal of Experimental Social Psychology*, 20, 409–24.

Gergen, K.J., Hepburn, A. and Comer Fisher, D. (1986) 'Hermeneutics of personality descriptions', *Journal of Personality and Social Psychology*, 50, 1261–70.

Gilbert, G.M. (1951) 'Stereotype persistence and change among college students', *Journal of Abnormal and Social Psychology*, 46, 245–54.

Gillis, J.S. and Avis, W.E. (1980) 'The male-taller norm in mate selection', *Personality and Social Psychology Bulletin*, 6, 396–401.

Goffman, E. (1959) *The Presentation of Self in Everyday Life*, New York: Anchor Books.

Goffman, E. (1963) *Stigma: Notes on the Management of Spoiled Identity*, Englewood Cliffs, NJ: Prentice-Hall.

Goldberg, L.R. (1981) 'Language and individual differences: the search for universals in personality lexicons', in L.Wheeler (ed.) *Review of Personality and Social Psychology*, Vol. 2, Beverly Hills, Calif.: Sage

Goldman, W. and Lewis, P. (1977) 'Beautiful is good: evidence that the physically attractive are more socially skillful', *Journal of Experimental Social Psychology*, 13, 125–30.

Guilford, J.P. (1936) *Psychometric Methods*, New York: McGraw-Hill.

Hall, C.S. and Lindzey, G. (1985) *Introduction to Theories of Personality*, New York: Wiley.

Hall, E.T. (1966) *The Hidden Dimension*, New York: Doubleday.

Hamid, P.N. (1968) 'Style of dress as a perceptual cue in impression information', *Perceptual and Motor Skills*, 26, 904–6.

Hamid, P.N. (1972) 'Some effects of dress cues on observational accuracy: a perceptual estimate, and impression formation', *Journal of Social Psychology*, 86, 279–89.

Hamilton, D.L. (1979) 'A cognitive-attributional analysis of stereotyping', in L. Berkowitz (ed.) *Advances in Experimental Social Psychology*, Vol. 12, New York: Academic Press.

Hamilton, D.L. and Gifford, R.K. (1976) 'Illusory correlation in interpersonal perception: a cognitive basis of stereotypic judgements', *Journal of Experimental Social Psychology*, 12, 392–407.

Hamilton, D.L. and Zanna, M.P. (1974) 'Context effects in impression formation: changes in connotative meaning', *Journal of Personality and Social Psychology*, 29, 649–54.

Hamilton, D.L., Driscoll, D.M. and Worth, L.T. (1989) 'Cognitive organization of impressions: effects of incongruency in complex representations', *Journal of Personality and Social Psychology*, 57, 925–39.

Hamilton, D.L., Dugan, P.M. and Trolier, T.K. (1985) 'The formation of stereotypic beliefs: further evidence for distinctiveness-based illusory correlation', *Journal of Personality and Social Psychology*, 48, 5–17.

Hastie, R. (1981) 'Schematic principles in human memory', in E.T. Higgins, C.P. Herman and M.P. Zanna (eds) *Social Cognition: The Ontario Symposium*, Vol. 1, Hillsdale, NJ: Erlbaum.

Hastie, R. and Kumar, P.A. (1979) 'Person memory: personality traits as organizing principles in memory for behaviours', *Journal of Personality and Social Psychology*, 37, 25–38.

Hastie, R. and Park, B. (1986) 'The relationship between memory and judgement depends on whether the judgement task is memory-based or on-line', *Psychological Review*, 93, 258–68.

Hastie, R. and Rasinsky, K.A. (1988) 'The concept of accuracy in social judgement', in D. Bar-Tal and A.W. Kruglanski (eds) *The Social Psychology of Knowledge*, Cambridge: Cambridge University Press.

Hatfield, E. and Sprecher, S. (1986) *Mirror, Mirror, On the Wall*, Albany, NY: State University of New York Press.

Heider, F. (1958) *The Psychology of Interpersonal Relations*, New York: Wiley.

Heider, F. and Simmel, M. (1944) 'An experimental study of apparent behaviour', *American Journal of Psychology*, 57, 243–59.

Heilman, M.E. and Saruwatari, R.L. (1979) 'When beauty is beastly: the effects of appearance and sex on evaluations of job applicants for managerial and non-managerial jobs', *Organizational Behaviour and Human Performance*, 23, 360–72.

Helson, H. (1964) *Adaptation-Level Theory*, New York: Harper.

Hensley, V. and Duval, S. (1976) 'Some perceptual determinants of perceived similarity, liking and correctness', *Journal of Personality and Social Psychology*, 34, 159–68.

Hess, E.H. (1972) 'Pupilometrics', in N. Greenfield and R. Sternbach (eds) *Handbook of Psychophysiology*, New York: Holt, Rinehart & Winston.

Hewstone, M. and Jaspers, J. (1987) 'Covariation and causal attribution: a logical model of the intuitive analysis of variance', *Journal of Personality and Social Psychology*, 53, 663–72.

Hogarth, R.M. (1981) 'Beyond discrete biases: functional and dysfunctional aspects of judgemental heuristics', *Psychological Bulletin*, 90, 197–217.

Hovland, C.I., Janis, I.L. and Kelley, H.H. (1953) *Communication and Persuasion: Psychological Studies of Opinion Change*, Westport, Conn.: Greenwood Press.

Howitt, D., Billig, M., Cramer, D., Edwards, D., Kniveton, B., Potter, J. and Radley, A. (1989) *Social Psychology: Conflicts and Controversies*, Milton Keynes: Open University Press.

Hull, C. (1928) *Aptitude Testing*, New York: Harrap.

Hull, J.G. and West, S.G. (1982) 'The discounting principle in attribution', *Personality and Social Psychology Bulletin*, 8, 208–13.

Humphreys, L.G. (1957) 'Characteristics of type concepts with special reference to Sheldon's typology', *Psychological Bulletin*, 54, 218–28.

Hunter, J.E. and Coggin, T.D. (1988) 'Analyst judgement: the efficient market hypothesis versus a psychological theory of human judgement', *Organizational Behaviour and Human Decision Processes*, 42, 284–302.

Huston, T.L. (1973) 'Ambiguity of acceptance, social desirability, and dating choice', *Journal of Experimental Social Psychology*, 9, 32–42.

Jackson, D.N. and Stricker, L.J. (1982) 'Is implicit personality theory illusory? Armchair criticism vs. replicated empirical research', *Journal of Personality*, 50, 240–4.

Jackson, D.N., Chan, D.W. and Stricker, L.J. (1979) 'Implicit personality theory: is it illusory?', *Journal of Personality*, 47, 1–10.

James, W. (1890) *The Principles of Psychology*, New York: Dover.

Johnson-Laird, P.N. and Byrne, R.M.J. (1991) *Deduction*, London: Erlbaum.

Jones, E.E. and Davis, K.E. (1965) 'From acts to dispositions: the attribution process in person perception', in L. Berkowitz (ed.) *Advances in Experimental Social Psychology*, Vol. 2, New York: Academic Press.

Jones, E.E. and Harris, V.A. (1967) 'The attribution of attitudes', *Journal of Experimental Social Psychology*, 63, 302–10.

Jones, E.E. and McGillis, D. (1976) 'Correspondent inferences and the attribution cube: a comparative reappraisal', in J.H. Harvey, W.J. Ickes and R.F. Kidd (eds) *New Directions in Attributional Research*, Vol. 1, Hillsdale, NJ: Erlbaum.

Jones, E.E. and Nisbett, R.E. (1971) 'The actor and the observer: divergent perceptions of the causes of behaviour', in E.E. Jones, D.E. Kanouse, H.H. Kelley, R.E. Nisbett, S. Valins and B. Weiner (eds) *Attribution: Perceiving the Causes of Behaviour*, Morristown, NJ: General Learning Press.

Jones, E.E., Davis, K.E. and Gergen, K.J. (1961) 'Role playing variations and their informational value for person perception', *Journal of Abnormal and Social Psychology*, 63, 302–10.

Jourard, S.M. and Secord, P.F. (1955) 'Body-cathexis and personality', *British Journal of Psychology*, 46, 130–8.

Kahneman, D. (1991) 'Judgement and decision making: a personal view', *Psychological Science*, 2, 142–5.

Kahneman, D. and Miller, D. (1986) 'Norm theory: comparing reality to its alternatives', *Psychological Review*, 93, 136–53.

Kahneman, D. and Tversky, A. (1972) 'Subjective probability: a judgement of representativeness', *Cognitive Psychology*, 3, 430–54.

Kahneman, D. and Tversky, A. (1973) 'On the psychology of prediction', *Psychological Review*, 80, 237–51.

Kahneman, D., Slovic, P. and Tversky, A. (eds) (1982) *Judgement under Uncertainty: Heuristics and Biases*, Cambridge: Cambridge University Press.

Kahney, H. (1986) *Problems Solving: A Cognitive Approach*, Milton Keynes: Open University Press.

Kaiser, S.B. (1985) *The Social Psychology of Clothing and Personal Adornment*, London: Collier Macmillan.

Kalick, S.M. (1988) 'Physical attractiveness as a status cue', *Journal of Experimental Social Psychology*, 24, 469–89.

Kaplan, M.F. (1971) 'Context effects in impression formation: the weighted average versus the meaning change formulation', *Journal of Personality and Social Psychology*, 19, 92–9.

Kaplan, M.F. (1974) 'Context-induced shifts in personality trait evaluation: a comment on the evaluative halo effect and the meaning change interpretations', *Psychological Bulletin*, 81, 891–5.

Kaplan, M.F. (1975) 'Evaluative judgements are based on evaluative information: evidence against meaning change in evaluative context effects', *Memory and Cognition*, 3, 375–80.

Karlins, M., Coffman, T.L. and Walters, G. (1969) 'On the fading of social stereotypes: studies in three generations of college students', *Journal of Personality and Social Psychology*, 13, 1–16.

Katz, D. and Braly, K.W. (1933) 'Racial prejudice and racial stereotypes', *Journal of Abnormal and Social Psychology*, 30, 175–93.

Keating, C.F. (1985) 'Gender and the physiognomy of dominance and attractiveness', *Social Psychology Quarterly*, 48, 61–70.

Keating, C.F., Mazur, A., Segall, M.H., Cysneiros, P.G., Divale, W.F., Kilbridge, J.E., Komin, S., Leahy, P., Thurman, B., and Wirsing, R. (1981) 'Culture and the perception of social dominance from facial expression', *Journal of Personality and Social Psychology*, 40, 615–26.

Kelley, H.H. (1950) 'The warm–cold variable in first impressions of persons', *Journal of Personality*, 18, 431–9.

Kelley, H.H. (1967) 'Attribution theory in social psychology', *Nebraska Symposium on Motivation*, 15, 192–238.

Kelley, H.H. (1971) *Attribution in Social Interaction*, Morristown, NJ: General Learning Press.

Kelley, H.H. (1972) *Causal Schemata and the Attribution Process*, New York: General Learning Press.

Kelley, H.H. (1973) 'The processes of causal attribution', *American Pychologist*, 28, 107–28.

Kelly, G.A. (1955) *A Theory of Personality: The Psychology of Personal Constructs*, New York: Norton.

Kendrick, D.T. and Gutierres, S.E. (1980) 'Contrast effects and judgements of physical attractiveness: when beauty becomes a social problem', *Journal of Personality and Social Psychology*, 38, 131–40.

Kenny, D.A. and Albright, L. (1987) 'Accuracy in interpersonal perception: a social relations analysis', *Psychological Bulletin*, 102, 390–402.

Kerckhoff, A.C. and Davis, K.E. (1962) 'Value consensus and need complementarity in mate selection', *American Sociological Review*, 27, 295–303.

Kernis, M.H. and Wheeler, L. (1981) 'Beautiful friends and ugly strangers: radiation and contrast effects in perception of same-sex pairs', *Personality and Social Psychology Bulletin*, 7, 617–20.

Kerr, N.L. (1978) 'Beautiful and blameless: effects of victim attractiveness and responsibility on the judgements of mock jurors', *Personality and Social Psychology Bulletin*, 4, 479–82.

Kerr, N.L., Bull, R.H.C., MacCoun, R.J. and Rathborn, H. (1985) 'Effects of victim attractiveness and disfigurement on the judgements of American and British mock jurors', *British Journal of Social Psychology*, 24, 47–58.

Kim, M.P. and Rosenberg, S. (1980) 'Comparison of two structural models of implicit personality theory', *Journal of Personality and Social Psychology*, 38, 375–89.

Kleinke, C.L. (1986) 'Gaze and eye contact: a research review', *Psychological Bulletin*, 100, 78–100.

Kleinke, C.L. and Staneski, R.A. (1980) 'First impressions of female bust size', *Journal of Social Psychology*, 110, 123–34.

Kretschmer, E. (1925 [1921]) *Physique and Character*, trans., W.J.H. Spratt, New York: Harcourt.

Kruglanski, A.W. (1989) 'The psychology of being "right": the problem of accuracy in social perception and cognition', *Psychological Bulletin*, 106, 395–409.

LaFrance, M. and Mayo, C. (1978) 'Cultural aspects of nonverbal communication', *International Journal of Intercultural Relations*, 2, 71–89.

Landy, D. and Sigall, H. (1974) 'Beauty is talent: task evaluation as a function of the performer's physical attractiveness', *Journal of Personality and Social Psychology*, 29, 299–304.

Langer, E.J. (1978) 'Rethinking the role of thought in social interaction', in J.H. Harvey, W. Ickes and R.F. Kidd (eds) *New Directions in Attribution Research*, Vol. 2, Hillsdale, NJ: Erlbaum.

Langer, E.J., Blank, A. and Chanowitz, B. (1978) 'The mindlessness of ostensibly thoughtful action: the role of "placebic" information on interpersonal interaction', *Journal of Personality and Social Psychology*, 36, 635–42.

Langlois, J.H. and Roggman, L.A. (1990) 'Attractive faces are only average', *Psychological Science*, 1, 115–21.

Lawson, E.D. (1971) 'Hair colour, personality, and the observer', *Psychological Reports*, 28, 311–22.

Lay, C.H. and Jackson, D.N. (1969) 'Analysis of the generality of trait-inferential relationships', *Journal of Personality and Social Psychology*, 12, 12–21.

Lay, C.H., Birron, B.F. and Jackson, D.N. (1973) 'Base rates and informational value in impression formation', *Journal of Personality and Social Psychology*, 28, 390–5.

Leary, M.R. and Kowalski, R.M. (1990) 'Impression management: a literature review and a two-component model', *Psychological Bulletin*, 107, 34–47.

Lerner, M. (1980) *The Belief in a Just World: A Fundamental Delusion*, New York: Plenum.

Lerner, M. and Miller, D. (1978) 'Just world research and the attribution process: looking back and ahead', *Psychological Bulletin*, 85, 1030–51.

Liggett, J.C. (1974) *The Human Face*, New York: Stein and Day.

Lippmann, W. (1922) *Public Opinion*, New York: Harcourt, Brace.

Loftus, E.F. (1979) *Eyewitness testimony*, Cambridge, Mass.: Harvard University Press.

Lombroso, C. and Ferrero, G. (1896) *La femme criminelle et la prostituée*, Paris: Germer Bailliere.

McArthur, L.Z. (1972) 'The how and what of why: some determinants and consequences of causal attribution', *Journal of Personality and Social Psychology*, 22, 171–93.

McCaul, K.D., Veltum, L.G., Boyechko, V. and Crawford, J.J. (1990) 'Understanding attributions of victim blame for rape: sex, violence, and foreseeability', *Journal of Applied Social Psychology*, 20, 1–26.

McGarty, C. and Penny, R.E.C. (1988) 'Categorization, accentuation and social judgement', *British Journal of Social Psychology*, 27, 147–57.

Macrae, C.N. and Shepherd, J.W. (1989) 'Do criminal stereotypes mediate juridic judgements?', *British Journal of Social Psychology*, 28, 189–91.

Mayer, J.D. and Bower, G.H. (1986) 'Learning and memory for personality prototypes', *Journal of Personality and Social Psychology*, 51, 473–92.

Miller, D.T. and Ross, M. (1975) 'Self-serving biases in the attribution of causality: fact or fiction?', *Psychological Bulletin*, 82, 213–25.

Mills, J. and Aronson, E. (1965) 'Opinion change as a function of communicator's attractiveness and desire to influence', *Journal of Personality and Social Psychology*, 1, 173–7.

Mirels, H.L. (1976) 'Implicit personality theory and inferential illusions', *Journal of Personality*, 44, 467–87.

Mirels, H.L (1982) 'The illusory nature of implicit personality theory: logical and empirical considerations', *Journal of Personality*, 50, 203–22.

Mischel, W. (1968) *Personality and Assessment*, New York: Wiley.

Mischel, W. (1973) 'Towards a cognitive social learning reconceptualization of personality', *Psychological Review*, 80, 252–83.

Morris, D. (1977) *Manwatching*, London: Cape.

Morris, D., Collett, P., Marsh, P. and O'Shaughnessy, M. (1979) *Gestures: Their Origin and Distribution*, London: Cape.

Morse, S.J., Gruzen, J. and Reis, H. (1976) 'The eye of the beholder: a neglected variable in the study of physical attractiveness?', *Journal of Personality*, 44, 209–25.

Mueser, K.T., Grau, B.W., Sussman, S. and Rosen, A.J. (1984) 'You're only as pretty as you feel: facial expression as a determinant of physical attractiveness', *Journal of Personality and Social Psychology*, 46, 469–78.

Mullen, B. and Johnson, C. (1990) 'Distinctiveness-based illusory correlations and stereotyping: a meta-analytic integration', *British Journal of Social Psychology*, 29, 11–28.

Mummendey, A. and Schreiber, H.-J. (1984) 'Different just means better: some obvious and some hidden pathways to ingroup favouritism', *British Journal of Social Psychology*, 23, 363–8.

Murstein, B.I. (1972) 'Physical attractiveness and marital choice', *Journal of Personality and Social Psychology*, 22, 8–12.

Murstein, B.I. (1977) 'The Stimulus-value-role (SVR) theory of dyadic relationships', in S. Duck (ed.) *Theory and Practice in Interpersonal Attraction*, London: Academic Press.

Newcomb, T.M. (1961) *The Acquaintance Process*, New York: Holt, Rinehart and Winston.

Newcomb, T.M. (1968) 'Interpersonal balance', in R. Abelson, E. Aronson, W. McGuire, T. Newcomb, M. Rosenberg and P. Tannenbaum (eds) *Theories of Cognitive Consistency: A Sourcebook*, Chicago: Rand McNally.

Newcomb, T.M. (1981) 'Heiderian balance as a group phenomenon', *Journal of Personality and Social Psychology*, 40, 862–7.

Nisbett, R.E. and Ross, L. (1980) *Human Inference: Strategies and Shortcomings of Social Judgement*, Englewood Cliffs, NJ: Prentice-Hall.

Norman, W.T. (1963) 'Towards an adequate taxonomy of personality attributes', *Journal of Abnormal and Social Psychology*, 66, 574–83.

Nystedt, L. and Smari, S. (1987) 'Conception of interpersonal trait and action categories', *Journal of Personality*, 55, 711–27.

Osgood, C.E. (1962) 'Studies on the generality of affective meaning systems', *American Psychologist*, 17, 10–28.

Osgood, C., Suci, G.J. and Tannenbaum, P.H. (1957) *The Measurement of Meaning*, Urbana, Ill.: University of Illinois Press.

Ostrom, T.M. (1977) 'Between-theory and within-theory conflict in explaining context effects in impression formation', *Journal of Experimental Social Psychology*, 13, 492–503.

Passini, F.T. and Norman, W.T. (1966) 'A universal conception of personality structure?', *Journal of Personality and Social Psychology*, 4, 44–9.

Pavelchak, M.A. (1989) 'Piecemeal and category-based evaluation: an ideographic analysis', *Journal of Personality and Social Psychology*, 56, 354–63.

Peterson, K. and Curran, J.P. (1976) 'Trait attribution as a function of hair length and correlates of subjects' preferences for hair style', *Journal of Personality*, 93, 331–9.

Petty, R.E. and Cacioppo, J.T. (1985) 'The elaboration likelihood model of persuasion', in L. Berkowitz (ed.) *Advances in Experimental Social Psychology*, Vol. 19, New York: Academic Press.

Posner, M.I (1978) *Chronometric Explorations of Mind*, Hillsdale, NJ: Erlbaum.

Pratto, F. and Bargh, J.A. (1991) 'Stereotyping based on apparently individuating information: trait and global components of sex stereotypes under attention overload', *Journal of Experimental Social Psychology*, 27, 26–47.

Quattrone, G.A. (1982) 'Overattribution and unit formation: when behaviour engulfs the person', *Journal of Personality and Social Psychology*, 42, 593–607.

Reeder, G.D. and Brewer, M.B. (1979) 'A schematic model of dispositional attribution in interpersonal perception', *Psychological Review*, 86, 61–79.

Reis, H.T., Nezlek, J. and Wheeler, L. (1980) 'Physical attractiveness in social inter-action', *Journal of Personality and Social Psychology*, 38, 604–17.

Reis, H.T., Wheeler, L., Spiegel, N., Kernis, M.H., Nezlek, J. and Perri, M. (1982) 'Physical attractiveness in social interaction: II. Why does appearance affect social experience?', *Journal of Personality and Social Psychology*, 43, 979–96.

Rips, L.J. and Marcus, S.L. (1977) 'Suppositions and the analysis of conditional sentences', in M.A. Just and P.A. Carpenter (eds), *Cognitive Processes in Compre-hension*, Hillsdale, NJ: Erlbaum.

Roll, S. and Verinis, J. (1971) 'Stereotypes of scalp and facial hair as measured by the semantic differential', *Psychological Reports*, 28, 975–80.

Romer, D. and Revelle, W. (1984) 'Personality traits: fact or fiction? A critique of the Shweder and D'Andrade systematic distortion hypothesis', *Journal of Personality and Social Psychology*, 47, 1028–42.

Rosch, E. (1978) 'Principles of categorization', in E. Rosch and B.B. Lloyd (eds) *Cognition and Categorization*, Hillsdale, NJ: Erlbaum.

Rosch, E. and Mervis, C. (1975) 'Family resemblances: studies in the internal structure of categories', *Cognitive Psychology*, 7, 573–605.

Rosch, E., Mervis, C., Gray, W., Johnson, D. and Boyes-Braem, P. (1976) 'Basic objects in natural categories', *Cognitive Psychology*, 8, 382–439.

Rosenbaum, M.E. (1986a) 'The repulsion hypothesis: on the nondevelopment of relationships', *Journal of Personality and Social Psychology*, 51, 1156–66.

Rosenbaum, M.E. (1986b) 'Comment on a proposed two-stage theory of relationship formation: first, repulsion; then, attraction', *Journal of Personality and Social Psychology*, 51, 1171–2.

Rosenberg, S. (1977) 'New approaches to the analysis of personal constructs in person perception', in A.W.Landfield (ed.) *Nebraska Symposium on Motivation 1976*, Lincoln: University of Nebraska.

Rosenberg, S. and Jones, R.A. (1972) 'A method for investigating and representing a person's implicit theory of personality: Theodore Dreiser's view of people', *Journal of Personality and Social Psychology*, 22, 373–86.

Rosenberg, S. and Sedlak, A. (1972) 'Structural representations of implicit personality theory', in L.Berkowitz (ed.) *Advances in Experimental Social Psychology*, Vol. 6, New York: Academic Press.

Rosenberg, S., Nelson, C. and Vivekananthan, P.S. (1968) 'A multidimensional approach to the structure of personality impressions', *Journal of Personality and Social Psychology*, 9, 283–94.

Ross, L. (1977) 'The intuitive psychologist and his shortcomings: distortions in the attribution process', in L. Berkowitz (ed.) *Advances in Experimental Social Psychology*, Vol. 10, New York: Academic Press.

Ross, L., Greene, D. and House, P. (1977) 'The "false consensus effect": an egocentric bias in social perception and attribution processes', *Journal of Experimental Social Psychology*, 13, 279–301.

Rothstein, M. and Jackson, D.N. (1984) 'Implicit personality theory and the employ-ment interview', in M.Cook (ed.) *Issues in Person Perception*, London: Methuen.

Ryckman, R.M., Robbins, M.A., Kaczor, L.M. and Gold, J.A. (1989) 'Male and female raters' stereotyping of male and female physiques', *Personality and Social Psychology Bulletin*, 15, 244–51.

Schank, R.C. and Abelson, R.P. (1977) *Scripts, Plans, Goals and Understanding: An Inquiry into Human Knowledge Structures*, Hillsdale, NJ: Erlbaum.

Scherer, K.R. (1986) 'Vocal affect expression: a review and model for further research', *Psychological Bulletin*, 99, 143–65.

Scherer, K.R. and Giles, H. (eds) (1979) *Social Markers in Speech*, Cambridge: Cambridge University Press.

Schneider, W. and Shiffrin, R.M. (1977) 'Controlled and automatic human information processing: I. Detection, search, and attention', *Psychological Review*, 84, 1–66.

Schul, Y. and Bernstein, E. (1990) 'Judging the typicality of an instance: should the category be accessed first?', *Journal of Personality and Social Psychology*, 58, 964–74.

Schuler, H. and Berger, W. (1979) 'The impact of physical attractiveness on an employment decision', in M. Cook and G. Wilson (eds) *Love and Attraction*, Oxford: Pergamon.

Scribner, S. (1977) 'Modes of thinking and ways of speaking: culture and logic reconsidered', in P.N. Johnson-Laird and P.C. Wason (eds) *Thinking: Readings in Cognitive Science*, Cambridge: Cambridge University Press.

Secord, P.F. (1958) 'Facial features and inference processes in interpersonal perception', in R.Taguiri and L.Petrullo (eds) *Person Perception and Interpersonal Behaviour*, Stanford, Calif.: Stanford University Press, pp. 300–15.

Secord, P.F. and Backman, C.W. (1974) *Social Psychology*, 2nd edition, Tokyo: McGraw-Hill.

Secord, P.F. and Muthard, J.E. (1955) 'Personalities in faces: IV. A descriptive analysis of the perception of women's faces and the identification of some physiognomic determinants', *Journal of Personality*, 39, 269–78.

Secord, P.F., Dukes, W.F. and Bevan, W. (1954) 'Personality in faces: I. An experiment in social perceiving', *Genetics Psychology Monographs*, 49, 231–79.

Semin, G.R. (1980) 'A gloss on attribution theory', *British Journal of Social and Clinical Psychology*, 19, 291–300.

Semin, G.R. and Greenslade, L. (1985) 'Differential contributions of linguistic factors to memory-based ratings: systematizing the systematic distortion hypothesis', *Journal of Personality and Social Psychology*, 49, 1713–23.

Semin, G.R. and Manstead, A.S.R. (1983) *Accountability of Conduct*, London: Academic Press.

Seyfried, B.A. (1977) 'Complementarity in interpersonal attraction', in S. Duck (ed.) *Theory and Practice in Interpersonal Attraction*, London: Academic Press.

Shanteau, J. and Nagy, G.F. (1984) 'Information integration in person perception: theory and application', in M.Cook (ed.) *Issues in Person Perception*, London: Methuen.

Shaver, K.G. (1985) *The Attribution of Blame*, New York: Springer-Verlag.

Sheldon, W.H. (1940) *The Varieties of Human Physique: An Introduction to Constitutional Psychology*, New York: Harper.

Sheldon, W.H. (1942) *The Varieties of Temperament: A Psychology of Constitutional Differences*, New York: Harper.

Sherman, S.J., Presson, C.C. and Chassin, L. (1984) 'Mechanisms underlying the false consensus effect: the special role of threats to the self', *Personality and Social Psychology Bulletin*, 10, 127–38.

Shoemaker, D.J., South, D.R. and Lowe, J. (1973) 'Facial stereotypes of deviants and judgments of guilt or innocence', *Social Forces*, 51, 427–33.

Shotter, J. (1975) *Images of Man in Psychological Research*, London: Methuen.

Shweder, R.A. (1975) 'How relevant is an individual difference theory of personality?', *Journal of Personality*, 43, 455–84.

Shweder, R.A. (1977) 'Likeness and likelihood in everyday thought: magical thinking in judgements about personality', *Current Anthropology*, 18, 637–58.

Shweder, R.A. and D'Andrade, R.G. (1979) 'Accurate reflection and systematic distortion? A reply to Block, Weiss and Thorne', *Journal of Personality and Social Psychology*, 37, 1075–84.

Sigall, H. and Landy, D. (1973) 'Radiating beauty: effects of having a physically attractive partner on person perception', *Journal of Personality and Social Psychology*, 28, 218–24.

Sigall, H. and Ostrove, N. (1975) 'Beautiful but dangerous: effects of offender attractiveness and nature of the crime on juridic judgment', *Journal of Personality and Social Psychology*, 31, 410–14.

Simpson, J.A., Gangestad, S.W. and Lerma, M. (1990) 'Perception of physical attractiveness: mechanisms involved in the maintenance of romantic relationships', *Journal of Personality and Social Psychology*, 59, 1192–201.

Singer, M.S. and Singer, A.E. (1985) 'The effect of police uniform on interpersonal perception', *The Journal of Psychology*, 119, 157–61.

Sissons, M. (1971) 'The psychology of social class', in *Money, Wealth and Class*, Milton Keynes: Open University Press.

Skowronski, J.J. and Carlson, S.E. (1987) 'Social judgement and social memory: the role of cue diagnosticity in negativity, positivity, and extremity biases', *Journal of Personality and Social Psychology*, 52, 689–99.

Skowronski, J.J. and Carlson, S.E. (1989) 'Negativity and extremity biases in impression formation: a review of explanations', *Psychological Bulletin*, 105, 131–42.

Smeaton, G., Byrne, D. and Murnen, S.K. (1989) 'The repulsion hypothesis revisited: similarity irrelevance or dissimilarity bias?' *Journal of Personality and Social Psychology*, 56, 54–9.

Snyder, M. (1974) 'The self-monitoring of expressive behaviour', *Journal of Personality and Social Psychology*, 30, 526–37.

Snyder, M. (1979) 'Self-monitoring processes', in L. Berkowitz (ed.) *Advances in Experimental Social Psychology*, Vol. 12, New York: Academic Press.

Snyder, M., Campbell, B.H. and Preston, E. (1982) 'Testing hypotheses about human nature: assessing the accuracy of social stereotypes', *Social Cognition*, 1, 256–72.

Snyder, M., Tanke, E.D. and Berscheid, E. (1977) 'Social perception and interpersonal behaviour: on the self-fulfilling nature of social stereotypes', *Journal of Personality and Social Psychology*, 35, 656–66.

Spears, R., van der Pligt, J. and Eiser, J.R. (1985) 'Illusory correlation in the perception of group attitudes', *Journal of Personality and Social Psychology*, 48, 863–75.

Spillman, D.M. and Everington, C. (1989) 'Somatotypes revisited: have the media changed our perception of the female body image?', *Psychological Reports*, 64, 3, 877–90.

Stewart, R.H. (1965) 'Effect of continuous responding on the order effect in personality impression formation', *Journal of Personality and Social Psychology*, 1, 161–5.

Storms, M.D. (1973) 'Videotape and the attribution process: reversing actors' and observers' points of view', *Journal of Personality and Social Psychology*, 27, 165–75.

Stricker, L.J., Jacobs, P.I. and Kogan, N. (1974) 'Trait interrelationships in implicit personality theories and questionnaire data', *Journal of Personality and Social Psychology*, 30, 198–207.

Stroebe, W. (1977) 'Self-esteem and interpersonal attraction', in S. Duck (ed.) *Theory and Practice in Interpersonal Attraction*, London: Academic Press.

Swann, W.B., Jr. (1984) 'Quest for accuracy in person perception: a matter of pragmatics', *Psychological Review*, 91, 457–77.

Swap, W.C. (1977) 'Interpersonal attraction and repeated exposure to rewarders and punishers', *Personality and Social Psychology Bulletin*, 3, 248–51.

Swede, S.W. and Tetlock, P. (1986) 'Henry Kissinger's implicit theory of personality: a quantitative case study', *Journal of Personality*, 54, 617–46.

Symons, D. (1979) *The Evolution of Human Sexuality*, New York: Oxford University Press.

Taft, R. (1955) 'The ability to judge people', *Psychological Bulletin*, 52, 1–23.

Tajfel, H. (1969) 'Cognitive aspects of prejudice', *Journal of Social Issues*, 25, 79–97.

Tajfel, H. (1981) *Human Groups and Social Categories*, Cambridge: Cambridge University Press.

Tajfel, H. and Turner, J. (1979) 'An integrative theory of intergroup conflict', in W.G. Austin and S. Worchel (eds) *The Social Psychology of Intergroup Relations*, Monterey, Calif.: Brooks-Cole.

Tajfel, H. and Wilkes, A.L. (1963) 'Classification and quantitative judgement', *British Journal of Psychology*, 54, 101–14.

Tajfel, H., Sheikh, A.A. and Gardner, R.C. (1964) 'Content of stereotypes and the inference of similarity between members of stereotyped groups', *Acta Psychologica*, 22, 191–201.

Taylor, S.E.(1982) 'The availability bias in social perception and interaction', in D. Kahneman, P. Slovic and A. Tversky (eds) (1982) *Judgement under Uncertainty: Heuristic and Biases*, Cambridge: Cambridge University Press.

Taylor, S.E., Fiske, S.T., Etcoff, N.L. and Ruderman, A.J. (1978) 'Categorical and contextual bases of person memory and stereotyping', *Journal of Personality and Social Psychology*, 36, 778–93.

Tetlock, P.E. and Manstead, A.S.R. (1985) 'Impression management versus intrapsychic explanations in social psychology: a useful dichotomy?', *Psychological Review*, 92, 59–77.

Thibaut, J.W. and Kelley, H.H. (1959) *The Social Psychology of Groups*, New York: Wiley.

Thibaut, J.W. and Kelley, H.H. (1978) *Interpersonal Relations: A Theory of Interdependence*, New York: Wiley.

Thorndike, E.L. (1920) 'A constant error in psychological ratings', *Journal of Applied Psychology*, 4, 25–9.

Thornton, G.R. (1944) 'The effect of wearing glasses on personality traits of persons seen briefly', *Journal of Applied Psychology*, 28, 203–7.

Trzebinski, J. (1985) 'Action-oriented representations of implicit personality theory', *Journal of Personality and Social Psychology*, 48, 1266–78.

Tversky, A. and Kahneman, D. (1973) 'Availability: a heuristic for judging frequency and probability', *Cognitive Psychology*, 4, 207–32.

Tversky, A. and Kahneman, D. (1974) 'Judgment under uncertainty: heuristics and biases', *Science*, 185, 1124–31.

Tversky, A. and Kahneman, D. (1982) 'Judgments of and by representativeness', in D. Kahneman, P. Slovic and A. Tversky (eds) (1982) *Judgment under Uncertainty: Heuristics and Biases*, Cambridge: Cambridge University Press.

Tzeng, O.C. (1982) 'The artificial dispute over implicit personality theory: an answer to Jackson, Stricker and Mirels', *Journal of Personality*, 50, 251–60.

Tzeng, O.C. and Tzeng, C. (1982) 'Implicit personality theory: myth or fact? An illustration of how empirical research can miss', *Journal of Personality*, 50, 223–39.

Volpp. J.M. and Lennon, S.J. (1988) 'Perceived police authority as a function of uniform hat and sex', *Perceptual and Motor Skills*, 67, 815–24.

Walster, E. and Festinger, L. (1962) 'The effectiveness of "overheard" persuasive communications', *Journal of Abnormal and Social Psychology*, 65, 395–402.

Walster, E., Aronson, E. and Abrahams, D. (1966a) 'On increasing the persuasiveness of a low prestige communicator', *Journal of Experimental Social Psychology*, 2, 325–42.

Walster, E., Aronson, V., Abrahams, D. and Rottman, L. (1966b) 'Importance of physical attractiveness in dating behavior', *Journal of Personality and Social Psychology*, 4, 508–16.

Warr, P.B. and Knapper, C. (1968) *The Perception of People and Events*, Chichester: Wiley.

Watkins, M.J. and Peynircioğlu, Z.F. (1984) 'Determining perceived meaning during impression formation: another look at the meaning change hypothesis', *Journal of Personality and Social Psychology*, 46, 1005–16.

Weber, R. and Crocker, J. (1983) 'Cognitive processes in the revision of stereotypic beliefs', *Journal of Personality and Social Psychology*, 45, 961–77.

Wedell, D.H., Parducci, A. and Geiselman, R.E. (1987) 'A formal analysis of ratings of physical attractiveness: successive contrast and simultaneous assimilation', *Journal of Experimental Social Psychology*, 23, 230–49.

Weiner, B. (1979) 'A theory of motivation for some classroom experiments', *Journal of Educational Psychology*, 71, 3–25.

Weir, S. and Fine-Davis, M. (1989) '"Dumb blonde" and "temperamental redhead": the effect of hair colour on some attributed personality characteristics of women', *The Irish Journal of Psychology*, 10, 11–19.

Wells, W. and Siegel, B. (1961) 'Stereotyped somatotypes', *Psychological Reports*, 8, 77–8.

Wilson, P.R. (1968) 'Perceptual distortion of height as a function of ascribed academic status', *Journal of Social Psychology*, 74, 97–102.

Winch, R.F. (1958) *Mate Selection: A Study in Complementary Needs*, New York: Harper & Row.

Wishner, J. (1960) 'Reanalysis of "impressions of personality"', *Psychological Review*, 67, 96–112.

Wyer, R.S., Jr. (1974) 'Changes in meaning and halo effects in personality impression formation', *Journal of Personality and Social Psychology*, 29, 829–35.

Wyer, R.S., Jr. and Martin, L.L. (1986) 'Person memory: the role of traits, group stereotypes, and specific behaviours in the cognitive representation of persons', *Journal of Personality and Social Psychology*, 50, 661–75.

Wyer, R.S., Jr. and Watson, S.F. (1969) 'Context effects in impression formation', *Journal of Personality and Social Psychology*, 12, 22–33.

Yang, K. and Bond, M.H. (1990) 'Exploring implicit personality theories with indigenous or imported constructs: the Chinese case', *Journal of Personality and Social Psychology*, 58, 1087–95.

York, M.W., Wilderman, S.K. and Hardy, S.T. (1988) 'Categories of implicit interpersonal communication: cross-cultural responses', *Perceptual and Motor Skills*, 67, 735–41.

Zajonc, R.B. (1968) 'Attitudinal effects of mere exposure', *Journal of Personality and Social Psychology Monograph Supplement*, 9, 1–27.

Zanna, M.P. and Hamilton, D.L. (1977) 'Further evidence for meaning change in impression formation', *Journal of Experimental Social Psychology*, 13, 224–8.

Zebrowitz-McArthur, L. (1988) 'Person perception in cross-cultural perspective', in M.H. Bond (ed.) *The Cross-Cultural Challenge to Social Psychology*, London: Sage.

Name index

Subject index